# Keeping Kids Reading

Also by Mary Leonhardt

*Parents Who Love Reading, Kids Who Don't:
How It Happens and What You Can Do About It*

# Keeping Kids Reading

## How to Raise Avid Readers in the Video Age

# Mary Leonhardt

CROWN PUBLISHERS, INC., NEW YORK

Copyright © 1996 by Mary Leonhardt

Published by Crown Publishers, Inc., 201 East 50th Street, New York, New York
10022. Member of the Crown Publishing Group.

Random House, Inc. New York, Toronto, London, Sydney, Auckland

CROWN is a trademark of Crown Publishers, Inc.

Printed in the United States of America

Design by Lenny Henderson

Library of Congress Cataloging-in-Publication Data
Leonhardt, Mary.
Keeping kids reading: how to raise avid readers in the video age
/ Mary Leonhardt.—1st ed.
Includes bibliographical references and index.
1. Reading   2. Children—Books and reading.   3. Reading—Parent
participation. I. Title
LB1050.L453   1996                                          96-4
428.4′3—dc20                                                CIP

ISBN 0-517-70114-6

10   9   8   7   6   5   4   3   2   1

First Edition

# Contents

• • • • • • • • • • • • • • • • • • • • • • • • • • • • • • • • • •

# Acknowledgments

• • • • • • • • • • • • • • • • • • • • • • • • • • • • • • • • • • • • •

Many thanks to my husband, Dick, and my children, Julie, Tim, and Molly, for their enthusiastic support.

A special thanks to my editor, Peter Ginna, for his thoughtful, insightful suggestions.

Thanks to my agent, Dick McDonough, for his continuing work on my behalf.

Special thanks to the many students who consented to be interviewed for this book.

# Introduction

In my first book, *Parents Who Love Reading, Kids Who Don't: How It Happens and What You Can Do About It,* I explained that parents are rarely to blame for a kid's dislike of reading; it's schools that manage to turn reading into a dreaded chore. I still believe that. But since that book was published, I've been lucky enough to travel around the country and talk to many parents. They tell me that their kids don't really dislike reading, they just never seem to have time to do any. They'd rather play sports, work at a job, talk on the phone . . . or rent a movie. Somehow, their kids are not making time for reading.

Teachers around the country tell me the same things. Kids don't read. They read only what they have to read, if that. The sad thing I found was that many teachers are very distressed by this state of affairs, but don't know how to change it. Driven by curriculum guidelines and new state mandates, those teachers don't see any way of nurturing a love and habit of reading in their schools. If anything, the idea that a child should *love* reading is even more of a foreign idea to policy setters and educational administrators now than it was when I wrote my first book.

And so, for now, keeping kids reading is still up to parents and the very brave individual teachers who are willing to push back all of the increasing curriculum mandates. Keeping kids reading is also up to librarians, who, in many of the places where I traveled, seemed to be the only professional adults even *interested* in nurturing a love of reading. Hence I have gained an incredible respect for librarians.

For parents, teachers, and librarians, the question is, How do we keep kids reading? In a culture dominated by emerging computer technology and elaborate video systems, how do we foster a love of books? How do we ensure that kids become avid readers?

I've been interested in those questions for years. During the first days of a class, I always ask my new students to write a reading history for me. "If you like to read, great!" I tell them. "Describe for me the kind of reading you do. Write down anything you can remember—titles, authors, kinds of books, anything. And if you don't like to read, that's okay too. Tell me the bad news. Let me know what I'm up against!" Once I know who the avid readers are, I always keep a special eye on them, chatting with them about their special likes and dislikes, as well as the reasons they read so much.

In addition, I occasionally get the opportunity to survey students whom I don't have in my own classes. This spring I got almost four hundred other students from my own district, as well as seventy-seven students from a district in Wisconsin, to write a summary of their likes and dislikes about reading—which books, especially, they liked or disliked, and what kinds of school activities made them like reading, and which ones made them dislike reading. The surveys confirmed the conclusions I'd already formed concerning what kinds of activities nurture a love of reading.

But probably the most valuable research I did for this book was to interview at length thirty high school juniors and seniors who had scored over 600 on the verbal section of the Scholastic Aptitude Test, a score that puts them in the top 7 percent of seniors headed for college nationwide. They were all avid readers. I wanted to know why they continued reading when most of their classmates chose other, more enticing activities. Most of these students I knew very well: I'd had them in class, I'd chatted with them outside of class, I was involved in activities with them.

Our discussions ranged from how they got started reading, to the books they read, to their writing, to how they did in school. Mostly I wanted to find out what was *different* about their experience. What did their parents do to nurture such avid readers? How did they avoid being turned off by school assignments?

The kids were wonderful about talking to me. They gave up exam-studying time to tell me about their experiences; they chatted with me by phone over the summer. "How did it happen that you started writing poetry?" I'd ask. Or, "Where did you *get* all the books you read?" They were unfailingly polite, perceptive, and helpful: they really made this book possible.

This book, then, is the result of those interviews and surveys, and of my informal conversations over the years with all of my students. It has also been strongly influenced by my experiences with my own three children.

The first chapter describes how those sophisticated readers I interviewed are different from their classmates, and why you should try so hard to ensure that your children keep reading. Chapter 2 describes four goals of reading instruction that should help you make decisions about books and activities you might try with your children. Chapters 3 and 4 contain concrete suggestions for ways to ensure that your preschoolers and elementary-school-aged children develop a love and habit of reading. Chapter 5 is about writing, because I've found that my very best readers were almost always kids who also wrote for fun. The independent writing they did really seemed to support their reading. Chapters 6 and 7 are on what I call reading paths, so you can get some idea of the kind of reading each of your children might like. I've found, over the years, that kids who initially like one kind of book will usually, though not always, progress along a path to another predictable type of reading. Chapter 8 is about the special problems of keeping teenagers avidly reading. Chapter 9 offers an overview on dealing with schools and with specific school problems, as well as a variety of other reading problems. It also contains a compilation of many of the questions I've been asked. The appendix comprises partial transcripts of some of my interviews with avid readers.

I hope you find this book helpful. You'll see, as you read, how at odds my suggestions are with current educational practices. But you might keep in mind also that, according to the 1994 National Assessment of Educational Progress report ("The Reading Report Card"), reading scores have declined from the already low scores of 1992. This has been the case in every area of the country, and across every demographic group. Currently, only 34 percent of high school seniors test at a level of proficient or above in reading. Twenty-five percent of high school seniors test *below a basic reading level.* We can't wait for schools to change. We can't entrust reading to the professional education establishment. Whether as teachers, parents, or librarians, we have to take care of the children entrusted to us now. For now, at least, we have to keep our own children reading.

I'd love to hear comments or additional suggestions from readers. You can reach me % Crown Publishers, Inc., or on e-mail at maryl@tiac.net. You can also visit my *Keeping Kids Reading* page on the World Wide Web at http://www.tiac.net/users/maryl/.

# The Best Readers of All: How Avid-Reading High School Seniors Are Different

What differentiates top readers from mediocre, everyday readers? And what is the key ingredient of a top reader?

After twenty-five years of teaching high school English, in schools all across the country, I'm very sure of the answer. The top readers are the avid readers, the students who are always reading books of their own choice, above and beyond the requirements of any high school course. It doesn't seem to matter very much *what* they read, although over their years of reading they tend to gravitate to more complex authors and books.

In my classes I insist that all of my students become avid readers. If they want to get an A on their weekly reading, they have to read at least two hundred pages a week of a book of their own choice. I became curious to see what effect, if any, this reading was having on their SAT verbal scores, and to this end I acquired a list of student SAT scores for my high school for the last four years. We have about five sections of American Literature, and five sections of British Literature—the courses most college-prep juniors take—and about ten sections of sophomore English, a course everyone takes. Students usually take the SAT exam at the end of their junior year or the beginning of their senior year, and I was curious to see how many of my students had been among the high scorers.

I was pleased to see that, even though I teach only two sections of tenth grade each year, and only one or two sections of American and British Literature a year, in three out of the four years I checked, the majority of students who scored above 600 on the verbal section were ones who had been in my classes. For one year—the year I had two American Lit. sections—two thirds of the high scorers were my students.

I know this isn't a scientific study, but it does indicate to me that turning students into avid readers, even if one does it at a fairly late date, can have a highly significant positive effect on their reading ability. And if they've been reading avidly since they learned to read, as was the case with some of my students, they are fundamentally different from their classmates. The avid reading they have done has shaped them more powerfully than any school experience or peer experience they have had.

It's hard to describe all the subtle differences in ability between avid readers and kids who rarely read, but after they've written a few papers and participated in a few class discussions, it becomes obvious that certain kids are always getting the A's. Certain kids are just doing much better in English.

"It's not fair," students argue passionately with me. "I spent hours and hours on that paper and only got a B. What do you want me to do? What's *wrong* with the paper? And I know you give A's. You just favor some kids."

An extremely intelligent, conscientious, but not particularly avid-reading boy explained ruefully to me one day the difference between him and his avid-reading brother. "I spend hours and hours on homework. I work so hard to get everything done perfectly, and I don't even know when my brother *does* homework. I think he sneaks in the bathroom for a few minutes and sits on the toilet seat and scribbles his papers out. And he gets all A's." What follows is my attempt to explain to my classes the *reason* why avid readers are different. Afterward I'll explain in detail what the major differences are.

"Pretend you're at a tennis match," I tell my students. "And pretend one player loves tennis, and has played for a couple of hours every day almost since he could walk. The other player likes tennis okay, and has had a few lessons. But that's really it. Who's going to win that match?"

Easy answer, I'm told: the player who loves the game and has played his whole life. And even if, by some fluke, the other player manages to win a game, the first player will play much better. Even if he's having a bad day, he'll play much better than the other player. He'll move better. He'll anticipate better when the ball is coming. He'll know where to be on the court, how to hit the ball back. There are all kinds of subtle aspects to the game that he'll just *know*—aspects that it's almost impossible to teach someone directly.

"And there's something else," I tell them. "Someone who doesn't understand the game well—someone like me—won't even be able to *appreciate* how much better that excellent player is. I'll miss the subtle moves, the strategy, the anticipation."

They agree with me. They know that when you really understand a game—especially if you're an accomplished player—it's much more fun to watch the game. You get much more out of it, because you just see things that uneducated viewers don't.

"It's like reading," I then tell them. "Kids who have read every book they could get their hands on, from the age of six onward, are just going to be much better readers. They're going to see things you don't see. And if, in addition, they've written poems and stories and letters, they're going to *write* much better. Practice is everything."

"But I couldn't read all the time," one girl argued. "I was playing soccer so much—and that's really important for college—so I just didn't have time."

That argument always used to stop me cold. How could I explain the importance of reading to a student who really thought that colleges preferred excellent soccer players to excellent readers? Of course, what I've finally realized is that, to some extent, she's right. Colleges, like everyone else, know that a player's best effort, combined with the best coaching, isn't nearly enough to produce a winning soccer player. The player has to be terrific to start with—and being terrific means hours and days and years spent practicing on the soccer field. There's no shortcut.

Similarly, a student's best efforts at literary tasks—combined with the best teaching—aren't nearly enough to produce a top-achieving English student. The student has to walk into my high school class having already spent hours and days and years reading and writing. Again, there's no shortcut.

I don't think many students, parents, or even teachers understand this. Somehow they think performance in academic subjects, including English, is largely the result of effort on the student's part and excellent instruction on the teacher's part. The one other variable they'll throw into the pot is native intelligence. If a student is trying hard and being taught well, but not achieving, the student must be dumb—or, perhaps, learning disabled.

This is usually wrong. The core academic ability—not just in English but in any subject—is reading, and students who work hard and still struggle in school are almost always kids who have never done much reading for pleasure. Avid reading changes students. Avid reading changes everything.

Specifically how are students who have kept reading different? What abilities have they acquired during all the hours they spent curled up with X-Men comics and Baby-sitters Club series books?

They're different in the ways I described in my last book, *Parents Who Love Reading, Kids Who Don't.* Avid readers read better, write better, concentrate better—and seem to be better able to weather personal trauma with their academic credentials intact. But since I wrote that book, I'm seeing more subtle differences between long-term readers and kids who have never really developed a lifelong habit of reading. Briefly, I'm also seeing these differences:

## Avid readers have many interests and do well in a wide variety of subjects.

About a year ago I attended Awards Night at our high school. What quickly became apparent was that the same students were getting all the awards. As they trooped up on the stage, again and again, some people started to laugh. It seemed ridiculous that the same person would be winning awards in English, physics, math, and a foreign language. But that's what we saw happening—not always, of course, but often. There were about four or five kids who were winning a whole cluster of awards—and every one of those kids was an avid reader.

Afterward I spoke to the mother of one, a girl who wrote wonderful poetry. The girl had showed much of her poetry to me, and I had helped her pick what I thought was the best of her best to enter into the writing contest. It turns out she hadn't even entered any of her poetry in the writing contest; instead she'd entered some fiction she'd written, which was also exciting and strong. Then her mother told me that her daughter's real interest was science! Hence all of the science awards.

This is something I see again and again. While children often *enter* reading through a particular interest—they read everything they can find about sports, for example—through years of reading they develop many, many other interests.

The corollary to this is that students who have interests in many areas can master new academic areas with much more ease. They've picked up bits and pieces of history from their wide reading—the Little House books by Laura Ingalls Wilder, for example, provide a vivid picture of life in the United States in the nineteenth century; Anne Rice's vampire books range from the old South to medieval Europe in setting—so students who read these books have a framework in their minds that makes learning very easy.

This idea of a learning framework is the principle behind the very popular E. D. Hirsch books: *What Your Third Grader Needs to Know*, *What Your Fourth Grader Needs to Know*, and so forth. And he's right that if a child knows a little about an era of history or a field of science, the rest of his learning is easier. Of course, I don't think that teaching children a large number of unrelated facts is the way to build these frameworks—I've only seen such frameworks firmly in place in the minds of avid readers—but I think his *principle* is right.

I had quite a discussion about this topic with an assistant professor at Harvard who was teaching a group I was in how, supposedly, to teach reading skills. She was telling us to teach framework before having a student read a book. Before giving a student *Catch-22*, for example, you would teach him about the Italian campaign in World War II. She had all kinds of ideas about how to teach these frameworks: have kids write down what words come to mind when they think of war, and so on.

I have two problems with this approach. One is that it usually doesn't work. You can teach frameworks until you're blue in the face, but if a student is not yet ready to read that book, nothing you do is going to help very much. And even the rare times when teaching frameworks does enable a student to get through a difficult book, what have you gained? How have you helped that student to become an independent reader? Every time he's given a difficult book, is he going to have to find someone to go through a dog-and-pony show for him, teaching him frameworks? The concept is ridiculous.

And, of course, the other problem is that if you're continually assigning reading that kids can't understand on their own—reading that you have to coach them through—you have pretty unhappy, discontented readers on you hands.

So, by high school age, we want students who have already developed these learning frameworks in their minds. And these kids are, without exception, avid readers.

Interestingly, a writer who is wildly successful at developing science frameworks in kids' minds is Michael Crichton. Over dinner one night, my eleven-year-old nephew described to me with great glee all of the havoc dinosaurs could cause. Of course, he'd just finished *Jurassic Park*, and was now eager to read Crichton's other books. Robin Cook's books provide interesting medical frameworks; and books about the legal profession are proliferating like, well, like lawyers! Even books that don't seem to have any relevant factual content—a fantasy series, perhaps—often show how governments or other power structures work. Kids who start out loving fantasy and science fiction often go on to read history and political science.

So the frameworks that kids develop are crucial to further learning. And the only kids who, by high school age, have these wide-ranging, factual frameworks in place are the avid readers.

That's one reason why avid readers do so well over a large variety of academic subjects. But along with these frameworks is another crucial ability: to see the relative importance of the information one is acquiring.

## Avid readers acquire the ability to sift information and to understand how unrelated facts fit into the whole field of learning.

This is a crucial ability. Avid readers are more likely to acquire a sense of proportion; they can see the forest for the trees.

This comes up in obvious ways in class. Once I had a class reading *Catch-22*. One character is Major Major's father, a farmer who "advocated thrift and hard work and disapproved of loose women who turned him down." He was cruel to his wife, and showed his sardonic sense of humor by naming his son Major, instead of Caleb, as his wife wished. When I asked the class what they thought he was like, most students thought he was all right; he was a farmer, he went to church. It was only my avid reader who said disgustedly, "He's scum, slime." He could see through the details of the description to the bitterly sarcastic tone underneath—and understand what the author was really saying.

This is probably the major reason why it's so hard for mediocre readers to write a really wonderful paper. Their style isn't good because they haven't yet acquired sophisticated written language structures—but even more important, they miss tone and nuance. They'll miss the warm affection in which Salinger obviously held Holden Caulfield—and decide that Holden's just a whiner.

This inability to distinguish forests from trees hurts them in every subject. What were the important reasons for the Civil War? They can memorize lists, but can they come up with creative thinking on the subject? No. In every subject area, the ability to distinguish the critically important from the surrounding facts is what distinguishes the excellent students from the mediocre students.

Of course, I think this is exactly what's happened in the field of reading. Many professors and researchers have, for years, overlooked the single most crucial fact of teaching reading: if a kid hates reading and never willingly reads, *nothing* will help him become a better reader until you change that. A love of reading is everything. A love of reading is the crucial factor in reading success. A sense of perspective is everything.

How does avid reading develop a sense of perspective? To start with, I think avid reading gradually gives kids a sense of how complex many situations are. Early formula fiction—comic books and Nancy Drew, for example—is written in a simplistic tone, with good characters and bad characters. But as kids continue reading, and wander into more complicated authors, authors start making them aware of the complexities inherent in most situations. Even fairly simple series books, like the Sweet Valley books, have characters who start out looking pretty bad, but end up looking a little better. Stephen King is very good at describing complicated parent-child relationships. Read *Christine* and you'll see an achingly real description of a kid who doesn't get along with his parents—and why.

Seeing situations in their true complexity is the beginning of acquiring a sense of proportion. Some people actually take pride in their unwillingness to see complexities. Anyone who brags that she always speaks her mind, for example, is usually someone who lacks a sense of when a statement is not appropriate to a situation. She's the person who will tell an acquaintance that her brand-new dress makes her look fat.

By reading many authors with many viewpoints, kids gradually acquire a sense of reality that, I think, is much more complex and layered than that of nonreaders. And with that complex sense of reality can come a sense of proportion.

The real test of a sense of proportion is a person's sense of humor—which is, after all, just the ability to see things suddenly in a new perspective. A funny comment or situation usually juxtaposes expected realities with unexpected ones. Other children have this ability sometimes too, of course, but I see it much more often in avid readers.

In my British Literature classes we usually read *The Importance of Being Earnest* by Oscar Wilde. The kids who are avid readers always love the play. It's very funny to them—and to me! When Lady Bracknell reports that she called on Lady Harbury, a recent widow, and says, "I never saw a woman so altered; she looks quite twenty years younger," Algernon responds casually, "I hear her hair has turned quite gold from grief." The play is funny because the avid readers instantly understand both viewpoints: a woman whose husband has just died should look older, and her hair should have turned gray from grief. But this woman is really delighted her husband has died, and has dyed her hair gold. The unexpectedness of the widow's reaction—and perhaps the honesty of it—is what is so funny to us. And, of course, underlying the funny lines is Wilde's really savage satire of the upper class in England. Again, usually only the avid readers understand this.

Related to avid readers' ability to recognize important concepts without getting lost in the details is their ability to see beyond surface reality. This may be the most critical difference between avid readers and kids who rarely pick up a book.

**Avid readers develop an ability to understand how other people think and feel.**

It took a student to explain this to me. She was reading *The Color Purple* by Alice Walker, and really loved the book. She told me that she had already seen the movie, but it wasn't nearly as good.

"I couldn't tell what Celie was thinking," she told me. "I could see what she was doing, but I couldn't understand why. Now I can see what she was thinking all the time."

I started to think then about the relationship between violent books and violent kids. One thing I know: avid readers are almost never violent kids. Kids can read war books and horror books and science-fiction thrillers and still be gentle, peace-loving students. But there is research showing at least some relationship between the amount of violent movies and television kids see, and the violence they engage in.

The crucial difference is that when we watch a movie, we are outside of the minds of both perpetrator and victim. We only see what actually happens; we don't see the feelings and thoughts of the people involved. So it's fairly easy to harden our hearts to the victim's plight.

When we read, on the other hand, we are inside the minds of the characters. We understand their confusion. We feel their suffering. While movies can desensitize us to violence, I think reading can make us more sensitive to it. We understand, in a much deeper sense, the impact of violence on a victim's life.

I've always thought that this is why many avid-reading kids are not in the most popular social groups during late elementary and junior high school. The social scene is pretty brutal during those years. There are popular kids, and there are others who definitely are not popular. A child can't be a charter member of the popular group if he keeps feeling sorry for his less popular classmates. And avid readers are likely to empathize with victims. They may have read *Blubber* by Judy Blume, and have some understanding of what it's like to be fat. They may have read stories of kids from abusive homes. They understand the pain of others too well to really have the killer instinct necessary to shine in a preadolescent social situation.

Almost any type of reading develops this sensitivity in children. They read *Charlotte's Web* and learn to feel sorry for spiders and pigs. In fact, I can still see my younger daughter, at the age of about five or six, throwing a neighborhood boy's candy all over his front lawn because he was drowning spiders. "Spiders are our *friends*!!" she screamed at him. The five-year-old boy just stared at her, dumbfounded. He was a little boy. Little boys like to throw spiders in ponds. It is their God-given right. This little boy, as it turned out, grew up to be a wonderful reader and a gentle, peaceful young man. But, of course, many young people today are growing up violent. It's always seemed to me that there is a direct correlation between the violence some of our inner-city youths display on the streets and the low reading scores they display in school. According to the National School Board Association, 93 percent of urban school districts reported student assaults and fights as the most frequent form of violence in 1992; 91 percent of urban districts reported problems with weapons in schools. At the same time, the National Center for Education Statistics, in its 1992 Reading Report Card, reports that over 90 percent of the students in what it calls "disadvantaged urban" schools failed to achieve a proficient level in reading by eighth grade. Ninety percent! By twelfth grade, after as many as one third of the students have dropped out, the figure isn't much better. Eighty percent of the eighteen-year-olds who are still in school test below a proficient level.

Teaching these disadvantaged kids values—the popular solution at the moment—isn't working. And I don't think it will work as long as kids see other kids as objects. Our very difficult goal is to try to sensitize these young violent offenders to the feelings of their victims. Being raised in loving homes with loving adults is certainly the best way to raise children who can care about other people. Unfortunately, as a society, we don't seem able to guarantee loving, gentle families to all of our children. Trying to turn kids into avid readers is clearly not a panacea, but I think it might help. Being pulled into the minds of thousands of narrators in thousands of different books might help neutralize the paranoid, violent reactions characteristic of youthful offenders.

Avid reading tends to make kids more aware of other people *as people*—it helps them develop a heart. And this leads me to my final difference—perhaps the greatest difference between avid readers and people who get all of their information from electronic media and friends.

**Avid readers tend to be more flexible in their thinking, and more open to new ideas.**

When you're reading a good book, you're continually being pulled into the author's viewpoint, whether it's through a character's eyes or through the voice of a third-person narrator. You're continually seeing reality as the author wants you to see it. You sympathize with the characters that he makes sympathetic. You're angry at the happenings he shows as cruel. And, after reading many, many books, by many, many writers with different viewpoints, an avid reader gradually becomes aware of the complexity of reality. And I think an avid reader becomes suspicious of dogmatic statements, and less apt to buy into closed systems of thinking.

Seeing events on a screen is fundamentally different. While a director can try to choose his events, and portray them in a certain way to control the viewer's reaction, there is no strong "voice" interpreting events for a viewer. And so a viewer can much more easily put his own interpretation on events. Books don't allow you this leeway. You're pulled to see events as the author wants you to. And so readers are drawn out of their own mindset into the mind of another.

Books are powerful. Religious or political groups who want to impose their belief systems on our country are probably right to be nervous about books. Their mistake is that they are only nervous about certain books. But if you're part of a group that wants to completely control the thinking of its children, you need to go after all books that are not written specifically by members of your group to teach your worldview, because any other reading will draw children into other worldviews and—sooner or later— your children will become more flexible and creative in their thinking. I'm not saying that wide reading will necessarily change children's beliefs, but it will help them understand and respect others' beliefs.

Of course, as a pluralistic country, we need citizens who are flexible, open, and accepting of others' beliefs. We also need citizens who are gentle and peace-loving, and worried about the welfare of their neighbors. And we need leaders with wide-ranging minds, leaders who can separate the nonessential from the critical—leaders who have competence in a wide range of areas. We need avid readers.

How do we produce lifelong avid readers? That's the next chapter.

# Overall Strategy: Four Goals for Readers

A difficulty that arises in discussions on how to develop readers is that we have many different goals for our children. Yes, we want them to love reading and form a habit of reading. But we also would like them to think critically about their reading, certainly as they grow older. We don't want our twenty-four-year-old daughter still thinking that Sweet Valley High books are perceptive, realistic descriptions of high school life. We'd like our children to begin reading complex, well-written novels and detailed, thoughtful nonfiction. We'd like them to have some knowledge and appreciation of the classics. How can we accomplish this?

I've thought about this for a long time, and have finally concluded that it makes sense to look at our reading goals in a hierarchical way. I'm proposing four goals, and that we make the first of these goals absolute. Nothing must interfere with it. The second goal is absolute unless it interferes with the first; in which case the first goal takes precedence. The third goal is only absolute if it doesn't conflict with the first or second goal. And the fourth goal is absolute if it doesn't conflict with the first, second, or third.

## First Goal: Children must love reading.

This goal is absolute. No one—teachers, parents, librarians, curriculum directors, book reviewers—must do or recommend anything that puts in jeopardy children's love of reading.

The implications of this statement are enormous. It means that all of the skill exercises that children dislike—but are "good" for them—are not allowed if they cause a child to dislike reading. It means that parents and teachers must be very creative and empathetic in teaching kids to read. Anything children do that has the "reading" tag affixed to it must help children to love the subject.

Actually, reading experts are starting now to give lip service to the concept that children need to love reading. But they act in a schizophrenic way. They *say* it's important for children to love reading, but give no guidance and helpful hints on how teachers can accomplish instilling a love of reading. No, the reading experts are too busy insisting that teachers use multicultural literature and only "good" children's literature. Also, teachers should be teaching critical thinking skills—and probably even moving kids through a programmed reading series. And what if all these other activities make kids dislike reading—as well they might? Well, somehow that's not important.

At heart, few education experts really *believe* that it's crucial for children to love reading. What's crucial to them is that they get their own programs in place, their articles published, their place in the reading establishment secured. Does this happen by worrying about a child's feelings toward reading? Unfortunately, no.

I think my first goal would be a good place for all of the state committees creating school standards to start. *Children must love reading.* How do you find out if the children in a school district love reading? Easy—ask them, in an anonymous questionnaire: Do you (a) hate to read; (b) think reading is okay but not great; or

(c) love to read? Unless 80 percent of the school's children choose *c*, the school fails. Let me tell you, that would get schools interested in developing a love of reading.

And how important is this love of reading? The extensive survey of adult literacy that was released in 1993 showed that almost half of the adult population of our country can't read well enough to hold down a decent job. According to the 1994 results of the National Assessment of Educational Progress (the NAEP Reading Report Card) released in August of 1995, 25 percent of all twelfth graders scored *below* a basic reading level, and 66 percent scored below a proficient level. The figures are even worse for eighth grade; by twelfth grade a large percentage of poor readers have dropped out.

These figures are so horrifying that, as a country, we have to look past ideological barriers and resolve to do whatever it takes to nurture in our children a passion for reading, for learning. Our economic viability and our ability to function as a democratic country depend on our having a literate citizenry.

Maybe the heart of the issue is that we need the courage to trust our children: to trust that if we encourage their love of Doctor Who books and John Grisham thrillers, they'll also grow to love more difficult literature. We need the courage to trust that if we open up the world to them, by giving them a love of reading, they'll grow into thoughtful, literate, independent adults.

I've never been surprised that we have trouble helping children to love the multiplication tables—but *reading*? We're raising a generation of children whose last thought, when they're looking for entertainment, is to find a good book.

But you can change that—in your own house, at least. And the first step toward changing it is to keep your priorities straight. A love of reading is the greatest educational gift you can give your children—better than a private-school education, better than a networked computer, better even than a degree from Harvard.

A love of reading changes everything.

## Second Goal: Children should form a habit of reading.

In my previous book I gave many suggestions for helping children form a reading lifestyle. I talked about how to get kids reading who used to hate books, how to set up a reading-friendly house, finding that first wonderful book, and other tips. I was essentially talking about how to help your child form a habit of reading. But, considering the questions I've been asked by parents over the last year, I see that I wasn't clear about one point: when helping your children form a habit of reading, you must never put in jeopardy their love of reading.

I saw this when many parents told me they were setting up reading times for their children: after dinner, for example, their children would have to read for an hour.

While the goal—helping children form a habit of reading—is laudable, the means are risky. Many kids have told me they were turned off to reading by such tactics. And that means you're breaking the absolute, first law of reading.

A main focus of the present volume is to suggest ways of building a habit of reading while still encouraging a love of reading. For example, one way to help your children form a habit of reading, without trying to regiment their reading, is by encouraging series books. Avid readers tear through series books. Some avid readers reported to me that they read one a day. They are wonderful, and I think essential, for building up a habit of reading, and further developing a love of reading. Another way is to figure out your child's reading "path." After your daughter finishes the Baby-sitters Club books, what book might she like next? There are many practical things you can do to encourage a habit of reading.

Schools do very little to develop a habit of reading in children. In fact, many teachers actively discourage the kind of "binge reading" that develops a lifelong habit. You know the drill; it's probably happened to one of your children. Your daughter is in love with horses, and is currently racing (so to speak) through the Saddle Club series. The teacher, concerned that her interest seems too narrow, tells her no more horse books. Enough! Read something else!

Something else? Your daughter is at a loss. What else is there worth reading but horse books? Now, if your daughter's love of reading is strong enough, it may well survive this dictum. She may discover the Anne of Green Gables books and decide they're wonderful too. But she may not. She may be too angry at not being able to continue in her favorite series that she doesn't read anything. So I think the risk is too great. Let her binge her way through the Saddle Club books, and the Walter Farley books, and the Marguerite Henry books and, if she's a little older, the Dick Francis books. By then she's reading really well, and has a firm habit of reading. She'll be more than happy to try something else.

Besides discouraging binge reading by children, schools have one other fatal flaw when it comes to nurturing a reading habit. The following story is an illustration of this flaw:

My older daughter, Julie, is soccer coach at the University of New Hampshire. During summers she coaches at sports camps. Last summer she took her soccer team to a very wealthy camp in Maine for a tournament. The camp had everything: endless tennis courts, soccer fields, riding stables. They were even planning a nice lunch by the lake for the soccer players after the tournament.

It was during a New England heat wave, and temperatures were around ninety-five degrees, with comparable humidity. Julie's team was scheduled to play first, but there was no water on the field.

"We'll wait," she told the other coaches.

Twenty minutes passed, and a camp director jogged up. "What's the problem? Why the delay?"

"There's no water on the field," Julie said simply.

"Well," he pointed out brusquely, "there's a drinking fountain right across that other field."

"It's ninety-five degrees," Julie said. "If one of my players comes off the field with heat exhaustion, I'm not going to send her jogging across two fields to stand in line at a drinking fountain. My team won't play without water on the field."

Of course, she got her water when the director saw that she meant it. However, no one bothered to refill the water for the other teams.

"We won, of course," Julie told me later. "Mine was the only team that wasn't dying of thirst."

What does this have to do with reading? To me, the connection is clear:

There are no books in the schools.

Oh, there are *some* books: textbooks, class sets of a few fiction titles, and a small selection of library books. But the amount of high-interest, reading-habit-forming books in a school is about equivalent to one drinking fountain across two soccer fields during a heat wave.

As I interviewed my avid readers, one point came up again and again. They had all grown up either surrounded by books in their homes, or living within biking distance of a library. Not one of my avid readers got any but a small fraction of his reading material from school.

Few schools understand the crucial importance of having stacks and piles and bookshelves overflowing with comics and magazines and series books and joke books and every other kind of reading that kids can instantly love. Instead, schools put their money into computers and CD-ROMs and satellite hookups and camcorders and audiovisual libraries and everything you can imagine—except the one thing crucial to education: *books.* They don't understand that kids won't form a habit of reading without easy, instant access to huge quantities of enthralling reading material. So another key to forming a reading habit is to make sure your children have easy access to irresistible reading material. I'll talk about this more in later chapters.

My second suggestion to state standards committees concerns this need for children to form a habit of reading. Again, on that anonymous questionnaire, they should ask children how much time they spend, after school, doing reading they are really enjoying: (a) no time; (b) under fifteen minutes; (c) fifteen minutes to an hour; or (d) over an hour. At least 80 percent of the children have to circle *c* or *d* for the school to pass. A question like the above might persuade schools to spend a larger portion of their budgets on such truly crucial items as books.

But until this happens, you're going to have to be the supplier of endless reading material for your child.

Let's say you've done all this. Your child loves reading, and has formed a habit of reading. Your house is full of books she loves; she can get to the library any time, and she spends a good chunk of time every day reading just for her own pleasure. Things are chugging along very well. Even if you do nothing else, sooner or later your child will become an adult with very sophisticated literary skills.

But let's suppose that you'd like to do a little more. You want to make sure your child becomes a sophisticated reader. You want your child to learn to appreciate some of the more subtle aspects of literature, like imagery and theme. How can you go about this?

## Third Goal: Children should learn to read with a critical eye.

Keep in mind that this is the *third* goal; it only holds if it doesn't conflict with the first or second goals. In encouraging your children to develop critical reading skills, you must never put in jeopardy their love or habit of reading.

Of course, schools routinely put in jeopardy a student's love of reading and habit of reading. Actually, that isn't exactly true. So few students today are *developing* a love of reading and a habit of reading that schools aren't destroying a love of reading so much as preventing it from ever happening.

Kids who are not accomplished readers are usually very bored with the endless analyzing that teachers love to do. That's why an overwhelming majority of high school students will report to you that they hate poetry—their teachers are always making them go through every poem, line by line.

But here's the interesting thing: accomplished readers often love to talk about their reading. They *like* to discuss theme and character development and tone and narration. They like to compare a current book they're reading with other books they've read. They like to read the same book with other students so they can have better discussions.

In my course evaluations, I consistently find that my accomplished readers want to do more in-common reading with their classmates so they can discuss the reading in depth, while my less accomplished readers are bored even by the relatively small amount of in-common reading we do, and especially dislike discussing reading in depth.

It's a problem that, as a teacher, I'm always struggling with. As a parent, your job is a little easier, since you're only dealing with a couple of kids.

If your son has a love of reading and a habit of reading firmly in place, then it's perfectly all right to engage him in discussions of his reading. I'll give you many suggestions in later chapters on how to do this. For example, if he's a science-fiction reader, ask him what he thinks about Isaac Asimov. Is his writing dated now? How does he compare to Robert Heinlein and Arthur C. Clarke? What about writers who seem to combine fantasy and science fiction, as Piers Anthony does in his Cluster series?

Ask your daughter how Barbara Kingsolver's books compare to those of V. C. Andrews. They both feature strong heroines: how are they alike? What about Danielle Steel? Do her books have enough realistic detail to carry the somewhat improbable stories?

Even when your children are very young, you can start discussing their reading with them in such a way that they begin thinking critically.

To do this well, you should be aware of the stages of analysis kids go through. When kids are just starting to enjoy reading, I find that they do very little analysis. I always have students keep an account of their reading. Typically, in these reading journals, I'll get a bit of literal summary, and if I insist on some comment that goes beyond simple summary, I'll get something like this at the end of the summary: "Comment: Good."

After a bit, some more life works its way into kids' writing about books, but what you get is still mainly summary and personal response. The following journal entry deals with the first sixty-five pages of *Led Zeppelin: Hammer of the Gods*, by Stephen Davis. The underlining was done by the student:

> This is the hardest book I've ever read <u>that I love</u>. I've read every page of this book with a smile on my face. It's just basically been about Jimmy Page and how he was raised and the little unknown rock band's he's played with. Then it started describing the other members of led Zeppelin, and how they grew up. Now it's all come together, Now I know how Led Zeppelin was formed. I'm really into this book.

When kids become comfortable about giving their personal responses to books, adults should never belittle their enthusiasms. "It sounds wonderful," I always say. "You're really getting good at finding interesting books."

I really can't stress strongly enough the importance of validating your children's response to books. It's obviously unlikely they'll love the same books you do. But if you want them to have the self-confidence to keep thinking critically about their reading, you have to respect their opinions. Their opinions will change and develop, but only if they have the self-confidence to keep forming opinions.

I have one line I always use with the kids who read so poorly that they have real trouble finding a book they'll enjoy. When they finally find one, I'll say, "Wow, it *must* be a really good book, if you like it." And when they're ready for another book, I'll give them the book that's my best shot, and say, "I wish you'd try this one. I'm not sure if kids will like it. But I know how particular you are, and I figure if *you* like it, it's really a great book." I can get them almost every time.

After a reader becomes confident that his personal response to books is accepted and valid, you can start pushing for a little more. I tell the students in my American and British literature classes, for example, that they need to write more than summary and personal response; they need to talk about such things as character development, theme, narration, and imagery—or perhaps compare this current book with others that they've read.

When kids first start doing this, they typically write a summary, and then, after the summary, they'll write a short paragraph trying to analyze the book a bit. What follows is a typical example. The young man is writing about a Spenser mystery by Robert P. Parker, called *The Judas Goat*. After his summary he writes:

> I think that Mr. Dixon learned that revenge is not as sweet as he thought it would be. And I think that the blond learned that crime doesn't pay, no matter how much is at stake. And finally I think that Spenser just reaffirmed how much he loves Susan. I liked this book a lot and I would give it an 8.

He makes some nice, insightful comments, but doesn't really deal with the book in a comprehensive critical fashion.

But after students have done a good deal of reading, and have gotten used to talking or writing about their reading in a critical fashion, I get wonderful, insightful comments embedded all the way through their summary. That's when I know they're reading, at least much of the time, with a critical eye. What follows is a summary of one week's reading from an American Literature student I had. The journal entry was much too long to reproduce in its entirety here—hence all of the ellipses—but I think you can get the flavor of it:

> Nov. 23rd.
> This week I finished <u>Lasher</u> by Anne Rice (277 pages) and I read all of <u>The Accidental Tourist</u> by Anne Tyler (342 p.)
> One of the really good things about Anne Rice is that after I've finished her book, I really <u>believe</u> her, whereas with Stephen King and Dean Koontz, I'll say to myself, "Ho-hum, that was an okay story," and of course I'll never think that anything like it could actually happen. I think I believe Anne Rice because she textures everything so well, and puts in significant detail in all the right places. For example, an "Anne Rice" detail would be that Rowan Mayfair's Aunt Evelyn was having an affair with her [Aunt Evelyn's] cousin Stella. A "Dean Koontz" detail would be that [if he wrote the

plot of Lasher] Aunt Evelyn has wispy gray hair. . . . Anne Rice has a sneaky way of getting you to believe her darkly luscious tales. If I had to make a food analogy of Anne Rice's books, I would say that her novels are like cherry cordials— dark chocolate with ruby red, luminous cherries hidden inside. Yum . . .

I really enjoyed reading The Accidental Tourist. If The Accidental Tourist was a kind of food, it would be a chocolate sundae. Sweet and satisfying, and very easy to swallow.

Of course, the writing of this student is wonderful, but it's not unique: I probably had about ten students this last year that wrote with all of her insight, if not with her embedded imagery and metaphor. You can see how sophisticated her response to literature is—she's simply light-years ahead of the kid who read the Led Zeppelin book, or even the kid who read the Spenser novel. (Actually, I always had, with her, the sinking feeling that she was light-years ahead of me.)

But I think you can see that the foundation she has—her delight in reading, the amount of reading under her belt—isn't something that can be shortcut with any skills teaching. At least, not with any skills teaching I've ever heard of. With a student like this, all I know to do is draw her out and discuss her insights to help her gain confidence and become motivated to do some critical thinking and comparing that she otherwise might not do. Ironically, a student with this kind of dazzling insight often becomes quiet in class discussions—reluctant to take on a more impassioned speaker who is arguing a much more simplistic viewpoint. I don't know why, but often students who hold more one-dimensional views on issues (usually the mediocre readers) argue their views more forcefully. So children and teenagers who are acquiring large frameworks of knowledge, and starting to see how complex most situations are, really do need support from an interested adult.

Therefore I think you should work a bit on drawing your children out, and helping them to start reading with a critical eye. Just make sure that nothing you do interferes with their love of reading or their habit of reading—especially since only avid readers have the foundation to read with critical acumen in any case. Turning kids off to reading by insisting on too much analysis and criticism is winning a battle only to lose the war.

So let's say your kids are reading with a critical eye, and still maintaining their love and habit of reading. What's next?

## Fourth Goal: Children should learn to appreciate classical and multicultural literature.

In addition to our extremely rich tradition of American and European literature, outstanding works from all around the world are now becoming easily available to us in translation. We hope, of course, that our children will someday read and appreciate this great reservoir. I've always thought that literature afforded a much more accurate and compelling view of different eras and cultures than a history book could ever do.

But keep in mind that this is the *fourth* goal of reading. Helping a child appreciate the world's great literary works must never put in jeopardy her love of reading, her habit of reading, or her willingness to read with a critical eye.

This is something schools do *routinely*—without any thought at all. Everyone in a class, for example, may be assigned to read *Great Expectations*. Never mind that only about one tenth of the class reads well enough to be able to enjoy a long, somewhat rambling, nineteenth-century novel. Your son stares at the thick book in dread, a knot in his stomach. How is he ever going to get through it?

We want our kids to read either classical or other "good" literature or—the latest wrinkle—multicultural literature. Never mind that only competent readers can really understand and enjoy classical literature. Never mind that most multicultural literature pushed in the schools is boring even to the group it showcases. And, especially, never mind that by forcing kids to read literature they dislike—literature they aren't ready for—we ensure that they will *never* love reading, and *never* become avid, independent readers. None of these considerations is as important as our belief that kids *should* read the *Odyssey*, and *shouldn't* read *Salem's Lot*, by Stephen King. And we conveniently overlook the harsh irony that it is only kids who read books like *Salem's Lot* who will ever be ready to read such great literature as the *Odyssey*.

How many students are really capable of reading, with enjoyment and excellent understanding, complex, classical works? Only 7 percent of the twelfth graders in this country test as advanced readers, according to the NAEP, which matches perfectly with the 7 to 8 percent of twelfth graders who scored over 600 on the college board exams before the scores were recalibrated upward.

I think this is what many teachers—and curriculum directors and principals and school committees and standards committees, since teachers often have very little say about what they teach—don't understand: a student who is an avid, sophisticated reader will easily love complex, classic works of literature; a mediocre reader will not—cannot! You just can't take a kid who has never read anything but school-assigned reading, and expect him to be able to read with the fluency and skill required to read difficult works of literature.

The horror stories of adults not understanding this are legion, ranging from the required summer reading lists to the recommended reading lists that book critics publish, to the assigned reading in junior high and senior high school English classes. It's my own feeling that this drive to control what kids read—to ensure that they read literature the adult community approves of—is a major factor in the reading crisis today.

Once, at a rather slow book signing, I spent some time looking through various school summer reading lists at Barnes & Noble. Wow. Every single boring, difficult book that I had ever seen in schools was on those lists, including some newer titles to make the lists multicultural. There were, of course, a few classic titles that most kids enjoy—*Of Mice and Men* and *East of Eden* by John Steinbeck, and *To Kill a Mockingbird* by Harper Lee, and these make sense to recommend, but the lists I saw were filled with sure losers: *The Old Man and the Sea* by Ernest Hemingway (only good for older, philosophical students), *Ethan Frome* by Edith Wharton (I haven't found any students who reliably like this book), *A Separate Peace* by John Knowles (a wonderful book, but only for wonderful readers), and so on. Some of the multicultural titles were worse: *The Bluest Eye* by Toni Morrison (just too hard for any but sophisticated readers), *The Road to Coorain* by Jill Ker Conway, a book that has no dialogue for the first thirty-four pages. It's a lovely book, but not for a turned-off fifteen-year-old.

But suppose your son or daughter is ready for some complex, challenging books. What do you give your son after his three hundredth fantasy book, when he's expressed a willingness to try something else? What do you give your daughter when she's finally grown tired of Mary Higgins Clark?

The principle is this: Look for the kind of books your daughter is reading now, and then look for classics that are along the same line. For example, if your daughter has loved stories of families—the Little House books by Laura Ingalls Wilder, for example—you might give her *Little Women* by Louisa May Alcott, or *The Secret Garden* by Frances Hodgson Burnett. If she's a little older, and has raced through teen romances, encourage her to try *Pride and Prejudice* by Jane Austen. If your son has enjoyed war novels or historical fiction, he'll probably enjoy Dickens's *Tale of Two Cities* (he's a *good* reader, remember). If he's a very good reader, and loves history, you might even suggest Tolstoy's *War and Peace;* a couple of very good, avid-reading boys in my classes have enjoyed it. In chapter 7 I'll give you more ideas of the kinds of classics different kids might enjoy.

Of course, it may well happen that your daughter will pick up *Pride and Prejudice* and decide it's really dumb. You don't have to agree with her, but you have to respect and encourage her opinions. So you don't try to force her to read the book or argue her out of her dislike for the book.

I had a student who had read a Shakespeare play with a group at school, and was trying to decide what kind of paper to write.

"Why don't you do a review?" I suggested. "Something like 'The Best and Worst of *A Midsummer Night's Dream*'?"

"Oh, no, I couldn't do that," he said, horrified. "My teacher last year told me that I could never criticize Shakespeare, because he's a famous writer, and I'm just a kid."

What a terrible thing for a teacher to say! We can't pick and choose what we want our children to think critically about. If we won't let them think critically about Shakespeare, why do we think they'll react critically to the speeches of politicians—or of salesmen? Critical thinking isn't something one turns on and off.

My daughter had a similar experience in a course she was taking that dealt with minority writers. The teacher, who was African-American, told the white students that they couldn't criticize any black writers, since they (the white students) couldn't possibly understand the black experience. The result, inevitably, was that my daughter completely shut down in the course.

Let's briefly discuss so-called multicultural literature. I say "so-called" because *all* literature is multicultural to someone. For example, *A Separate Peace*, by John Knowles, is multicultural, and foreign, to an inner-city black teenager.

I find—no surprise—that children are hungry to read books that describe their own experiences.

The problem is that there are so few readable books that describe the experiences of minority youngsters. Many of the books written by minority writers are too sophisticated—written in too literary a manner—for most of the minority kids I get in my classes. And that is too bad, because these kids—all kids—long to read books that help them make sense of their own experiences. Note to publishers and writers: We need more *popular* black fiction. We need a black Stephen King, a black Danielle Steel, a black John Grisham.

One African-American writer that I can count on my kids loving is Terry McMillan. Her three books—*Mamma, Disappearing Acts*, and *Waiting to Exhale*—are read by virtually all of the young black women in my classes, and by a considerable number of the young black men. But because of the amount of profanity in her books, and the explicit sexual descriptions, I doubt that her books will ever show up in an official high school curriculum.

If kids grow up reading literature that reflects their own experiences, when they are avid, sophisticated readers, they will branch out and read about other cultures.

For many minority kids, it's a wonderful, breathtaking moment when they first read a book that really seems to come out of their own lives. A Chinese-American girl who read *The Joy Luck Club*, by Amy Tan, wrote, "I used to think my mother was crazy. Now I see she's just Chinese."

So whatever kind of parent you are—Irish-American, African-American, Japanese-American—try to find books first that come out of your own culture for your children to read. And after they've seen that literature can reflect their own lives, you can gently introduce them to books that reflect the lives of other groups.

In my experience, what happens with very good readers is that they start to identify with people from much broader backgrounds than their own. Many of my excellent-reading white, middle-class girls love *The Joy Luck Club* because they see something of their own mother-daughter relationships. When you try to move children to books that describe experiences foreign to them, I think it's helpful if, initially, there's some point of identification in the books. I had a refugee girl from Cambodia in my class a few years back, who, from the ages of six to twelve, had lived through the whole horror of Pol Pot's regime. In the camps she used to spend her entire days collecting single grains of rice; she watched her father being tortured, and eventually lost him in her escape. The book she fell in love with in my class was *Black Boy* by Richard Wright. Although it's the story of a black Southern youth during the early twentieth century in America, she could identify with the oppression he lived under, and the spirit he showed to overcome it.

I had another interesting experience with a group of refugees from terrifying circumstances. These were children who had fled Laos during the 1970s, and had swum across a river under Communist gunfire to reach a refugee camp. There they languished for a number of years before finally being admitted to the United States. The boys loved superhero comic books; they read all I could find. The girls loved Harlequin romances. I finally realized that they wanted to escape to a world where good always triumphed, a world where lives ended happily. And what was wrong with that? At that point in their lives, maybe *Batman* did them more good than *Ethan Frome* ever could have.

So I really think the key to helping children learn about other cultures through literature is to do it on an individual basis. Luckily, as a parent you can do that. Look for books that, although by an author of a different culture, speak in some way to your own children. Don't look at books as medicine that your children should take because it's good for them. Look for books they can easily love. As they become more and more adept as readers, the kinds of books they can easily love will multiply until they'll be able to find pleasure and excitement in the most complicated works of literature.

But you can't shortcut this process. You need to follow the hierarchy of goals, and watch your children grow naturally into avid, sophisticated readers. The following chapters offer suggestions for things you can do to help them along the way.

# Strategies and Tips for Preschoolers

## HAVE LOTS OF BOOKS

Books everywhere! That's your motto. The main similarity among my high school readers was that they all reported having had easy access to books while growing up. What follows are some tips for acquiring a book-filled house for your preschoolers.

### 1. Buy your preschoolers one book each on every shopping trip.

The great thing about picture books is they're so plentiful and cheap. And all kinds of stores are now carrying them: supermarkets, variety stores, music stores, pet shops, drugstores. Your children can choose the lucky books that will make it back to your house today.

Of course, you may have to put a dollar limit on which books they can choose from ("Today is small paperback day, kids. You can have any one of *these* books, but I can't afford the books on that other shelf today. Maybe next time!"). You might encourage your child to get a very *little* book on those days. They're cheap for you, and easy for toddlers to hold. I know that some days it will seem as if you just don't have even that extra two or three dollars, but consider all the advantages to buying each child a book every trip.

- Your children will see that you value books and reading as much as you value eggs and milk, a new dog collar, or plastic trash bags.
- Your children will get into the habit of looking at books with an eye to buying one. This becomes very important when they grow to be teenagers and have a bit of money to spend. Maybe it won't all go for CDs and video rentals if they are in the habit of buying books. Many of my teenagers don't even *think* of going to buy a book. When John Grisham books were sweeping my classes, they'd come to me and report that the library copy was out, and my copies were out. How could they do the reading for their reading journal for me? I'd explode, "Buy the book! Big deal—it's six ninety-five. How often to you spend six or seven dollars renting videos?" But it simply doesn't occur to many kids to walk into a bookstore and pick out a book.
- Your children will eventually acquire their own carefully chosen library. With any luck, they'll keep adding to it their whole lives.
- Your children can have their favorite books instantly available so that they (or you) can read them over and over again. Almost all of my avid readers mentioned having reread their favorite books many times.
- You'll find that having children absorbed in books while being pushed through a supermarket is infinitely preferable to having them absorbed in grabbing potato chips, or diving at large Campbell's soup displays.
- Your children, by choosing books they like, may help move the direction of the publishing industry away from acquiring children's books that might win awards (decided by adults) to choosing books that appeal to children. That's already happening with fiction for elementary-school-aged kids. Writers that ten-year-olds love, such as R. L. Stine and Ann Martin, are ruling the juvenile best-seller lists, and are encouraging publishers to look for other, similar writers. Money talks.

## 2. Buy books at garage sales and flea markets. Watch classified ads.

Children's picture books can be literally a dime a dozen at garage sales and flea markets. You should really stock up. Even if your children don't like every single book you bring home, that's okay. You probably only paid a quarter. Heck, an ice cream cone costs a lot more than that. And it's necessary—it's *crucial*—that you have a lot of books in your house. If your children came with you to the garage sale, I'd tell them you'll pay for any books they choose, up to whatever dollar limit you can afford. Be a sport! See how many books you can get for the price of one video rental. One mother of an avid reader described to me the books she used to buy: "I used to buy *so* many books. One day I looked around and was really shocked. Maybe I'd overdone it." But she didn't. Her daughter is a wonderful reader.

Here's why you want garage sale and flea market books:

- These are books you only paid a few cents for, so who cares if your kids get jelly all over them—or cut out the pictures to paper their room? It will keep you much more relaxed over the hard usage that avid readers sometimes mete out to their favorite books. One mother told me that she used to give old *Reader's Digest*s to her daughter when she was really tiny and was going through the tear-out-the-pages stage. The result was that her daughter grew up to love books.
- It will mean you will have a great *quantity* of books around—and living in houses with great quantities of books was the one constant I heard from my avid readers.
- You can try new kinds of books that a particular child doesn't like yet—but might grow to like if they're readily available.
- I think you'll find that some of the older out-of-print picture books are wonderful and impossible to find anywhere else.

## 3. Take your preschoolers regularly to the library.

Many of the avid readers I interviewed reported living close to a library. They all reported spending their summers going through huge stacks of library books. "I'd go and get about thirty books and take them all out and read them all that day. Then I'd take them back and get some more," one girl told me. I'm sure she was exaggerating a bit, but I started thinking it was more important to live close to a library than to live in a good school district.

Regular library trips are important because:

- Children can try out new books at no cost. If they find that one special book they really love, they can buy it on a shopping trip.
- Many new, beautifully written and illustrated hardcovers are really out of pocketbook range for most parents. But any child can have access to them in a library.
- You can start to build a *habit* of library attendance. It's easy to raise enthusiasm in preschoolers for a library visit, but it's harder when kids get older. So build the habit now.
- Most children's librarians are very friendly and warm to children, especially to preschoolers. It's important children learn early on to like and respect librarians, because older children—like many of my students—don't like, and even fear, librarians. "They *are* scary," one of my high school students wrote. It's ridiculous, but there is a stereotype of librarians (mean, abrupt, only interested in getting every book back on time) that kids not familiar with librarians often accept. And this keeps older kids out of libraries.
- Most libraries also have social activities such as story hours or book clubs. These are important because children see that reading isn't valued just in their own families. Lots of other people love reading too. Also, your kids may make other book-loving friends. And story hour is another chance to see librarians in a friendly role.
- You can use the library visits to stock up on books for yourself. It's important that your child see you reading too.

## READ BOOKS ALOUD

Much has been written about the importance of reading aloud to children. I just have a few points to add.

## 1. Your children must have absolute choice about which books they want to hear.

I know. I know. I really thought if I had to read *Curious George Goes to the Hospital* one more time, *I* was going to be ready for the hospital. But my kids all loved that book. So pretend that you find it a good book too. Smile and just *read* it. It's very important. Here's why:

- My poor readers report feeling very disenfranchised when it came to reading. They felt no one cared about their likes and dislikes, their tastes. By allowing your children to choose, you're validating their taste in books.
- You are also validating your children's ability to make critical judgments. Of course their taste is not your taste. They're *kids*. But if they don't feel that their opinions are respected now, they'll either become rebels or stop making critical judgments—both dead-end ways of operating.
- You often don't know why a particular book is so appealing to a particular child. My older daughter had frequent doctors' visits and hospitalizations owing to ear problems. I think *Curious George Goes to the Hospital* soothed her worries. Maybe your son *loves* the Richard Scarry books because he's lonely, and so loves the little animal friends that people Scarry's books.

## 2. Ham up the books when you read them aloud.

Many of my avid readers have very fond memories of certain books because they were read with such enthusiasm and gusto by adults in their lives. One girl recalled fondly a teacher who, when reading a book about witches, used different "witch" voices for the different characters. After that, she went on and read all of the witch books she could find. Here are some other reasons for being outrageous and silly when you read:

- Laughing together over a story with your children brings you closer together with them, and makes story time that much more pleasurable and memorable.
- Doing different character voices helps your children better to com-

prehend the tone and nuances of a story. One of the major differences between my avid readers and mediocre readers lies in their ability to understand subtleties of tone and theme in literature.
- Jazzing up a story helps keep you, the reader, awake too.

### 3. Use your special talents to make reading come alive for your children.

A mother of one of my avid readers told me that she used to act out the stories she read with her daughter. She loved doing it—they did it all the time, she told me—but she also cautioned me that parents shouldn't do this unless they really enjoy acting. She suggested that an artistic parent might want to draw pictures with her children.

I loved these ideas, although I never thought to do any of them with my children. The mother also mentioned that the daughter was very afraid of the wolf in *The Three Little Pigs*, so she had her daughter play the wolf's part when they acted that one. The daughter loved doing it, and even dressed up like a wolf for Halloween.

### 4. Talk through books to very young children.

One-year-olds and most two-year-olds don't have sophisticated enough listening skills to follow any but the most simple books. That is why books like *Goodnight Moon* are such classics. So no matter what book your one-year-old grabs, talk through the story. Like this:

- Point to a picture on the first page and say in a bright voice to your toddler, "Look, kitty cat!" Your toddler will probably pat the picture and might even repeat the word. That's fine. Audience participation is always good. With luck, maybe he'll point out the next riveting item: "Dog! Look, dog!"
- Move through the book at a pace dictated by your child's activity level. If he's squirming after two pages, flip to the end and say something like, "And now everyone goes to bed. Like you!"
- Gradually, as your child's attention span lengthens, start really reading parts of the story. But be ready at any instant to abandon

ship and and make up a good, snappy ending: "But the turtle didn't want to eat peanut butter anymore. He wanted to crash his Tonka trucks into the sandbox, just like you do! Want to go out back and play now?"

- Remember, the key thing is that your toddler enjoys story time. The instant you feel his enjoyment waning, wrap it up. He doesn't need to be able to listen to *War and Peace.* He's *two,* for heaven's sake. His attention span for stories will lengthen, but only if story time is always enjoyable for him.

## 5. Read comic books aloud.

This probably isn't something you think to do, but enough of my excellent readers report loving comics as kids, that I think you should try it. One of the all-time best English students to go through our high school described his comic book experience to me: "I loved comic books. Before I could read, my dad used to read comic books to me and show me the pictures. Spider-Man, The Incredible Hulk, X-Men, The Adventurers, you know, Daredevil, everything." You may be reluctant to read fairly violent superhero comics to preschoolers (although avid readers are almost never violent kids), but certainly there's no objection to Disney or Harvey comics (Casper the Friendly Ghost, Richie Rich, etc.). These are easy to find in dime stores and discount stores.

Here's why you should read them:

- Most children already feel friendly toward comic-book characters because they've seen them in cartoons on television. If they love cartoons, they'll like comics. And watching cartoons doesn't help a child acquire literacy skills. Reading, and being read to, does. So comics are better! Don't rent a Donald Duck video. Buy a comic! They're cheaper, more interesting, and more likely to help kids love reading.
- Comics usually have plot lines of much greater interest to children than most picture books. They motivate children to try to figure out what happens next from the pictures. They keep a kid's interest.
- Most comics suitable for young children are funny. Kids love anything funny.

## 6. Read or recite poetry.

Young children have a natural love for rhythm and rhyme, and I think thirty or forty years ago children had more exposure to poetry. I can remember that I, along with all of my friends, had a little record player and a selection of records. I'd sit on the floor, play my favorite records over and over again, and sing along. One of my sisters did that so often with her favorite song—which was *Bouncy, Bouncy Bally*, as I recall—that my older brother finally threw the record down the stairs until it broke. But I don't see kids listening to songs over and over again as much today. I think videos and organized play groups have pretty much supplanted such simple pleasures. And a love of rhythm and rhyme are the beginnings of a love of poetry.

I know you probably don't want to sit your two-year-old daughter down on the floor with your expensive CD player, but I think you should somehow work songs and poetry into her daily routine. Look for poetry books in the library, buy a sturdy child's tape recorder, some music or poetry tapes, and show her how to work it. Be sure to try Mother Goose books. Many children love them.

If you have a good auditory memory, and can easily memorize poetry, you might also recite poems for her as you move through the day. I used to do this with my kids, and we all really enjoyed it. I'd change the lyrics a little to fit the situation.

I remember that when my younger brother Jim was about two, and I was in high school, I used to change the lyrics of "Puff the Magic Dragon" for him. "Little Jimmy O'Grady loved that magic Puff!" I'd sing. One day Nancy, another sister, heard him singing it. "It's Jackie Paper!" she scornfully told him. "Not Jimmy O'Grady." I felt a little guilty—as though I'd set him up—but he did like poetry and songs then!

And it's important that your preschool children like poetry and songs. Here's why:

- Poetry and songs develop an ear for language. In poetry the sound and cadence of words are so important. Early exposure to different types of poetry can sensitize a child to nuances of language.

- Some children may take readily to memorizing poetry and songs also. I wouldn't push this—auditory memory is everything when it comes to memorizing, and many people are not so gifted—but if your child starts reciting songs and poems, be properly impressed and encouraging.
- Early exposure to poetry may help prevent the dislike of poetry that sets in when teachers insist that students all know what trochaic and iambic pentameter mean. Also, much of the poetry that your kids will be exposed to in school will be really dumb (Look at the train. Toot! Toot!) or just plain too hard and boring. If your son enters school with a real love of poetry, first of all, he may actually like some of the poetry other children find difficult and boring. Second, even if he doesn't like the school poems, he'll still know that he likes *poetry*.

A love of poetry, and a willingness to read it, helps make a kid a more careful and critical reader altogether.

### 7. Don't always be willing to read books on demand.

I've seen some preschoolers get fairly obnoxious about pestering parents for stories. Yes, it is important to read to children, but it's more important to raise children who realize the world doesn't revolve around them. I don't think parents should feel guilty when it's the end of a long day—the kids are bathed, dinner is finished, laundry is folded, lunches are packed, stories are read—and your children want yet one more story. No! Put the youngsters to bed with some books of their own to look at, put your feet up, and read the paper. Consider:

- No one—not siblings, teachers, friends, relatives—likes spoiled, whiny children.
- If you're always willing to read to your children, what's the incentive for them to learn to read themselves?
- Your goal in reading, as in everything else, is to produce joyous, independent children. When you always drop everything you're doing to read to your children, you risk sending them the message

that they are incapable of getting pleasure from books themselves. Provide the books, but, sometimes, give yourself a break.

## TEACHING KIDS TO READ THEMSELVES

In my first book, *Parents Who Love Reading, Kids Who Don't*, I went into a good deal of detail about how I taught my older daughter to read before she was in school—and why I wished I'd taught my other two children to read also. I recommended teaching easy phonics (first letter sounds, mostly), and using everyday activities to start building a sight vocabulary. I didn't—and *don't*—recommend buying expensive commercial phonics programs; I think it's much better to put your money into children's books and comics. So that's my first recommendation: Don't buy expensive phonics programs. Instead:

**1. Buy as many early-reader books as you can afford.**
My younger daughter finally taught herself to read. Here's her account: "I remember the first time I read a book. I was sitting on a swing set in the backyard and it was *Fox in Sox*. When I couldn't get a word, I'd run around to the front of the house 'cause you were sitting on the porch, and then go back. It seemed like a lot of fun to figure them out myself. Plus the idea of a fox in socks seemed so incredibly funny."

Here are some good reasons to give your children early-reader books:

- Kids find them funnier and more appealing than the programmed readers they'll get in school.
- Some early-reader books are really simple—they have only one or two words on a page—but the boost to a child's self-esteem when he can read a whole book, all by himself, is immeasurable. And so what if the whole book comprises only ten words? Who's counting?
- With any luck, your young reader will want to read stories to everyone, once she starts. That's great! Just listen in a rapt manner; don't correct mistakes or help figure out a word unless she asks.

Your job is just to be an enthralled, excited audience. The mistakes will clear up as she gains practice.

- Even when your beginning reader is getting a little smoother, you should still provide him with plenty of easy-reading books. It's how he'll build self-confidence in himself as a reader. *Never* say, "Oh, that book is too easy for you." One refrain I heard over and over from my avid readers was that they loved rereading easy childhood favorites.

## 2. Buy easy-reading comics.

There are two kinds of comics: the comic-strip variety, which are collected in large anthologies and sold in bookstores (e.g., Garfield and The Far Side), and the regular kind of comic books sold at newsstands and in comic-book stores (X-Men, Donald Duck, etc.). The rule of thumb is that funny comics are much easier to read than superhero or adventure comics. Look at the comics yourself. You should be able to tell. Obviously, for teaching children to read, you want the easy, funny comics. Garfield might be a good one to start with, or one of the Disney ones.

Start by reading the whole comic to your children. Then, gradually, have them start to take parts—initially the easiest, simplest parts—and read the comic like a play. As they start reading better, they can read the longer parts. Pretty soon they can be reading the whole comic without you. (When they're ready to do this, but lack the confidence, start them on the comic, and then pretend to get very sleepy, or busy. They'll finish themselves.)

Once you find a comic they like, buy as many as you can find. Buy in quantity, and leave them in all the places your children congregate. I used to read *The Want Advertiser*, a local newsletter, and buy up collections of Richie Rich comics that people were selling off.

## 3. Have a special book-looking-at time with your preschooler.

This was something another mother told me about. She really needed a time to rest every day, but her preschooler no longer napped (I'm sure we can all identify with this situation). So she'd tell him that he could either lie down in his room and rest or—if he was very good and quiet—lie in her room with her and quietly look at books while she rested. It worked for her, and the kid grew up to be a great reader. I have a feeling my own kids would have looked at books for about five minutes, and then would have started jumping on my bed. But it might work for you. It's worth a try.

And you could do this quiet, book-looking-at time in other places—in the kitchen while you're making dinner, in the car, in restaurants while you're waiting to be served. Certainly at night, after you've read your daughter a bedtime story, you can leave other books by the bed, or in the crib, so she can look at them a bit on her own. And then you might sit by her bed for a few minutes with a book of your own. You can have a close reading time together. There are three reasons why this is valuable:

- When children study books on their own, they sometimes find out that they can read a little. Maybe just a word here or there, but the feeling is intoxicating for kids. Of course, a lot of the time they'll have memorized the story after hearing it so much, but I think many kids really start out reading that way. They memorize the book, study the words, and then remember what some of the words look like. *Voilà!* They're reading.
- The other important thing you're doing by setting up regular book-looking-at times every day is building a habit of reading. If your children pore over books initially during close, happy times with you, I think they'll be much more likely to continue reading on their own. A habit of reading is the next most important thing to a love of reading, and if you can start building that habit in your preschooler, you're way ahead of the game. Of course, you would never push this if it made your children—in any way—dislike reading. But a habit of reading built by having close, happy reading times with you might help your children to continue the habit of reading later. A habit of reading is what most of my high school students who are mediocre readers lack. They never have time to read, they constantly complain to me. A firmly entrenched habit of reading, going back to their preschool days, would make all the difference.

Something else that can make all the difference, I think, is a preschooler having a number of friends who are also interested in books.

## MAKE BOOKS PART OF YOUR PRESCHOOLER'S SOCIAL SCENE

As I was interviewing the avid readers in high school, I noticed that many of them were good friends with one another. Of course, good readers tend to be in the highest classes, and so they were often in class together. But some of these friendships went way back; I had groups of two or three kids who had been friends since elementary school, or before. And they were kids who traded books with each other, and made recommendations for each other's reading. It seemed to me that having a reading friend or two helped keep some of these kids reading.

Conversely, a few of my avid readers were rather lonely as young children. I wasn't sure whether because they read so much they didn't have time for friends, or whether they spent so much time reading *because* they didn't seem to have the knack for easily making friends. I know in some ways I was kind of a lonely kid too, and loved books about groups of friends, such as the Betsy-Tacy books. I could pretend I was part of that warm, friendly group.

So, the more I thought about it, the more important it seemed, if possible, to try to bring preschoolers together with books *and* friends. We want our kids to read, and of course we also want our kids to have friends. Here are a few suggestions for trying to make that happen:

### 1. When friends come over, suggest reading games.
You might help your child and friends to play bookstore or library, for example. You can help them set up shelves, get a play cash register, that kind of thing. You can even make it the kind of bookstore with tables and refreshments. The kids can sit at the little tables munching on snacks and chatting about which would be

the best books to buy. The point is, books would become topics of discussion; reading would be a social thing.

You can also suggest that your preschooler and friends pretend they are characters from some of their favorite books. They can pretend that they are each one of the Berenstain Bears, for example, or Clifford, the big red dog.

A thrift store is a great help in these pretend games. Maybe your daughter and her friends like fairy tales. At thrift stores or Goodwill stores you can usually get very fancy dresses, high heels, scarves, even costume jewelry sometimes—all of the necessities for playing fairy princesses. And the playing and the reading will support each other. The more they play at being princesses, the more eager they are to hear, and look at, books about princesses. And vice versa. Witches are something else that little girls love to read about, and love to play.

Ultimately, this kind of play will help your children to be better readers in a couple of ways:

- They'll be used to talking about books with kids their own age. If they're playing bookstore, and deciding which books to buy, they'll be thinking about books in an evaluative manner. This is a skill that it's very hard for some high school kids to acquire. All they seem to be able to do with books is recount plot summaries. If you can get your preschoolers to work book discussions into their play, you'll be setting a good basis for later critical thinking. Of course, you're not going to push this. The *crucial* thing is that preschoolers enjoy any activity related to books or reading. That is much more important than their having literary discussions.
- Pretending to be book characters also makes your children sensitive to character differences. One of the magical things about reading, as I've said, is that it draws kids into understanding characters who are very different from themselves. And trying to act out favorite characters has *got* to be much more beneficial than sitting on a floor watching characters on a television screen.

I'd really encourage *any* pretending that your children do.

## 2. Plan teddy bear picnics.

A friend of mine told me about this idea, which is popular among the nursery school crowd. For a daughter's fifth birthday, they invited her friends to bring their favorite teddy bears, and have a picnic in the park together. The kids had a lot of fun putting the teddy bears on swings, flinging them down slides—that sort of thing. You could just add the element of books. My local library lists more than a hundred juvenile fiction books that feature teddy bears! So ask everyone to bring their favorite teddy bear *and* their favorite teddy bear book. After the teddy bears have had their wild fling on the playground equipment, everyone could gather for refreshments and teddy bear stories. And the party favors would be—of course—a variety of teddy bear paperback books.

Mostly, of course, you would plan something like this just for fun, but it would also help kids to see that books can be compared and put into categories. Many of my high school kids are completely oblivious of this fact.

"How are those two books alike?" I'll say.

"Well, they're not!" they'll tell me. "There's nothing alike about them. They're about two different kids."

"Well, both kids are growing up . . ." I'll gently push.

"Well, yeah . . ."

You get the idea. It takes a while, but I can usually push them to start seeing similarities. It would be a lot easier, I know, if I had kids who were used to finding similarities in their reading. But again, this would just be a nice side benefit of social/book parties like this. Mostly they are to bring your child together with books, friends, and fun.

## 3. Make sure there are plenty of books around the areas where your preschooler hangs out with friends.

The kitchen is probably the most important place, since preschoolers eat almost as continually as teenagers. They eat much less, true, but it seems to me that my three- and four-year-olds were continually having little snacks. So while your son and his friends are perched on their chairs waiting for their crackers and juice, make sure there are some enticing picture books on the table. With any luck, your son's friend will grab one to look at—since it's probably new to him—and all of a sudden those old books will acquire a new glamour in your son's eyes. If they're really getting into reading—or talking—the books to each other, dawdle a bit over the snack preparation.

Cars are another key place to have books. We all know how much time we spend in cars, driving kids around. (A friend of mine said, wistfully, that a cleaning lady would be nice, but what she really *needed* was a chauffeur.) Again, on the principle that kids like anything they haven't seen before, your child's books will probably be very attractive to his friends. And surely kids looking through books while they're all buckled up in the backseat is preferable to almost anything else they might try to do—like taking off their shoes.

Why does reading alongside friends help develop a love of reading?

Even preschoolers are very aware of the "in" thing to do. My son, at the age of three, started a new nursery school and noticed on the first day that he was the only one who napped with a pacifier. Well, forget using that pacifier. He wouldn't take it to school anymore. Of course, that meant he didn't *nap* anymore—which I, along with his teachers, thought was a bad trade-off. But our opinion didn't matter. None of the other guys used pacifiers. He wasn't about to, either.

So try to make *reading* be the "in" thing for your child to do with his friends. Since the advent of the VCR, I think movie watching has become the social glue holding together many social occasions for kids. And that's fine. There are some wonderful movies—and some wonderful peaceful moments parents can have while kids are watching these wonderful movies. But try, at least some of the time, to be looking at books with your children.

### 4. Technology can be an aid in developing a love and habit of reading.

There are some very good computer programs available now that teach beginning reading skills. For very active children who need to be *doing* something every minute, it might make sense to try them with one of these programs. They are very good at engaging and keeping an active youngster's attention. Computers aren't critical—it's always more important to have a house full of books—but if you can afford one, why not try it?

Books on tape are much more low-tech, but are still popular with many kids. They can follow along with the reader on the tape, turning the page when the signal is given. I know that many children love these tape-and-book combinations, but my own kids always—immediately, it seemed—lost their place and would yell for me to figure out what page the reader was on. If they work for your children, fine. If they don't, you can still read the book to your child without the tape. That's what I finally did.

The VCR has revolutionized television viewing for children. Now you can rent wonderful children's movies, and usually these much-loved films will motivate children to read about their favorite movie characters as well. Some of the best-selling children's books are adaptations of movies, and children will often want to hear these stories over and over again. I do have a caveat here. It might be better if you didn't *buy* too many of the movies. Rent the movie, buy the book adaptation, and then have the book continually available for reliving the story. If the movie is also available, perched permanently by your television, your child might demand the movie rather than the book.

My general rule for technology is this: If it results in a greater interest in reading, it's fine. If computers and VCRs are supplanting books, put them aside for a while. It's *reading* that's important. Preschoolers don't need to be computer-literate.

## WORK ON WRITING

I didn't discuss writing much in my first book, except to point out that only children who are avid readers are excellent writers. Avid readers acquire a sense of language that kids who rarely read never get. That's still true, but I didn't explain that not all children who are avid readers are excellent writers. Some avid readers are very reluctant writers. That's something to keep in mind.

And I've realized the reading/writing link is very important. The avid readers who also love writing are usually the readers who read with the most critical intelligence. I think perhaps the act of writing helps develop both critical and creative thinking.

So I think you should work on writing too. Not a lot, at first, but some. Here's how:

## 1. Provide lots of blank paper and pencils and markers.

I used to buy blank paper at flea markets and discount stores for my kids. Be sure you buy lots, and buy it cheap. Because kids go through it like water. A two-year-old will make one grand sweeping mark on a page, and then reach for another sheet.

Also, look for very cheap markers, because kids are genetically programmed to leave the tops off. Then the markers dry up after one or two days of use. (Most important: you want washable markers. Every single one of my kids, at one time or another, wrote on the walls. No matter what we said! No matter how we threatened! We'd get up in the morning and there, in tasteful green and brown colors, would be marker ink all over their walls. Aaagghhh!)

With your selection of cheap markers and cheap paper, you're in business. Keep a stash in the car, in the kitchen, on the front porch—anywhere you and your children spend time. When things get slow, just hand out the supplies and be prepared to admire whatever they commit to paper. Here's why this is important:

Many of my high school students seem to have a strong, emotional reluctance to write. Getting anything down on paper is agony for them. Surely if they had been used to communicating, via paper, from a very early age, they would show more confidence and zip in their writing now. I think maybe this stage of scribbling on paper is equivalent to the very early reading stage, where little kids start just looking through books—sometimes even holding them upside down. It's a starting-to-feel-friendly stage with reading. I think that early scribbling on paper is a starting-to-feel-friendly stage with writing.

## 2. Spend as much time as you can listening to your children's daily accounts of their adventures.

In my last book I described the technique of active listening. The principle is not to judge what your children say, but to affirm what they say by thoughtfully repeating it, or by asking a sympathetic question, or by commenting on how the experience must have affected them.

For example, say you pick your daughter up at nursery school, and she tells you that Melissa hit her. Don't say, "That's terrible! I hope you told the teacher!" Right away, you're evaluating her actions. She'll get tired of being evaluated, and not tell you much after a while. Instead, say something like, "You must have felt really bad when she hit you." Then wait a minute. She'll probably say something like, "I cried. It wasn't fair. She always gets all the cookies."

Hmm. You see the situation now. Your daughter took one of Melissa's cookies. But don't jump on her, or on anyone else. You want to keep her talking to you, remember. So say something like, "It doesn't seem fair that she gets all the cookies." And wait. You'll probably hear something like, "I gave mine to David, but Melissa wouldn't share."

So now it's easy. You just say, "How great you were to share with David! I always knew you were a really generous kid!" And give her a hug, and let the matter drop. She's had the experience of telling you about a happening, and the experience was positive. This kind of experience of talking and being sympathetically listened to is really important when it comes to developing writers:

- The most common hangup with writing is that many kids feel they have nothing important to say. These are kids who write in tight little handwriting, and are terrified to show anyone their work. I had one student who walked around every day with his shoulders hunched, looking at the ground. He had no self-confidence, and that carried over to his writing. His handwriting was so small and self-effacing that I couldn't read it, so I finally got him writing on a Macintosh computer. He immediately set up the print size so it was even smaller than his handwriting. He then took the further precaution of erasing his file every day when he was finished. The next day he'd come to me and say, "I can't work. Something happened to my file. It's trashed." I'd take his disk to our very sympathetic computer room supervisor, who'd run the software that would bring his file back. Then he'd work that day, and trash the file again.

I finally figured out that he was afraid someone would take his disk from the computer room file box and read what he'd written. (Some things take me a while.) So I offered to keep his disk in my office desk. That finally satisfied him enough that he stopped erasing it every day.

An interesting thing I've noticed about kids is that when they're going through an emotional crisis, writing is often the first thing to go. They'll manage to do other homework, but not writing. Unfortunately, it's these students who really need someone to listen to them.

But you're going to draw out and listen to your preschoolers as much as you can, so they know people are interested in what they have to say, and so they know what they say is compelling and worthwhile. I know most parents are very aware now of the importance of developing self-confidence in kids, but you may not realize how necessary it is to good writing.

- You also need to listen to your preschoolers so they get the hang of developing their accounts of happenings and ideas. After being afraid, the next biggest block to good writing is a failure of kids to add the necessary detail to make the account rich and interesting. So when your four-year-old son starts telling you about the frog he saw in the backyard, listen sympathetically. Draw out the details he saw. Listen while he tells you as much as he remembers about the whole experience. And then the next time he sees something exciting, he may notice more details to tell you, since he knows he has an interested audience. When he's writing later, in school, this ability to organize and remember detail will really pay off.

- The other reason to draw out your preschooler to tell you about his experiences is to encourage him to develop a "voice" in his writing. A voice is a distinctive tone that identifies the work of good writers. Remember the journal excerpt I quoted earlier by the girl who wrote so fluently. Here's another little sample:

In addition to the many poems that I read, I also read Henry David Thoreau's essay "Economy." I won't pretend that it was easy for me to read—it wasn't. Essays in general are hard to read because they're so dense . . . the pages are simply jam-packed with ideas, and no conversation or plot to break up the downpour of the author's ideas.

Notice the voice in her writing. You can sense her excitement, her interest, her confidence that what she's saying is right, and important. Now notice the lack of interesting voice in this journal excerpt, from a boy who is just her age, although a grade behind.

Tex, S. E. Hinton p. 5 9/10/93 (about)
    This book is about two boys that live in the country. One boy has a horse and the other boy has a motorcycle. Johnny has the motorcycle and he brings Pet to school. He is the boy that has the horse and father and brother and him ride in the rodeo.

You can see that this young man has no confidence in his writing. He puts no interest or excitement into it. Just the facts, ma'am.
- After all of my years teaching, I'm starting to think that confidence is almost as crucial to writing as is a good sense of language. So get your children to feel, early on, that what they say and feel is important. That, plus a lot of reading, almost guarantees they'll be very good writers.

### 3. Encourage make-believe play.
Make-believe play is really the beginning of writing fiction. When kids are making up scenarios ("You be the spaceman and I'll be the monster"), they are, essentially, developing plots and characters. And I think kids do this naturally if we don't organize their activities too much.

You can help make-believe play by providing the kinds of toys that encourage it. Dolls, little action figures, and dress-up clothes are all props that kids use to create their own exciting worlds. My younger daughter went through a pretty intense "My Little

Pony" stage, where she paraded her ponies around the house and had them talking to each other, and her, and us, all day. And I wouldn't worry if the action is full of make-believe violence. At that time, my two older children were involved in some huge, ongoing, neighborhood war scenario—they even named our cat Sergeant, I remember—and I would catch them every so often up on our porch roof (strictly forbidden territory) hurling water balloons at the enemy below. They built forts, held battles . . . and are now lovely, peaceful, gentle adults—with very good imaginations.

So try to get your kids away from the television and computer games, and more involved in creating their own worlds.

- Dreaming up characters and pretending to be them will make character creation much easier when they start writing. They'll already have the experience of trying to think how another character would talk and act in a situation.
- The entire assortment of objects they bring together to set the scene—blankets for forts, boxes, clothes—is helping them see the importance of using detail and description in their writing. Creating a believable world that fits your characters is one of the hardest tasks of fiction writing. Your kids will have a big head start if they do this activity often as children.
- This isn't really related to reading or writing, but you sometimes get a real insight into the world of your children by watching the kinds of worlds they create in play. I used to find out what was happening at Molly's nursery school by watching her play with her little toy animals in the bath at night. She'd line them up around the tub, and have them doing and saying all kinds of school things. "Oh, good, Rabbit, you shared your snack. You can go out to play first." It was one of the ways I knew that her school was a good place for her to be.
- The make-believe play in which children engage sometimes can help them diffuse and make sense of the trauma that is happening in their real life. Virginia Axline wrote a book called *Dibs in Search of Self* that described this idea of play therapy. If your child is really

in need of professional therapy, of course, you should get it, but pretend play can help any child cope with the problems in his day-to-day life. Also—very important—the habit of creating imaginary worlds to help make sense of real ones will benefit your children immensely when they reach the angst-filled teenage years. You want them home writing poetry and stories when they're troubled—not looking for the nearest drug dealer. One of the best writers I've ever had told me that she had an incredibly unhappy ninth-grade year, but, she remarked ruefully, "High school was good for my writing because it was so painful." She just immersed herself in reading and in writing poetry as a way to cope with, and sometimes escape from, the high school pressures.

And now, before we leave the preschool section, I want to say a word about nursery schools.

## Don't make the teaching of reading your major criterion for a nursery school.

Nursery schools, for years, were a big part of my life. I feel like something of a mini-expert on nursery schools, having had kids in one kind or another of nursery school or day care, for about eighteen years, all over the country. So this is my take on it.

The big question is, Should you look for a nursery school that will teach your three-year-old how to read? I know there are some nursery schools that specialize in this, such as Montessori, and I do think it's wonderful if kids do learn to read early. But I'd be cautious. In fact, I think I'd judge nursery schools in a hierarchical way, as I judge reading programs. The primary thing is to find a nursery school that your child is happy attending. Second, it would be nice if your child learned some social skills. And finally, a little reading head start would be nice, as long as the reading instruction didn't interfere with your child's enjoyment of school, or acquisition of social skills. You're going to be working a bit with reading at home anyway, remember? If you follow the suggestions in my earlier book, you should be able to pull your child along in reading, as far as he is ready to go at this time. The problem with a nursery school's attempt to teach reading is that it can't gear its teaching to each individual child. You can.

As I write this, I'm trying to remember if any of my avid readers told me they learned to read in nursery school. I can't remember any. I do remember one girl who told me that her parents specifically enrolled her in a nursery school because they wanted her to read early. The experience wasn't a happy one, and she has confused memories of one teacher telling her to do one thing, and another telling her to do something else. Finally, one day in frustration she remembers, "I started to cry, and that was it. I stopped learning to read after that."

So before you look for a nursery school to teach reading, be sure it has these other qualities:

## 1. A nursery school has to be warm and nurturing.

When we'd move to another town, and I'd have to find day care again, I used to visit all of the nursery schools within a certain radius of where I would be working. I wouldn't call ahead of time; I'd drop in unannounced. Here's what I learned to look for:

*Friendly, happy teachers.* This is the absolutely essential quality. You want teachers who laugh easily, who aren't strict, who don't have hard-and-fast rules about child-raising. Since this is your child's first experience with school, you want it to be a happy one. I think kids forget details of preschool experiences but somewhere, deep in their psyche, they remember the emotion.

*A low student-teacher ratio.* Little kids need a lot of attention, and one adult's time can only be stretched so far. If a teacher is too stressed out, trying to supervise a large number of kids, she'll be more likely to be grouchy and inflexible. And your child will be more likely to be unhappy.

*Lots of kid-friendly toys.* I wouldn't be too impressed with a school that is overstocked with educational games. Look for a school with old dress-up clothes, blocks, dolls, trucks—the tried-and-true favorites. Also—a necessity—look for a school that has plenty of art supplies. When you arrive home tired, after work, you're not going to want to set up finger painting for your child. Look for a school that encourages all that messy stuff. Weekends, sure, you can do it. But during the week, look for a school with paste and scissors and glitter and paint. I was sold on one nursery school because, on the hot day when I walked in, all of the kids were standing around in their underwear, playing at a big sand-and-water table. They couldn't have been messier—or happier.

## 2. Look for a school that teaches social skills.

If you have a couple of warm, nurturing schools to choose from, then you might notice what kind of job the schools do with teaching social skills. Actually, a warm, friendly school, just by being warm and friendly, teaches by example the essence of social intercourse—caring about another person. But some schools really do a wonderful job with this—emphasizing sharing and supporting one another's efforts. One of my daughters told me how, in her nursery school, they'd all go to the bathroom and applaud when a classmate finally mastered toilet training.

Probably the worst thing a school can do, in regards to social skills, is park the kids in front of a television for a good portion of the day. I wandered into a school like that once. All the toys were on a high shelf, and all the children were sitting on the floor in front of a large TV screen. When you see a situation like that, just make a U-turn and walk right out. Your children aren't getting any chance to play or pretend or have fun with any of the other kids. (Also, realistically, you'd probably like to be able to put your child in front of "Sesame Street" when you get home, since you're tired and have to do the breakfast dishes and make dinner and do a million other things. You don't want television-watching time used up in nursery school.)

By high school age, a lack of social skills is really devastating to a kid. A student who is unhappy socially is probably not going to be able to concentrate well on schoolwork—along with his many other problems. Of course, most social skills are acquired in warm, loving families, but nursery schools can make a big difference too.

### 3. It's great if kids can get a little head start on reading in nursery school.

You're only going to consider a school that teaches reading if it is also, and primarily, a happy, loving place. *That's* what's most important. Not just because having a joyous, well-adjusted child is your primary goal—at least I'm assuming that's your primary goal—but because an unhappy school situation that teaches reading will probably make your child hate reading rather than love it. So you won't even achieve your educational goals.

But suppose that you've found a happy, nurturing school that helps kids get along with each other—and teaches reading! What should you look for?

Make sure the primary emphasis is on helping the children love books. Just as in your home, you want there to be books everywhere in the school. Children should be encouraged to look at the books, to "read" them with each other, and to even use them to build forts and castles. If children love books, they will grow to respect them—and you don't love things that people are always yelling at you not to touch.

This would be a school where the teachers read stories often to the children—but children who were not ready to sit and listen would be allowed to play elsewhere. Children have to enjoy story time.

The nursery school my younger daughter attended would take the children on weekly library trips. I thought that was a great idea; it got the kids used to going to the library with friends. It was also an inexpensive way to keep a fresh supply of books around.

And, finally, if the school uses the low-key ways of teaching reading that I suggested in my earlier book—games, tagging objects, writing down kids' stories, writing lists, teaching first-letter sounds—and these activities are only done as long as the children are enjoying them—then it sounds like you've found a wonderful school.

## What if it looks as though you're going to have major academic problems ahead?

First, I should explain my general theory about children with disabilities that will, most likely, interfere with reading. Look at it this way: Some people are born tall, well coordinated, and quick. I'm short, slow, and not very well coordinated. If being able to play basketball well were necessary to success in life, any of these tall, well-coordinated people would have a huge advantage over me. However, if I loved the game of basketball, and spent countless hours playing it, I might get to the point where I could play a pretty good game—certainly a better game than almost all of my friends, and a better game than that played by tall, well-coordinated people who never practiced. Just by practicing all the time, I'd develop more coordination; my sense of timing would improve. Also, I'd know the game so well that I would know how to use my strengths in playing, and avoid my weaknesses. On the other hand, if I never practiced, and hated the game, of course I'd be hopeless at it. (I *am* hopeless at it.)

Luckily for me, basketball isn't necessary to succeed in life, but I think reading is. So if you have a child who, it appears, will have academic difficulties, it's *critical* that you help her develop an early love of reading. An early love of reading may be enough of a head start to level the playing field. That's my general advice. Here are some suggestions on dealing with specific problems:

### 1. What do you do if you have a child diagnosed with ADD or ADHD?

ADD is short for attention deficit disorder. The *H* in ADHD means attention deficit disorder with hyperactivity.

When my older daughter was two, and being tested by a speech pathologist (my daughter had a cleft palate), the pathologist told us she was hyperactive. I was a little upset, but my mother-in-law just said, "*All* two-year-olds are hyperactive!"

I'm not sure if she would fit the definition today, but, let me tell you, she was very, very active. I couldn't take her shopping for clothes—she'd run under all of the changing-room walls. My husband was in Vietnam when she was two, and since I was teaching and had to leave her with a baby-sitter when I was in school, I didn't want to leave her with a sitter any other time. I started doing all of my clothes shopping by catalog. And forget supermarkets. We bought all our food, a few things at a time, from a corner grocery store. When we had to move across the country, we sold two cars rather than try to endure three days in a car with her. She was absolutely always on the move.

Here's how I coped. I decided that I wouldn't put her into situations where I knew she'd misbehave. Hence the catalog shopping, the small, personal stores we could hurry in and out of. We spent a lot of time at a wonderful park in Monterey, called the Dennis the Menace Park. It had a huge, real train locomotive for the kids to climb on—Julie was pirouetting along the very top ridge of it before her second birthday. The highest slides, the rope bridges—she knew no fear. I think I was too stupid to be afraid. I'd sit on a bench with a magazine and think, Oh, well, if she falls, the ground is all sand. She probably won't get hurt too badly.

We were very happy together. My friends used to tease me that they never heard me yell at her. I guess I never did. No reason to. She couldn't sit still at the table? That was okay. I used to sit her on top of the dishwasher (she always liked heights) with snacks while I was cooking. That amused her; she'd eat, and then run around and play while I ate.

I know the experts always recommend lots of structure and behavior-modification techniques to deal with ADD or ADHD. And maybe they're right. I just found with my own children, and later with the children I've had in my classroom who definitely were diagnosed as having ADD or ADHD, that I did best with them by essentially doing with them what I've just described: I gave them lots of warm affection, and placed them—as often as I possibly could—only in situations where they'd do well. This means that, as far as reading went, I gave them only books they'd chosen and that I was sure they'd like. I set up the classroom so they usually had a choice of activities. They could read in the classroom, or go to the computer lab and write. If they wanted to write using a pen and paper, that was okay. Maybe they wanted to write at home on their own computer, and spend all of their class time reading. That was fine. They just needed to bring in drafts every so often so I could see how they were doing.

To me, structure seems less important than giving children the feeling that they are in control of themselves. I just read a new book called *Helping Your Dyslexic Child*, by Eileen M. Cronin, Ph.D. (Prima Publishing, 1994), in which the author says that what she calls learning-handicapped children "need the security of knowing how to enter a room at home or at school, how to greet one another, where their supplies are kept, how to put materials away, and other school-related details. They must learn routines step-by-step until they master them." Well, yes. Kids need to know where things are, but kids who have academic problems aren't idiots. I find that empowering kids to make as many of the routine decisions every day as possible does more toward calming them down and getting them working than does all the regimentation I could possibly devise. As with all kids—and all grown-ups you have a relationship with—it's only when you give up control that you get control.

So introduce books to your very active child in a warm, friendly setting—a setting he feels he has much control over. Play the reading games with him—but again, always keep him in control. If he has trouble paying attention, ruthlessly shorten the stories you read, so you can praise him for being a good listener. If he goes wild in bookstores, pick out books for him and bring them home. The crucial element in ensuring academic success with high-risk kids is making them feel like *good* kids, and successful kids. Don't let anything jeopardize that.

And don't worry that you need to *teach* your four-year-old very active daughter how to behave in a mall. She'll pick it up, all on her own. By the time she's sixteen she'll be more at home in a mall than you are. And your five-year-old son who's careening through supermarket aisles at a hundred miles an hour now? Don't teach him to behave there. Somehow get someone to watch him when you need to shop—to keep your relationship with him warm and friendly—and by the time he's sixteen he'll be more comfortable in a store full of food than you can imagine. Misbehaving in stores is something kids grow out of—if they don't have other problems that make them angry and lead them to do destructive things.

So relax. You want at least the first four or five years of your very active child's life to be hassle-free and enjoyable, because school may be difficult. But I think it will be much less difficult if you send your child to school feeling empowered and successful, and having good beginning reading skills. So make sure he knows initial letter sounds. (You do this by playing games, of course.) Have him help you write up tags for objects he cares about, so he starts to gain a sight vocabulary. Read comic books with him— they have short selections and are full of action, perfect for kids always on the run—and gradually see if you can get him to start reading some of the parts. Praise him effusively for any little reading gain he makes.

If you can make your ADD son into an early reader, his whole school experience will be different. Teachers are much more tolerant of "smart" kids who fool around than they are of "dumb" kids. Also, he won't have the bad feelings about schoolwork that lower-achieving students do, and so he'll have less reason to act out in school. And—I know this sounds odd, but it's true—kids diagnosed as having ADD often seem to read with *more* concentration. It's like they're hyperactively reading. I wouldn't be surprised if some of our greatest researchers weren't kids who today would be labeled ADD because of their incredible energy and curiosity.

But early love of books, and early reading, is the key.

### 2. What if your child has hearing difficulties, or is slow in learning to talk?

Kids who acquire language slowly are probably at greatest risk for reading failure, and so these are kids who probably require the greatest direct teaching. You want them to enter first grade caught up with everyone else. You don't ever want your child to be one of the "dumb" kids.

If, for example, your daughter isn't making nice little jargony sounds in her crib by six or seven months, or isn't starting to talk in one- or two-word sentences by eighteen months, you should definitely get her hearing checked. It can't *hurt* to get her hearing checked—there are really effective ways of doing it now, even with young babies—and you may find she has a hearing loss. Even a slight loss will affect speech.

My older daughter was late in talking, and had poor articulation, so I kept asking about a hearing test. "Oh, she hears what she wants to," my doctor kept saying. When I finally prevailed, and got the test, she *wasn't* hearing very well. The audiologist explained to me that children with losses of 30 to 40 percent—her loss—are perceived as hearing well because, if you walk right up to them and speak directly to them, they hear you. You've overcome the 40 percent hearing loss.

So we had tubes put in her ears to correct the hearing loss, and then we arranged for speech therapy. Then I taught her to read so she'd have a visual picture of the words. I thought it would help her speech. And the good news is that, with all of that help, she did just fine in school. In fact, she majored in English in college. Early help was the key.

Some children don't have an actual hearing loss, but don't process language well. This is usually what people mean when they talk about a specific learning disability. If, for example, your son doesn't discriminate sounds well, he's going to be slower in figuring out how to read. A tipoff to this kind of disability usually appears in the child's early speech. If he's very late in starting to talk, or if, when he starts talking, he is very slow to acquire standard forms, you might be concerned. While most kids start out over-regularizing verbs—saying "throwed" for "threw," for example—you might have a problem if he is still doing this far past the age that his friends are doing it. You might have him tested, if you're really concerned, but you should certainly make sure that he's getting as much reading help from you as he'll accept. Do the things I have suggested above for ADD children and, in addition, really make sure this kid has plenty of books and comics around.

Because a child with a language disability is so much at risk for doing poorly in school, you might even go all out and ditch the television set for a few years. A couple of my very top readers reported growing up in houses without television sets; it really motivated them to turn to books for excitement and stories. With a kid who is learning language normally, I don't think you really need to ban television. But with a seriously language-impaired child I'd consider it. As with an ADD child, if you can send a language-impaired child off to school with a love of books and a beginning competence in reading, you'll have changed his whole school career.

### 3. What if your child has had a traumatic past?

I've had parents call me who have taken in foster children, or have adopted children from very sad, chaotic backgrounds. These children are very needy, and you can't count on them just moving into first grade and doing well. Or perhaps there has been a very sad happening in your own family: a death, an abusive spouse, or serious illness. Traumatic past events put a child greatly at risk for educational failure. But again, with all the emotional support you can give these youngsters—which should probably include professional counseling—early, avid reading is the magic bullet that can mean the difference between a school career that is unhappy and frustrating, and one that is happy and productive.

There is an incredibly moving book titled *A Hole in the World* by Richard Rhodes (Simon and Schuster, 1990) which is about the early death of the author's mother, and his father's remarriage to an abusive stepmother. The abuse was all-encompassing and horrific. He talks about riding his bike through the streets to see how normal families lived: "Everywhere I bicycled I stopped to watch people going about their lives, families in particular, fascinated with their quaint and alien normality. Numbed, adapted to such extremity that I was hardly even jealous, I felt like a man from Mars." But, he says, "Most of all I read . . . I escaped into books. Not exactly books in those years. Pulp science fiction . . . a world where underdogs triumphed, a world where even the most cunning and malevolent monsters were always outwitted in the end and destroyed." The reading not only ensured that he excelled in school, but, as you can see, also helped him deal with the present terrors of his living situation.

So if you have these youngsters while they're preschoolers, do everything you can to make sure they enter first grade loving books and reading. As with a language-delayed child, pull out all the stops, even if that means getting rid of your television. I really think reading is a key to saving these kids. Do whatever you have to do—and don't be surprised if their stories of choice, even as preschoolers, are books or comics you would consider really trashy. Kids deal with trauma in different ways, and while you may not think the stories they love are appropriate for them, those stories may deal with their needs in a way you never thought of, just as pulp science fiction helped show Richard Rhodes that evil could be overcome. It's absolutely crucial that these kids enter school loving reading—and learning.

## A FINAL NOTE

If you have a preschooler now, who's ready to start first grade but doesn't yet love books—and isn't even close to beginning to read—that's okay. Don't panic. Believe me, the game isn't up by the time a kid's five. I've had wonderful readers who didn't start reading until rather late in elementary school. It's easier, of course, if they read earlier, but not all kids do. One of my all-time favorite kids, who got a 680 on his verbal SATs, told me that he didn't learn to read until the third grade. He only learned then because his mother unexpectedly had twins—and had no more time to read to him. He taught himself to read using Tolkien's Ring Trilogy—I know it's hard to believe, but he was a very truthful kid—and it took him until seventh grade to finish that trilogy. Then he went on and read everything.

So if your child has not yet fallen in love with books, relax, and read the next chapter on how to help your elementary school children to become wonderful readers.

# Strategies and Tips for Elementary School Kids

## ACQUIRING BOOKS

Your child has started elementary school, and you've got a house full of picture books. That's okay! You'll find your kids still reading these books for months, maybe for years, to come. So hold on to them. If room is a problem—and room is always a problem in my house—you might try to hold on to them until your child is ten or eleven, anyway. I remember my daughter, at the age of fourteen, tearing the house apart to find one of her favorite picture books, *Chilly Billy*.

But you'll want to start getting more books, especially as your children move up to the second and third grades. This is a *critical* time in the reading life of children. If children develop into avid, independent readers by third or fourth grade, they should be prepared to be excellent high school students and candidates for top colleges. Note that they won't necessarily be terrific high school students, but at least they'll have the ability, unlike kids who arrive in high school without ever having done much independent reading.

So how do you go about creating a book-filled home for these kids? Here are some tips drawn from my own experiences, and from those of my students:

### 1. Try to arrange time to take each of your children individually on lunch and book-buying trips.

When your kids were preschoolers, they usually went along on most of your shopping trips anyway. What else were you going to do with them? But once kids start school, you'll find they aren't tagging along so often. They're in school or, within a few years, old enough to stay home alone for a few hours. So I think you should make a point of specifically arranging book-buying trips.

I used to take my older daughter, when she was around eight or nine, on comic-buying trips in Norfolk, Virginia. We'd go downtown to a little newsstand that carried cheap, out-of-date comics and magazines (cheap, out-of-date comics was what I could afford at that time in my life). We'd spend some time looking through the piles of Richie Rich comics, trying to find some that she didn't already have. Then we'd go to lunch.

We had a great place to eat lunch, and we ate at the same place every time. It was a grand old Norfolk department store, which was right across from the newsstand. On its mezzanine was a coffee shop, and the tables were set next to the balcony railing, so you could sit at your table and look down at everyone shopping on the first floor. I remember it as a very happy time, and I feel it's probably one of the reasons that she so loved reading comic books.

There are a number of reasons why special book-buying trips are important:

- You are telling your child in yet another way that books are important, and that her tastes are important. In the rush of elementary school activities, this sense is easily lost. Of course, you're also telling your daughter that *she* is important, and that you value time with her. This is good for all kinds of reasons, but the reason that matters in the present context is that you're connecting an important, pleasurable activity (lunch with you!) with reading.

- Conversations about reading and books can happen naturally on these outings. You probably won't have the budget to buy out the bookstore, so you can have serious discussions with her about which books she wants to choose. Which books are her favorites? Which books does she really want to own? In the rush of our daily lives, sometimes it's hard to have serious, in-depth discussions with our children, so this would be a chance to do so. Remember, though, that fostering a critical response to literature is the third reading law, and must never put in jeopardy the first two laws.

- As with your preschoolers, these shopping trips should keep your children in the habit of walking into bookstores and buying books. They'll be starting to have a little money of their own now. Perhaps they want to save some of it for these book-buying trips, since your budget will be limited. I probably sound like a broken record on this subject, but I can't tell you the great number of high school students I have who never think of buying a book! They practically live in video stores—they're always telling me about all of the movies they've rented—but buy a book? It just doesn't occur to them until I mention it.

## 2. Haunt flea markets and garage sales for collections of series books.

A comment that came up again and again when I was interviewing avid readers was that someone gave them a box filled with books of one series—usually Nancy Drew or Hardy Boys, but occasionally something else. Kids got these boxes of books from cousins or an older brother, or occasionally from a parent who had been to an auction or flea market. When I was about eight, my family moved into a house that had a whole collection of books, written around the turn of the century, about a young woman named Patty. I *loved* those books. I carefully arranged them on shelves, I made covers for them, and I read them again and again.

My students told me that they read every volume of these windfalls of series books, then usually went on to buy the more recent titles. Sometimes they started collecting them. For a number of kids, they were a big factor in keeping them reading. (And, as I reported in my last book, most of my avid readers reported liking the earlier Nancy Drews—the ones they got from relatives or flea markets—better than the updated versions that bookstores carry.)

I go to flea markets all the time—I get most of my classroom library there—and lately I've been noticing that people are selling off collections of Baby-sitters Club books and Sweet Valley books and even, occasionally, Goosebumps (by R. L. Stine) books. These collections are pure gold, and I can hardly bear to pass them up. But I no longer have an elementary-school-aged child, and my high school students have moved on to other reading. But sometimes it will be ten or eleven o'clock in the morning when I see these books—which means they've been there for hours—and still no one has bought them. I just can't believe it.

So go and buy up these collections! Here are some reasons:

- There's no kind of reading that develops a love of reading and a habit of reading for children as well as series books. If your son reads one Goosebumps book and loves it, he'll love the next thirty-two—because they're all exactly alike. And that's okay. After reading thirty-two books he'll be reading a little better, and he'll be able to move on to something else—such as R. L. Stine's Fear Street series for older kids, or some Stephen King books! But he'll be forming a firm habit of reading—something to keep him reading through all the lure of soccer leagues and rollerblading and fort building.
- Having large collections of series books in your house means your children's friends will come over to read them or borrow them. And that's great! As much as preschoolers need reading friends, school-aged children need them even more. Someone to discuss and trade books with, and read with.

### 3. Buy up collections of magazines of interest to your children at flea markets and garage sales.

Magazines are a great deal at flea markets—usually they go for a quarter or even a dime apiece. If your son or daughter has a special interest, and if you see a collection of magazines there that deals with it, go wild. My husband always tells the story of the *National Geographic* collection that a librarian gave him. He lovingly read them, arranged them, collected them—for years! In fact, our attic is *still* full of old *National Geographic*s.

Flea markets will often have great collections of car magazines, doll magazines, *Highlights* magazines, even *Mad* magazines. (*Mad* magazines tend to be expensive—like comic books; unfortunately, they've become collector's items.) And since most magazines are usually so cheap, even if your children are not interested in them when you bring them home, you can just recycle them, or donate them to a charity.

Here are some reasons to buy up collections of magazines:

- Magazines provide a good introduction to nonfiction reading for children. Because most magazines are written in a very reader-friendly fashion, kids find out that they can learn really interesting information through *reading*. There's a good chance their textbooks at school are very dull and proper and politically correct—and *boring*. Magazines provide an exciting entry into the world of gathering-information-through-reading.

- Wide reading of magazines is one of the fastest and easiest ways for children to acquire good knowledge frameworks. I was all ready for psychology classes in college because I had spent years reading features like "Can This Marriage Be Saved?" in my mother's women's magazines.

- Piles of old magazines are also good lures for neighborhood children. On rainy days your children and their friends can read through them, trade them, cut them up—do all kinds of reading-togetherness things.

### 4. Look for collections of comic books.

These are harder to find because, like the *Mad* magazines I mentioned, they've become collector's items. You rarely see a whole box of them for sale at a flea market for a reasonable price. It's much more likely you'll see a collection of them with each comic individually bagged and priced. And most of the people looking to buy them will be adults. It's too bad that the *real* value of a comic—teaching kids to love reading—has been forgotten in its value to collectors.

But that's the reality, so if you have a child who loves comics, you're probably going to have to spend a fair amount of money. Try flea markets, certainly, but also watch newspapers and any magazines that have large classified sections. Sometimes you can find large collections at a reasonable price there.

One warning: Since the main value of the comics you're buying is their ability to foster a love of reading and a habit of reading, don't start nagging at your kids to treat them like collector's items. Yes, if your son wears white gloves while he reads his X-Men comic, and puts it away in a little plastic bag afterward, it will be worth a couple of dollars in a few years. Big deal. Your insistence on this careful treatment may just make reading comics more of a chore than it's worth. Even looking at comics purely in a financial way, your son's becoming an avid reader is going to be worth a lot more money to him than a collection of pristine comics will ever be. So be casual about the comics. Don't worry if they end up on the floor, or covered with strawberry jam. If they're bringing your child to a love of reading, they've more than paid for themselves.

## 5. Buy subscriptions to your child's favorite comics and magazines.

You can't just stick with the old; you're going to have to pay for new issues as well. Buying subscriptions is good not only because the subscription price is usually lower per issue than the newsstand price, but a subscription keeps fascinating reading material coming into the house on a regular basis.

## 6. Keep your children going to the library.

If you live close to a library, you're lucky, of course. Just be sure to tell your kids that if they lose a book, or forget to bring one back, that's okay. You'll pay the fines. This is very important because so many of my less well read students tell me they don't use the library because they're afraid they'll lose a book. Or they did lose a book two years ago and can't afford to replace it. Or they owe money in back fines and they're afraid they won't be able to check out any more books—you get the idea. Kids really worry about this stuff. And even if your child builds up fines of one or two dollars a week—which is unlikely—that still probably doesn't touch what you pay on late fines for video rentals. And you didn't even have to rent the books in the first place! Even if you're paying late fines all the time, as well as an occasional charge for a lost book, the library is still, by far, the cheapest place to get such a huge variety of reading material.

At a library convention, one librarian told me about a girl who had lost a twenty-dollar book. The library told her that she'd have to pay for the book before she took out any other ones. So the girl's mother said, "I'm not paying for that book. To teach you a lesson, you'll just have to get along without the library."

The librarian and I were both floored. What kind of lesson was that mother teaching her daughter? That it's okay to lose something and not replace it? That the incredible privilege of taking home any book you want from a library isn't worth even twenty dollars?

"I'll bet that mother would spend twenty dollars on clothes and not even think twice about it," the librarian said sadly. The mother, however, somehow thought she was teaching her daughter responsibility.

My theory is to teach children responsibility for relatively unimportant activities—like doing dishes, or taking out the trash. If they fail to take out the trash one night, the world won't end. You can let natural consequences happen: the kitchen will probably smell of trash in the morning. But some things are too important to let natural consequences happen. Suppose your children's job was to feed the family dog, and they kept forgetting. Would you let the dog die of hunger to teach them a lesson? Of course not. But it seems to me equally terrible to restrict children's access to a library because they can't remember to bring books back on time.

If you don't live near a library, or if your children don't especially feel like going to libraries, you need to take a more active role. As one mother said in a letter to me, "Going to the library, disappointing as this is for me to admit, is a definite turn-off for them. So I have assumed the responsibility for making sure that they always have on hand library books THAT I HAVE TAKEN THE TIME TO SELECT, CHECK OUT, AND RETURN." [Emphasis in original.] This seems to be working well for her, and her children are avid readers. You also might try getting your children into libraries by making library trips part of other, more enticing excursions. Say casually, "Anyone want to go to Burger King for lunch?" And after the car is filled with your children and maybe some others, remark, "After lunch I have to stop at the library. You can look for any books you want while I'm finding mine."

However you do it, try to ensure that your elementary school children stay used to using a library—for all kinds of reasons:

- When kids become competent, fluent readers in elementary school, almost the only way to keep them continually in books is to keep them going to the library. "When I moved to Concord I would ride my bike down to the library every day," one student told me, "and so for a lot of that summer, when my mother was working, I'd end up reading a book or two a day." Since so many children's books are relatively short, and since some kids pick up reading so quickly, it's really impossible—unless you're independently wealthy—to keep them completely supplied with reading material from bookstores and flea markets.
- Kids are more likely to expand their reading repertoire with library books. They'll be more willing to try new writers and new subject areas, since they can immediately take the books back if they don't like them.
- The selection of books in good libraries is much larger than that in a bookstore, since a bookstore only carries in-print titles, and only a fraction of those. Also, with the networks many libraries have now joined, they can get books they don't have in just a few days from neighboring libraries. The only books for which a library really isn't useful are new best-sellers and children's series books, especially if your child insists on reading the series in order.

- A habit of reading library books will help keep your children reading when they first leave home, and have no money.

- One more note about libraries: Don't worry too much about the size of a library. My students who live near small libraries almost seem to do better. Maybe a small library seems friendlier than a large one. One girl described going to a small branch library in the summer: "There was one right up my block, which was really small. I used to love to sit there all day. It's cool, and there are all these books around, and it's musty and dark and you can imagine you're in a medieval library somewhere."

## READING ALOUD

A few parents wrote to tell me that I should have emphasized reading aloud more in my first book, particularly reading aloud to older children. As one parent put it, "I wish you had mentioned reading aloud in the learning-to-read years. A child from five to ten will enjoy books well above his reading level, and much longer than the easy books. He can and will read them to himself later, if you have them around, though I did deprive myself of the pleasure of reading some good read-aloud books that I thought [my son] could soon read for himself—I read him the Laura Ingalls Wilder books, because I thought he might miss them because of their being girls' books, but not the Narnia books, which I knew would be sure-fire when their time came." This mother then went on to make another excellent point: "Reading aloud to older children means that they get familiar with the idioms of past centuries and other areas by ear, in the natural way, and do not come to college with a language barrier against anything written more than a generation ago."

I wonder if reading aloud is more important for boys. For some reason, over the years, the excellent-reading high school students who have reported reading out loud, and being read to when older, have almost all been boys. One young man told me how his mother would pick him up at school with her Agatha Christie mystery in the car so he could read it to her on the way home.

Another talked about long car trips: "We'd go on car trips every year to North Carolina. We read, on the way down—I think I was in eighth grade—*The Unvanquished* aloud, me and my father switching off, and *My Ántonia* on the way back. I love to hear things read aloud, and I love to read them myself; those two books stuck in my mind."

It is really important to keep reading to your school-aged children. Here are a few suggestions:

## 1. Try plays.

Kids love reading plays. Libraries usually have a pretty good collection of plays, some especially for young people. Instead of always reading regular books at night, you might occasionally try some play scripts. I've found that comic ones work the best. A great one to start with is *You're a Good Man, Charlie Brown*. *Barefoot in the Park*, by Neil Simon, is another that might appeal to late-elementary-school-aged kids, as might a collection titled *How to Eat Fried Worms and Other Plays*, by Thomas Rockwell.

- When kids read parts in a play, they're more likely to read with expression. And reading with expression means they're paying attention to the nuances of character development. It's strange, but I've found it almost impossible to *teach* students to understand characters. An understanding of people, of characters, is something acquired over a lifetime, but my sense is that students who immerse themselves in fictional characters have a bit of a head start—especially if, as in a play, they're pretending to *be* those characters.

- Reading plays is an easy way to get kids started doing oral reading themselves for enjoyment. They can just read a short part at first, and then read longer parts as they gain confidence.

- A final note: You don't really need to read plays to have your children reading parts. Any books with a lot of dialogue will work. Generally, you should read the narrator role, and let your kids read the dialogue. I do this a lot with my classes. There are some scenes in *Catch-22* that are so funny when read aloud in parts, that sometimes we can barely keep reading for laughing. *Catch-22* is too sophisticated for elementary school kids, but Roald Dahl's books are hysterical when read aloud in parts.

## 2. Keep trying poetry.

I mentioned that it's important to read or recite poetry to preschoolers. It is, but it's even more important to try to get elementary school children interested in poetry. Usually at this age, kids are still open to poetry, and haven't yet been turned off by English teachers who insist that they analyze difficult poems they don't even like. And, let me tell you, after being made to analyze these poems, students don't just dislike them anymore; they hate them, and poetry in general. So work early on giving your child a love of poetry to try to prevent this kind of damage.

A very helpful librarian in San Francisco sent me the following list of "absolute favorite" poetry books for elementary school kids, so be sure to try them:

Shel Silverstein, *A Light in the Attic*
Helen Ferris, *Favorite Poems Old and New*
Jeffrey Moss, *The Butterfly Jar*
Eva Moore et al., *Sing a Song of Popcorn*
Jack Prelutsky, *The Random House Book of Poetry for Children*

You should also continue to encourage any interest your children have in songs. Purely for my own enjoyment, I used to tape all of my favorite songs from the 1960s, and play the tapes on the car radio. My children soon knew most of the lyrics—as did many of the neighborhood kids I was always driving around. We had a little 1960s enclave right on our street. And my kids, anyway, kept their love of poetry and music.

I don't think it really matters what music lyrics or poetry you expose your children to, as long as it's poetry you love. Chances are they'll love it too. (These are elementary school children I'm talking about, remember. You get no such assurances with high school kids.)

A student at my school described how his father used to help him memorize poetry: "Well, he would read them to me—actually, he wouldn't read them to me, he knew them by heart—and we would memorize them. He'd say one line and I'd say the next line and we'd go through the poem and then we'd start with the other person so each one got every line. . . . I learned a couple of Shakespearean sonnets that way." This young man went on to write poetry as well, so do try to keep your kids feeling friendly toward poetry.

### 3. Ask your child to read aloud to you.

This is something I didn't think much to do with my own children—although one of my kids used to ask me to listen while she read aloud—but enough of my excellent readers have reported doing this with parents that I can see I really missed something. They read aloud while a parent was driving, doing dishes, or doing a variety of chores.

Naturally, you should be completely appreciative and noncritical when you encourage your child to do this. When my students read aloud, confidence is everything—well, maybe 50 percent. The ability to *read* is pretty important too. And that is another funny thing I see about reading aloud: willingness to read aloud doesn't seem to have much to do with ability. Some of my worst readers are the most enthusiastic about taking parts or taking turns whenever we read something aloud.

When you ask your child to read to you, you might pick a book that you like, and that you think your child would like. Or you might just say, "Read me something you're reading that you think I'd enjoy"—and then, of course, be sure you enjoy it! Having your child read to you is good for a couple of reasons:

- It validates your child as a good reader. As in most other things in life, self-confidence and a sense of mastery make any activity much more enjoyable. Sometimes I even enjoy ironing just because I do it so well. And if your child has chosen the book, it also validates his taste in books—since, of course, you'll enjoy his choice.
- The practice your child gets reading aloud with you will help when she's asked to read aloud in school. I have some students who I know are very good readers, but they are extremely reluctant to

take part in any reading-aloud activity at school. If we're all just reading a paragraph or two of a story, taking turns going around the room, they'll pass (something I always allow; I never make a student read aloud). If we're reading in parts, they'll never volunteer. I know a lot of the reasons for this reluctance are social—the high school social scene has layers upon layers of issues that I often miss—but I think a lack of self-confidence in reading ability is a major reason too.

- Just on general principles, of course, it's good to have your children do things for you, rather than your doing everything for them. Reading aloud is no different from any other activity in this sense. When your child gives you enjoyment, when he is helping you, his feeling of self-worth increases, and his relationship with you gets better. We always love the people we help!

## 4. Read aloud from books your child might not choose, but would enjoy.

The mother I quoted earlier was right about getting children used to the kind of language used in books written a hundred years ago, although the language wasn't just different then, it was more complex and really harder. Sentences were longer, with more subordinate clauses; more description was used, and nuances of social situations were more carefully described. My guess is that the people who could read a hundred years ago (and I realize this was a much smaller percentage of the population than now) read better than the average reader does today. I think forty or fifty years ago—before the advent of television—people read better, since so much of their entertainment and information was gotten through reading. Look at a magazine published in the early 1950s, such as *The Saturday Evening Post*, and you'll be amazed at how much writing is in the magazine, how long the stories and articles are, and how *many* of them there are. I really think the average reader read more then.

And this means the average reader read better and faster. When you read well and fast, you can enjoy a more descriptive, leisurely style of writing. You don't get bogged down in the descriptions;

you can visualize the things described more clearly; you enjoy the added richness.

So today there are books your children can enjoy hearing—if you read them with a great deal of expression to overcome the language differences—before they can enjoy reading them. Reading some of these older books aloud enables your children to hear the stories at the time in their lives when the stories will be most thrilling to them. *The Secret Garden* and *Anne of Green Gables* are two books of this kind that come to mind. A number of my students—even some of my best readers—report having tried these two books when they were younger, and having been discouraged by the difficulty. Later they moved into more adult reading, and missed them altogether.

The other kinds of books that are much improved by reading aloud are amusing ones, particularly books that depend on a kind of quiet, warm interaction among the characters. *Charlotte's Web* is this kind of book. I think kids can better understand the kind of amused tenderness that Charlotte feels for Wilbur—and the amused tenderness the author feels for all of the characters— when it's read aloud. Books with broader comedy, like the Mrs. Piggle-Wiggle books, are even funnier when the kids hear the names of the characters pronounced aloud.

Here are some reasons to keep reading aloud:

- With the expression you put into your reading, you can help kids see nuances of meaning they might miss on their own. You can ham up the characters, and help them to understand the tone of the book better. Also, with older books that have long descriptive passages, you can edit (skip) as you go.
- If you have a child firmly entrenched in reading series books (which is *good*), reading aloud is a gentle, enjoyable way to introduce her to some more demanding literature.
- Finally, of course, reading aloud with a child is a wonderful, close, nurturing thing to do. Kids grow up so fast—you turn around and they're leaving for college. So enjoy reading aloud with your children while you can.

## READING WITH FRIENDS

Having reading friends becomes even more important in elementary school than it was during the preschool years. This is the age when kids have a lot of time to read—or a lot of time to watch television and play Little League baseball. It's easy to watch television and play baseball with friends—so try to think up ways that reading, too, can be social. Here are some suggestions:

### 1. Encourage your children to be very generous in loaning their series books and comic books.

One caution: It will be tempting for you to try to keep track of all of the books the neighborhood kids have borrowed from your house. Don't do it. If they return the books, fine. If they don't, those books have already made reading more attractive for your own children. And the minute you start acting like a librarian, they'll stop coming to borrow books. It's better, *much* better, to lose a few. Also, your kids will start hearing about good books from their friends—which kids always see as a more reliable recommendation than any they get from an adult. And eventually, when their friends become avid readers, your children can borrow books from them.

### 2. During sleep-overs, have plenty of comics and paperbacks around.

I know kids will all want to rent a movie and watch it, but perhaps you could do both. Let them watch a movie, and then tell them they have to start getting ready to sleep, but they can look quietly at books. It's worth a try. If the reading material is enticing enough, at least some kids are going to be tempted. And, luckily, there aren't *that* many good movies. There's a good chance the kids will be jaded by movies and be open to reading a bit.

### 3. Suggest a doll sleep-over for your daughter.

Mention that before your daughter and her friends can put their dolls to bed, they should read them stories. This would be a great time to take out all of the picture books you may have stored away, so the girls can read them to their dolls. Once they start reading their old favorite picture books, they'll have a wonderful time reading and rereading them to each other.

### 4. Suggest a joke-book party for your eight- or nine-year-old son.

Jokes are very easy to read—and there seems to be a time in the lives of most eight- or nine-year-olds when disgusting and really dumb jokes are seen as absolutely hysterical—so even if your son's friends are not very big on reading, they might be willing to risk this. The deal is that everyone reads his favorite jokes, and you have a contest for the funniest, grossest, or silliest joke. The party favors are, of course, more joke books!

Note: I don't think parents are really capable of judging the quality of jokes you'll probably get. You'll have to arrange some kind of voting system. And you'll probably want to be out of the room.

### 5. Suggest a ghost-story camp-out for your eleven- or twelve-year-old.

As at the joke-book party, all the kids can bring their favorite scary story to read, or you can provide the scary stories. Stephen King's book of short stories, *Nightshift*, would probably work well. Also, this can introduce your child's friends to Stephen King, just when they're starting to get tired of children's books. Most avid-reading children, boys especially, move to adult authors by eleven or twelve, and Stephen King is one author who helps bridge adult and juvenile fiction for kids. Or you might try a children's writer who is writing very popular teenage horror—R. L. Stine.

But you get the idea. Put the kids out in the backyard with a tent and flashlights—and no VCR or television—and provide them with lots of food and scary stories to read to each other. Will the kids get too scared at night? Well—camp counselors tell scary stories all the time with kids this age, and even younger. And there's something about kids this age—boys especially—that seems to revel in gory, awful stuff. They might as well pick up reading skills—rather than television-watching skills—while being scared, is my theory. And—I can't emphasize this enough—it's not the avid readers who become violent, scary adults.

## 6. Encourage an interest in Dungeons and Dragons games.

I know that this is a controversial recommendation—some people seem to think there is something wicked and occult about D&D games—but I've seen a number of boys develop reading skills and a love of reading through this game and the books spun off from it. In addition, TSR, the producer of the game, has responded to the criticism of its perceived occult and supernatural content by toning it down considerably in recent years. I think all of the worry over the game is ridiculous. It's a fantasy game, and kids who read don't usually have much difficulty distinguishing fantasy from reality. One young man—a wonderful student and reader—described to me the advantages he got from playing Dungeons and Dragons:

> It was also about that time I got interested in Dungeons and Dragons and those type of things really fired the imagination, and had a lasting impression on me. At home I have eleven [Dungeons and Dragons] books that are 300 pages each. Some of it is supplemental background that teaches us what is based on reality. Historical stuff about various cultures which inspired my interest in other cultures. Some of it is just game rule text which also inspired me to check out things along that line. There are books and novels and short stories that are attached to the mythos of Dungeons and Dragons. . . . You can find them in bookstores. Also things like the DragonLance series. . . . It's produced by TSR books, which is the producer of Dungeons and Dragons, and so in my early years—fourth to sixth grade—that's a lot of what I read.

By the time I got this young man in class in high school, he was reading everything—history, political writings, classics. He's an excellent student—and I thought it was interesting that he attributed his wonderful imagination at least partly to his early experiences playing Dungeons and Dragons.

By the way, the books that he mentions, the DragonLance series, produced by TSR and written by various authors, is a wonderfully addictive series for hooking kids into reading.

If you have a son interested in Dungeons and Dragons, you might check your local comic-book stores, because they sometimes have areas for game-playing. I know that one in my town does, and there's a group of boys who frequent it, become friends, and play games together. I was in a games store in Oxford, England, that had a huge table right in the front of the store with an ongoing game. The table was surrounded by excited kids playing and kibbitzing—and often needing to refer to some of the extensive manuals about the game. It was a great place for kids to get acquainted with reading friends.

### 7. When you think of summer camp, think of fun reading material.

When my daughter went to camp last year, I sent her a collection of teen magazines that immediately made the rounds of her cabin. It was interesting to me that this year she wanted to take a bunch of paperbacks—so we went to the bookstore, picked them up, paid fifty dollars . . . and I'm sure I'll never see them again. But that's okay. It's really good to have reading be a social thing. (Molly told me she was the only girl in her cabin who went to public school—since her brother was a counselor, she got the much-reduced sibling rate—yet she was the one providing reading material for the whole cabin. It's not that the other parents necessarily begrudged money spent on books; they just didn't think to do it.)

### 8. Show interest in what your children's friends are reading.

You'd probably like your kids and their friends to start defining each other in terms of what they like to read as well as by what position they play on the soccer team, and what kinds of movies they like to rent. The longer I teach, the more convinced I am that self-image is a big factor in creating excellent readers. You want your children and their friends to see themselves as intelligent, literate people. Then they'll *become* intelligent, literate people.

While writing this book, I was visiting Ireland. One night, in a pub, I was talking to a group of young men who were thinking of emigrating from Ireland to America. "What kinds of good jobs are there in America?" they kept asking me. "How can we make good money there and get ahead?"

"You need to go to college," I told them. "For all of the really good jobs in America, you need a college education."

"Oh, no," they told me. "We don't mean those kinds of jobs. We mean jobs for ordinary lads like us."

Even though they were obviously bright and verbal, they didn't see themselves that way. Going to college wasn't an option they would ever seriously consider. And when I asked them what kind of reading they did, they just looked at me blankly. Reading, in their view, wasn't for "ordinary lads" like them.

I had the same experience with a barmaid in London. She was from a little village in northwestern England. When I asked her what she liked to read, she also looked at me blankly.

"Well, what did you read in school?" I persisted.

"Oh, books with little stories and questions," she told me. In other words, all she read were school readers.

"But didn't you read regular books?" I asked.

"Oh, only the really smart ones did that," she said matter-of-factly. She was a charming, intelligent young woman, but certainly didn't see herself as part of a literate world.

So treating your children and their friends as literate, book-loving people right from the beginning is very important. You treat people as you want them to be.

The other reason for engaging kids in book discussions is that it helps them begin to read critically. You can discuss books with your own children anytime, but think how great it would be if your children and their friends started discussing books with each other. They talk about everything else—why not books? Don't expect them to have long, involved discussions about theme and plot devices, but even cursory comments about why they like—or don't like—a book helps them to form a habit of critical thinking.

## 9. Give bookstore gift certificates as gifts.

When the neighborhood kids are leaving your child's birthday party with their little bag of treats and party favors, solemnly hand them an envelope at the door and explain that it's a gift certificate that will enable them to pick out a favorite paperback book at your local bookstore. Tell them that you can't wait to see what they choose. If you've been talking to them about reading, you can even say something like, "I bet it will be another DragonLance book. I know how you love them. Or maybe you'll surprise me!"

When your children are attending other birthday parties, buy a regular present, and then attach a bookstore gift certificate to the front of the box as well. I think you need to get a regular present, because you don't want to risk having the birthday child, if he just gets a gift certificate for a book, making some disparaging comment. Unfortunately, in the world of today's ten-year-olds, books don't have the glamour of other presents, and you want children to be pleased at receiving these certificates. So make them an extra treat.

The certificate doesn't have to be for a lot of money; most paperbacks for children are very inexpensive, about the price of one or two video rentals. But the crucial reason for giving a gift certificate is that it will not only get your children's friends into a bookstore; it will get their *parents* into a bookstore. Now, many of these parents may be in the habit of frequenting bookstores anyway, but some may not be. My town is full of very well-to-do parents who spend big bucks on their kids for everything you can think of except the most important thing of all (outside of food)—books! And maybe while the child is making his choice, the accompanying parent will also see an irresistible book. If nothing else, that parent will be aware that his child *will* read if someone just buys him books.

## A WORD ABOUT SCHOOL PROBLEMS

I discussed children with school reading problems in my first book, *Parents Who Love Reading, Kids Who Don't*, and I will deal with the school issues of average and excellent readers later in this book. But I would like to mention here a few guidelines you might follow if one of your children—your daughter, say—is having serious problems in elementary school.

1. When possible, let your daughter be the one to make the final decision about her educational placement, and about the kind of help she receives. There are two reasons for this. If she makes the decision, she'll be much more likely to "buy into" any arrangement, and so work hard. Even more important, she needs to feel like a competent, in-control individual in as many areas of her life as possible.
2. Look for teachers who seem to care genuinely about children. Choose a school that has a culture of involved, caring teachers.
3. Keep your daughter reading at home, even if she's in fifth grade and still reading only comics or picture books. Keeping her reading is more important than insisting that she spend hours and hours on inappropriate homework.
4. Don't let her stay in a school situation that is making her desperately unhappy. *Somehow* get her out.

I mentioned in the previous chapter that my older daughter was a very active preschooler. Today she might be diagnosed as hyperactive. But because she could read, she did okay in school. She didn't do terrifically well—I think things moved a little slow for her, and she would occasionally get in trouble for doing things like sneaking on her sailor hat when the first grade nun wasn't looking—but she survived, and went on to do very well in high school and college.

Keep your daughter reading. Keep her in a child-friendly school. Leave her in charge as much as you can. And I think she'll be okay.

So now you're making sure your children have access to plenty of books, you're still reading aloud to them, you're encouraging reading friendships for them, you're keeping an eye on their school situation, but you can still do one more thing. You can encourage writing.

# Helping Children in Elementary School Write for Pleasure

Why should you be concerned that your children write for pleasure? Obviously, everyone needs to be able to read—but to write? Sure, kids will have to write reports for school, but what does scribbling poetry at the age of eight have to do with important high school history reports? And how does all of this fit in with reading?

In the chapter on preschoolers I mentioned that you can't assume that wonderful readers will be wonderful writers. Kids who dislike reading *won't* be terrific writers—you can count on that—but that doesn't mean you *can* count on kids who *do* love reading being terrific writers. They might or they might not.

And it's very important that your children become confident, fluent writers. Kids who write easily and well are much more likely to have an easy time in school. Most school assignments involve at least some writing. A child who has acquired sophisticated language structures through reading, and acquired a fluency and style through much practice writing, will be able to do a better job than his classmates on school assignments, and in a fraction of the time. Avid readers and writers have told me that they made a point of never starting a paper until the night before it was due, because they could always finish it so fast. And one of the kids telling me this went on to Yale. (I wonder if he can still do this.)

But there's another reason for encouraging writing. I've decided it can't be a coincidence that my very best readers—the ones with the incredible insights that take my breath away—are almost always the ones with active, independent writing lives. They write poetry and stories—some of them have huge folders of stuff they've written for fun over the years. I really believe now—and this isn't an original insight with me, but I *see* it now— that just as reading helps writing, writing helps reading. Continually trying to write makes kids more thoughtful, alert readers.

I'm convinced that, just as reading fairly schlocky fiction—such as Star Trek books and R. L. Stine's Goosebumps series—will enable a kid later to read complex, difficult fiction, doing enjoyable, silly writing will enable a student later to do serious, high-quality writing. As in much of life, practice is almost everything.

The good news about writing is that the education establishment—teachers, curriculum directors, college professors, textbook writers—really values good writing, probably because it's possible to *see* good writing. It's hard to see good reading, so most people aren't aware of the tremendous gulf separating excellent readers from poor or mediocre ones. But writing? It's right there in front of you, and no one can pretend that a poorly organized, ungrammatical essay showing little insight or development of thought is equivalent to a beautifully written, clear, perceptive piece of writing.

For a while I thought schools were doing pretty well with writing. A practice called "process writing" swept the schools about ten years ago. Its premise was that the end product—a piece of writing—was not the all-important part of the assignment; it was the *process* of writing that was important. So kids were shown how to brainstorm ideas, do rough drafts, rewrite, help each other, and then do final editing. Then they "published" by putting their work in class anthologies or on a bulletin board, or even on the shelf of their school library. Good schools would hold an occasional "authors' breakfast" at which students could show off their work to their parents.

While there is still much of this exciting support of student writing going on, there is a new twist on writing that is chilling to me. It centers around something that educators call "rubrics." Rubrics are a combination of models of excellent student writing, and a description of what different kinds of writing should contain. What, for example, does an excellent story by a fifth grader look like?

At first glance it seems very sensible to present a fifth grader, who has been assigned to write a story, with a model of a really good story written by another fifth grader. And it seems good to say, "Now, your story will need an interesting plot, good character development, descriptive details. . . ." So what's my problem with this?

I'm uneasy for two reasons. One is that reliance on rubrics seems to make writing akin to painting by numbers. Good writers naturally imitate different authors before they develop their own styles, but it's an imitation that creeps into their writing without, usually, their even being aware of it. They don't read a Hemingway short story and then say, "I'm going to write one just like that." Good writers are always trying to make that leap into the unknown, to wrestle an aspect of experience into sudden clarity. And wide, avid reading presents models enough.

My other problem with rubrics is that I think they take the fun out of writing. When little children are learning to talk, we don't present them with sophisticated speech and say, "Talk like this." When a two-year-old says, "Want cookie," we don't tell him, "You *should* say 'I want a cookie.' " We very naturally model a little better form back to him: "You want a cookie? But it's almost time for dinner." Or, if it's his lucky day, "That's a great idea! Here's a cookie." We respond naturally to what he's saying while surrounding him with more sophisticated forms of speech.

I think that's what good writers need. We must respond naturally and enthusiastically to their work, while surrounding them with all different kinds of reading. I don't like the idea of sitting down with an eight-year-old and telling her that she needs more description of the castle in her story—unless she's been writing for a long time and really wants that kind of feedback. I'd rather just be enthusiastic, tell her it's a great story, and let her develop her descriptive powers at her own speed.

The danger in rubrics is that when we are always showing kids how to make their writing better, we risk demoralizing them and turning them off to writing altogether.

The four goals of reading really work for writing also. First, you want your children to enjoy writing. Nothing must interfere with that. Next, you'd like your children to form a habit of writing. A child whose room is littered with notebooks filled with old stories and drawings and poems is almost certainly going to be a good writer. Third, you do want your children to develop advanced writing skills, but this teaching must never jeopardize their love of writing. And, eventually, it would be wonderful if your children started producing sophisticated, exciting, finished pieces of writing. But that will only happen, I think, if the first three goals are kept in mind. Using rubrics attempts to shortcut the process, and jump a student up to the fourth level—producing completed, accomplished pieces of writing—before he's had a chance to develop a love of writing, a habit of writing, and some early skill in writing.

Keeping all this in mind, what can you do to help your elementary-school-aged child to develop a love and habit of writing? I talked to my excellent readers and writers, and they helped me with the following ideas:

### 1. Start out by having your children tell you stories.
You could do this as a game. When you and your children are going for a walk and see a squirrel, start a story. Say, "Oh, wow, you know why that squirrel is upset? She's the only one in her first-grade squirrel class who hasn't lost a tooth yet. The squirrel

tooth fairy must have lost her address." Pause a minute and hope one of your children jumps in with something. If someone does, great, make a big fuss over how wonderful the addition is, and keep the story going. The idea is to encourage your children to make up stories on their own.

You might try asking an older child to make up a bedtime story for his younger brother or sister. One extremely literate student told me that he used to make up bedtime stories for his cousins. He didn't write them down, because he didn't really write well enough at the time, but he enjoyed making them up. A girl who is one of the best writers I've ever had told me that she used to elaborate on the stories she read her little brothers; she'd improvise her own additions to the books.

Another student—a wonderful reader and a very talented writer—told me her mother used to ask her to make up a story on the nights she couldn't get to sleep. So my student would lie in bed making up stories, waiting for her mother to come back and listen. Sometimes she'd fall asleep before her mother returned— proving, I guess, not only that her mother was smart enough to think of things that would develop her as a wonderful writer, but also things that would help her fall asleep painlessly.

I know it's very much in fashion to take children to see storytellers, and to spin stories yourself for your children. And I think telling children stories is wonderful. But surely it's even better to encourage children to make up their own stories, and to tell them to you. Here's why:

- Children will start to acquire confidence in their ability to dream up exciting events and happenings. Confidence isn't everything, but it counts for a lot in any endeavor.
- Storytelling is a way for children to move from the very concrete kind of playacting they did as preschoolers, to a more abstract form of storymaking. Rather than having dolls and ponies and water balloons to help in constructing imaginary worlds, in storytelling they just have words and facial expressions and gestures. When they finally move on to writing stories they'll have only words. Storytelling is a fine bridge.

- You want your children to enjoy making up stories. Helping them to do it in casual, everyday situations takes the mystery and pressure out of composing plots and characters. There's more chance that it will be fun for them.

Besides making up stories to tell their parents and friends in elementary school, my avid readers make up stories to tell themselves.

## 2. Encourage daydreaming.

A number of my excellent readers and writers reported living for a good part of the time in their own worlds in elementary school. When things got boring, they would make up a wonderful story in their heads, with themselves as hero or heroine. One student told me that this talent used to get her in trouble: one teacher slammed a trash can so hard to get her attention that she fell and cracked her head in surprise. The teachers kept telling her that she needed to concentrate harder. Of course, she *was* concentrating—but not on what teachers wanted her to.

It's my own theory that many of the books we really *love* as children are really elaborate daydreams. I know I wanted to be a detective like Nancy Drew, and drive a roadster (whatever that was) and eat "luncheons." I think daydreaming puts us in touch with our wishes and hopes. Kids are working out plots and characters and settings while they daydream. And a kid who's really good at plotting out wishes and dreams may be the next Danielle Steel, or tomorrow's Roald Dahl. A kid who's good at plotting nightmares, of course, could be the next Stephen King!

How do you encourage your children to daydream? You could make sure they have boring teachers—but I think that's too dangerous. Always go for the bright, exciting, sympathetic teacher. But what you can do is make sure your children have time to daydream, and make sure you don't yell at them for sitting around occasionally staring off into space. It's okay that they daydream. It's good. They're making up stories. They're leaving the harsh world behind for a while. Escape into stories is the best kind of escape there is.

You might even try doing a little daydreaming yourself. Suppose a rich uncle that you never knew you had, because he was the black sheep of the family and disappeared thirty-seven years ago, died and left you five million dollars on the condition that you relocated to Hawaii. . . . You get the idea.

### 3. Encourage your children to dictate stories to you.

A number of my very literate students remember doing this, either with a teacher or a parent. One girl remembers that her first story was about an imaginary friend.

Dictating stories seems to be an effective way for children to become engaged with writing *and* reading—since reading their own stories is the most interesting reading that children can do—of course! Also, since you'll be typing or carefully printing these stories, the stories will take on a professional look to your child. Her story will be just like the stories you read to her. Like the stories in bookstores! She's an author. She's part of the literate world.

When you're writing his story down, be sure to keep it *his* story. Don't edit any more than you have to to make it understandable. Be lavish with praise. What a wonderful story he's written! Show it to the rest of the family.

If you have time, you could really make this a project. Write the story so that your child can add illustrations. Bind the book together somehow with staples or glue. Give it an honored place on your bookshelf.

Keep in mind that a sense of accomplishment and mastery is one of the best natural "highs" anyone can have. By taking the time to help your children write books, you're connecting this intense pleasure with literary pursuits. And you're probably having fun.

### 4. Keep lots of writing materials available.

One of my best writers described to me how she loved notebooks and pens. She loved starting new notebooks; she loved having lots of pens with her. And, from the time she was too little to remember, she wrote all of the time.

There are lovely blank books available now. Take your children to a stationery store and encourage them to choose favorite notebooks, pens, pencils—whatever they like to write with. My younger daughter liked diaries with locks. That's fine. I really think that, initially, much of the writing good writers do, they do for themselves. Another student told me she too loved diaries; her childhood was littered with a succession of locked diaries. "I thought it was nice having something secret," she said. She'd write in them, lose the keys, and then pry the locks open with a pin. Think of all the different skills she was gaining all at once.

If you can, get a computer that's really easy to use. I'm always amazed at the difference access to a computer makes. I think those of us who now write quickly on a computer forget how long and laborious the writing process used to seem when we did it by hand. A computer doesn't make a student write better, but it certainly makes it easier for him to practice writing. Also, if possible, you want to get your children typing correctly, so they can pick up some real speed. One of my great writers told me she taught herself to type by using an instructional computer program; I'm not sure, however, that you can count on that.

One great thing about having your children write on a computer is that their writing will be very legible, so they're much more likely to share it with you and with their friends. And, of course, they can rewrite much more easily. With computer graphics they can also make their writing look very professional. I think it helps their image of themselves as writers.

I had a student this year who hadn't previously done much writing, but who started writing poetry in my Writing Workshop class. He had a wonderful time with the computer, doing different layouts and using various fonts. For his final exam he put together a collection of his best work and, with the help of the computer room supervisor, used a layout format that made it look like a real book. He was impressed; I was impressed; all of his friends were impressed! None of his baseball friends had thought of him as a *poet* before. But he definitely was.

So now your children have plenty of things to write with—

paper, computers, diaries, lots of pens and markers. But there's one other thing you should keep in mind.

## 5. Don't try to correct your children's spelling or grammar unless they request help.

Not worrying about perfect spelling and grammar has become accepted practice at many elementary schools. In these schools children are encouraged to write, and their spelling and grammatical mistakes are ignored in the early grades. If you hear the term "invented spelling," it refers to the spelling of five-, six-, and seven-year-olds when they first begin writing.

This movement, to allow children to begin writing unhindered by spelling and grammatical expectations, is provoking a backlash in some quarters. How can we allow children to misspell words and not correct them? How will they ever learn to spell correctly?

I think, again, we have to remember how children learn oral language. When a two-year-old mispronounces words, do we say, "If you can't say the word correctly, don't speak at all?" Of course not. Little children mispronounce words constantly. That's okay with us. We even think it's kind of cute. If we tried to insist they pronounce everything correctly right from the start, they'd probably never talk.

It's the same way with writing. Children's spelling and grammar will gradually improve as they read and write more. Fluency and an enjoyment of writing are the main things to worry about first.

If your child asks for help, quickly give it. Tell him how to spell the words he's interested in. What you'll probably find is that he'll ask about a couple of words, and then cheerfully misspell all the other ones.

Another reason to encourage your children to begin writing at home with you is that you can be flexible and encouraging about their early attempts, while some teachers may not be. And I can't think of any other academic skill in which confidence is so critical to performance.

So ignore all of their errors, and concentrate on the charming aspects of your children's writing. Before you know it, they'll be writing essays on college applications. Then you may need to help them proofread. But not now.

So, armed with writing materials and a good attitude about writing errors, how can you get your children started?

## 6. Try letters.

When we think of children writing letters, we often have an image of our ten-year-old reluctantly sitting down at the kitchen table, writing a thank-you letter to her grandmother for the Christmas sweatshirt she didn't really like. For many children, that kind of writing is the only kind of out-of-school writing they do. No wonder writing has such bad associations for them.

Forget the mandatory thank-you letters. I know what Miss Manners and Dear Abby and Ann Landers say about them—but that your children acquire a love of writing is more important than that they reluctantly, slowly, churn out mandatory thank-you notes. Have them make their thank-you's over the phone. Or buy some commercial thank-you cards and show them where to sign. But avoid requiring writing tasks that they will see as a dreaded chore.

You can, however, encourage letter writing. I never realized how much kids enjoyed writing to each other until, in my Writing Workshop class, I required everyone to write at least one business letter, so I'd know they understood the form. They could write the letter to anyone they wished, so they immediately started writing really funny business letters to each other, and to imaginary bureaus and agencies about each other. They loved writing letters! I was awash in letters all semester.

You could start by writing notes yourself to your kids. Keep a pad of paper and a pen next to your notes, and ask for a reply. After they've done this a bit, suggest they write to a friend, or a favorite animal, or a children's author, or a television star. There are all kinds of possibilities. One day I forgot, *again*, to sneak in at night and get my six-year-old's tooth and leave money. "Cover for me," I pleaded with my older daughter.

So Julie, writing as the Tooth Fairy, wrote and told Molly that, while helping the Toenail Fairy (whom you wouldn't know about unless your toenails fall off) clean out her closet, a whole box of lion's teeth fell on her head, and she had to be rushed to the hospital—in a "toe truck"—and so couldn't pick up Molly's tooth and deliver the money. Molly was charmed and excited with the letter—the rest of us were convulsed with laughter—and answered it. As I remember, this went back and forth for while, and I had the fun of seeing two of my children having a wonderful time writing.

If you can get your child to write a letter to Santa or the Easter Bunny, or any other stars in her life, I think you should be completely shameless about intercepting the letter and writing back. Ask (as Santa) for more details from her Christmas list. Mention that one of your elves wants to sit around all day reading comics instead of making toys. Ask for advice. Tell her you'd like to see a drawing or a poem—or anything else she might be willing to produce. Have some fun with the letters, and she will be enthusiastic and entertained also. And she'll be writing!

Children love humor, so any whimsical letter-writing projects you can think of might entice them into writing. If you can even have them draw pictures for a friend or favorite relative, it's a good start.

After your kids get past the writing-to-Santa stage, and start writing real letters to real people, you should make clear to them that you'll be glad to help—by buying stamps, envelopes, paper, by mailing the envelopes, even addressing the envelopes, if they wish. What you promise them you won't do—and this is a promise that you will, of course, keep—is read their mail, outgoing or incoming, unless they invite you to. I mention this because my younger daughter told me that she has friends whose mothers routinely open their mail and read it. Naturally, this exerts quite a chilling effect on any correspondence those kids have.

Another kind of writing you can encourage are letters answering ridiculous offers in magazines and comics. You know the kind. Your son sends two dollars and gets back a dragon that supposedly expands to life size when placed in a cup of water. Of course the whole thing is ridiculous, and probably a scam, but if it gets your son excitedly writing, why not? Yes, he may well be disappointed with the purchase when it arrives, but you can't, and shouldn't, protect your children from some aspects of life. It's better for him to learn now to read the fine print than learn it when he's twenty, and buying a used car. And writing for these kinds of offers will get him excitedly watching the mail for answers, and maybe looking for more offers. Having a bit of a disappointment now and then might even make him more cynical about television ads. Wouldn't that be great? The main thing to keep in mind is that anything—like letter writing—that helps him acquire sophisticated literacy skills will ultimately protect him from scams and ripoffs.

The newest kind of letter-writing is electronic mail, or e-mail, which requires only a computer, a modem, and some kind of access to the Internet. As I write this book, e-mail is still used mainly by adults, but is spreading so rapidly that soon it may be common even for children to have e-mail addresses.

This is good news and bad news. The good news is that children who would never dream of writing letters will probably get excited by sending messages over the computer. *Any* writing is good practice, and I think sending and receiving e-mail can help make children confident and prolific writers. The bad news is that the Internet may be a somewhat scary place for children: Not only can they easily talk to strangers, the pornography available is pretty overwhelming. I hate censorship, but even I would think twice before letting a ten-year-old have free access to all of the home pages and sex sites I've seen. I know that software is being developed that would allow parents to exert some control, and perhaps that's the answer.

But, regardless of your decision about e-mail, do try to get your children doing some informal, letter-type writing. And, in addition, look for more formal writing that might engage their interest.

So you have your children occasionally, at least, writing letters. Is there any other kind of writing that might easily engage their interest?

## 7. Suggest that your children start a neighborhood newspaper.

I'm hoping you have a computer with a good word-processing program on it (Claris or something similar). You don't need this—kids can certainly write newspapers by hand—but with a regular word-processing program it's very easy to make a newspaper that looks grown-up and professional.

Most programs have what are called templates built in, and there's probably one in your program for a simple newsletter. Your child could use one of these to write up his stories. If there isn't a template for a newsletter, there almost certainly is a page setting that will allow him to divide the page into two or three columns. Columns alone will make an ordinary page of typing look much more like a newspaper. I wouldn't recommend that you go out and buy a really professional program such as PageMaker. It's expensive and pretty complicated to use. I've been an adviser to my high school's newspaper for four years, and I still can't figure it out. Of course, I'm anything but a computer genius. If your child is really good on computers, you might want to reconsider.

But at any rate, let's say it's your daughter who wants to write a little newspaper. Explain to her the three kinds of newspaper writing: news stories, features, and editorials. News stories, tell her, are usually about something that just happened. The most important information comes first, and the paragraphs are short. You should always try to get quotes. Here's an example:

---

### SNAKES EVERYWHERE!

Jason Leeds's box of twenty snakes was overturned today by his two-year-old brother Monty. The snakes quickly scattered throughout the Leeds house.

"I spent hours and hours collecting them!" said a distraught Jason. "I'll never be able to find them all again. It's not fair. Some rolled out of the door and someone else will get to have them."

Jason's mother, who was barricaded in her upstairs bedroom, was unavailable for comment.

---

A feature is a story about a news story. Some people call it the news behind the news. A feature on the snake news story might go like this.

---

### No Luck With Pets

Jason Leeds, who lost a whole box of his pet snakes yesterday, has never had much luck keeping pets.

"I had a great turtle one time," he told this reporter, "but it kind of dried up and died. And the ants I got for my ant farm got out of the carton and ate my mother's chocolate cake."

Neighbors remember other of Jason's pets. Vivian Reed said that he used to catch frogs. "But the frogs never lived too long. Maybe it was because he only fed them Cheerios."

Jason is now planning to order a piranha from the We're Not the Ones Who Die Pet Company.

---

In an editorial, your daughter can give her opinion. A snake-story editorial might go like this:

---

### Kids Need More Education in Pet Care

The loss of Jason Leeds's snakes yesterday, and the deaths of all of the other animals that he captures and tries to care for, show that he doesn't know the first thing about caring for animals.

You shouldn't keep twenty snakes in a box. It's not fair to the snakes! And who will care for the snakes now that they're all over the house!

To let a turtle dry up is just plain cruel. The poor turtle!

Oh, well, at least the piranha will solve one of Jason's problems: what to do with all the dead animal bodies.

But, Jason, get a life! Read up on pet care before you try again.

---

You can tell your daughter that movie reviews and book reviews are also, essentially, editorials. Horoscopes? Well, no one is sure what they are, but she could have fun writing them.

After she writes up the paper, make enough copies so she can distribute it around the neighborhood. She should have fun doing this, and she'll also learn about the power of the press. It's amazing how much more attention people pay to something that is written down.

Your son, if he is really interested in sports, could write up a local sports sheet for his teammates. Again, sportswriting comprises news stories, features, and editorials. A news story gives the results of games played: BULLDOGS BEAT TIGERS 8 TO 1. A feature story gives background or a different slant: HOGAN PLAYING WELL THIS SEASON IN SPITE OF INJURIES. And an editorial, of course, gives an opinion: LITTLE LEAGUE FIELDS NEED BETTER MAINTENANCE. If your town has a local newspaper, it might even run some of his stories. Editors look for local sports news. Some of my high school students have become regular sports reporters of high school games for the local paper, and with all of the younger kids' baseball and soccer league activity, I wouldn't be surprised if the local editors wouldn't be glad of some help.

If you have children with a wry sense of humor, you might introduce them to supermarket tabloids, and suggest they try writing in this style. Every so often I have a student throw in a "ringer" story in tabloid style, and it always makes my day. Last spring a Japanese student submitted one to me with the headline SATAN REPORTS THAT HELL FREEZES OVER. Quoting Mr. Satan extensively throughout, he went on to write a news story, feature, and editorial on the event.

Here are some reasons to encourage newspaper writing:

- Writing newspaper articles may spark an interest in reading the newspaper. It's always fun to see what other professionals in one's field are doing.
- Your kids should be able to read a newspaper article much more critically after trying to write one themselves. If nothing else, they should notice when a supposedly objective piece of reporting is moving over into editorializing.
- The style for newspaper writing is clear, simple, and direct—not at all a bad style to practice.
- If your kids take reporting seriously, and really research stories, their knowledge frameworks will develop rapidly.
- If your kids try a supermarket tabloid style, they'll be getting practice using irony and satire. Also, they'll be developing a sense of the absurd, always a great asset for surviving life's slings and arrows.

But let's say you have a son who has no interest in writing newspapers. He's a more thoughtful type of kid, and not a bit interested in neighborhood politics or happenings. So try something else. Specifically:

### 8. Try poetry!

I find that poetry is a fairly easy way for children to start composing, since the finished piece can be very short. Also, children still tend to write with distinctive voices, which helps make the poetry charming and engaging. A child can get a real "high" from completing a first poem. I've also realized that the best way to get children to enjoy reading poetry is to get them writing it first.

Here's how I get my students started. I tell them to think of an experience—or maybe a person—that they remember vividly. Then I have them write for five minutes, without stopping, everything they can remember about that person or experience. I tell them not to worry about grammar or spelling or organization, but just to write whatever comes to their minds.

After they're finished, I usually have them write for five more minutes, but with younger children I think I'd stop after the first five. Then I tell my students to look at what they've written, and to circle the phrases that best seem to capture the experience. I tell them also to circle the words that seem the most vivid or interesting.

Then I tell them to write down their circled words on a piece of paper, and try to arrange them in such a way that the experience becomes clear. Usually I do one example on the blackboard to show them what I mean. Then I drift around the room helping them.

I think you could do this with your children. Emphasize that poetry doesn't have to rhyme or have a regular meter. It just has to capture an experience vividly, in as few words as possible. A Christmas poem, for example, might read like this:

> *Shivering, excited*
> *the gray morning light*
> *a sparkling bike*
> *under the warm hazy Christmas tree lights.*

The poems can be very simple—actually, for your purposes, the poems can be anything! You want your children to have the thrill of creating poetry, no matter what the quality of their writing. They'll get better. And meanwhile they're learning to enjoy poetry, and they're learning to think of themselves as writers. They are also learning to reflect in a mature way upon their experiences, which helps their reading ability and their critical thinking ability. One of my students theorizes that avid readers tend to be more reflective in general. She was also a prolific, exciting writer—and I think it might be the writing that encourages the reflection.

After poetry, you might consider stories.

## 9. Encourage your children to write stories.
Most of my excellent readers reported writing stories for fun as children. One of my best-ever students laughed when I asked her

if she'd written fiction as a kid: "I'd write really long stories. I wrote a hundred-page story in first grade. I loved Harriet the Spy—she writes about everything."

Don't ask your children to write hundred-page stories, but tell them what good imaginations they have, suggest they might like to write a story down, and tell them you'll help them if they like. If they start writing in the third person ("Once there was a little boy who . . ."), suggest they try to pretend that they're the person in the story, so that they're using a first-person narrator. Kids' stories are *much* more interesting when told with a first-person narrator, and the inherent liveliness of that structure might keep them going. Their stories will probably be "wish" stories—about friends they'd like to have, battles they'd like to fight, things they wish would happen. That's fine. If they keep writing, they'll move on to other subjects. Of course, they'll write out of their own experiences now.

Some of my students told me that they wrote long stories, but qualified it by saying that they only did that after they got a computer. And another thing—not surprising at all—is that kids seem to write the kinds of stories they are reading. Mystery fans write mysteries. R. L. Stine fans write horror. Kids reading the Shannara books write fantasy.

You'll be really enthusiastic about these stories because of all the skills and attitudes that writing long fiction narratives develops:

- If nothing else, your kids will end up as fast typists—an invaluable skill. Over the years—with all of the papers demanded in high school and college, and the computer work demanded in most businesses—your kids will save untold thousands of hours if they're fast typists. I'm a fast typist, and I owe most of my speed to all of the horrible, long novels I used to type out.
- Fiction writers also seem to acquire more quickly an appreciation of complex, difficult literature. My guess is that, as they're writing their long novels, they become very aware of the conventions of popular fiction and are no longer so easily daunted by complexity.

They need to move on to more complicated literature to stay engrossed.

- When kids are writing novels, they are also much more aware of character development, setting, tone, narrator—all of the elements of fiction. It means that when they get to a high school English class and are asked to analyze these elements, they're right at home with the assignment because they've been thinking in these terms for years.

So you have your children playing around, at least a bit of the time, with some kind of writing. They may be perfectly happy just writing for themselves, but I think you should suggest that they publish their work. Here are some ideas for ways to go about it:

## 10. Help your children publish.

One of my best writers told me that, in first grade, she and a friend started a publishing company. They wrote little books, stapled or glued them together, and then sold them to their mothers' friends for a nickel apiece. And she's been writing ever since.

I thought this was a great idea, really something to encourage. Your children don't have to sell all of their writing, but you should certainly display it around the house if they'll let you. When our kids are little, we all post their artwork and other things on the refrigerator door; later you might want to have a special area in the house for displaying writing.

If your kids don't want you to display their writing, don't. This is supposed to be an enjoyable experience, remember.

Besides offering to display or "publish" writing at home, you can invest in a book titled *Market Guide for Young Writers: Where and How to Sell What You Write*, by Kathy Henderson (Writer's Digest Books, 1993). It gives instructions for sending out material to editors, lists magazines and book publishers that are receptive to writing by young people, and even profiles some young writers. In the back is a list of contests, some for children as young as three years of age.

Here are a few reasons why you should encourage your children to start sending work off to editors and contests:

- Kids will work harder on their writing when they have an objective. They'll be more encouraged to write and rewrite, to make a piece really special.
- Books that list markets for young writers, such as the one mentioned above, will contain lots of writing ideas for your children. When they start looking through a book of markets, they'll see the wide variety of writing that is published for children. And I'm sure it will give them new ideas they'd like to try.
- Your kids will start to be aware of spelling and grammar—and in this context I think that's fine. Sooner or later they have to learn to use standard English forms. If they're working on a story to get it ready to enter into a contest, they'll probably be more than ready to let you do a little grammatical and spelling instruction with them.
- The biggest reason of all is self-image. Sending off work to professional publications and contests is a great way for your children to start to see themselves as writers. Even if they never get anything back but a form rejection, I still think they'll be more likely to see themselves as literate, writing people than they would if they kept all their stories in a shoe box in their room. And, with practice, they may well get more than a standard rejection letter. Maybe they'll even get published!

So you've been working on getting your children writing. But you don't want to forget reading. In the next chapter I discuss some of the more common reading paths I see kids taking, usually from around third or fourth grade up through high school.

# Reading Paths, Reading Hooks, and
# Genre Fiction: An Overview

I've been fascinated, for the last few years, with the reactions of kids to various books. Which kids will like which books? I know, for example, that there are books that almost all kids who read well enough to understand them will like. They are the ones I starred in the reading lists in *Parents Who Love Reading, Kids Who Don't*. For example, *To Kill a Mockingbird*, by Harper Lee, and *East of Eden*, by John Steinbeck, are books that most kids with adequate reading skills will really like. Stephen King is an author most kids like. A huge number of my high school readers tell me they went through a Stephen King stage.

But, on the other hand, there are books that some kids *love*, and other kids, with comparable reading skills, *hate*. The Baby-sitters Club books, by Ann Martin, are in this category. Many young readers, almost all girls, love these books. Many young readers, mostly boys, think they are incredibly dumb. Some kids love Terry Brooks's Shannara books; others find them tedious and dull—almost unreadable. While most good readers will enjoy *The Hobbit*, by J. R. R. Tolkien, not nearly as many will enjoy his entire Ring Trilogy. And those who do like the Ring Trilogy usually like it much better than *The Hobbit*. Why do some kids love Robert Ludlum's books, and others find them boring—and yet almost all kids like at least one or two of the John Grisham novels?

And so the question becomes, Is there a pattern? Is it possible to predict which kids will like which books? Is it possible to know what, exactly, kids like about various books—and what they dislike?

I've become very interested in this question because I think, to some extent, it's a matter of luck who becomes a great reader. I'm convinced that kids lucky enough to pick up a book early on that has a strong appeal for them have a much better chance of growing up to be avid readers. My guess is that if children find books early that they really love, books they read over and over again, books that contain some ingredient that reaches them on some deep, fundamental level—those kids have experienced reading in a completely different way from the child who is just plodding through a programmed reader, or is made to read a book he finds boring. Reading has acquired power for these children. It has meaning in their lives. And I'm sure these are the kids who will always be looking for that next wonderful book. Probably the worst thing that can happen to children in regard to reading is that someone insists that they read a book that they really dislike.

In this chapter I will try to give you an overview of the different types of reading that I see my students doing, and in the next chapter I give suggestions for figuring out where your child fits into these reading paths and categories.

And there's one other note I'd like to make before starting. I'm hoping that, as you read through these categories, you'll see that all books—yes, even teenage romances—have valuable and interesting ingredients. I can't really say that I see that one type of reading is better than another. Sometimes teachers or parents will comment to me that one of their children is reading "good" books, such as the Redwall books, while another is reading "junky" books, such as R. L. Stine novels. I don't see the clear distinction. True, some books demand a more sophisticated reader— but I'm not sure that makes them better books.

I think books are often judged on their genres. Science-fiction books, for example, are often judged to be better than romances. There's no rational reason for it: both are unrealistic, both follow genre conventions, both tend to deal with the same themes over and over again. As far as style goes, I've seen well-written and poorly written books in both genres. Is the problem that most critics are male, and so more likely to like science fiction? I really don't know.

But, anyway, do try to keep an open mind about the different categories of reading. Remember that *any* reading your child does is wonderful if it builds a love of reading and a habit of reading. So don't be concerned about books they're reading that they love; be concerned when they're assigned to read books for school that they dislike. That's where the harm comes in.

## THE TWO BASIC READING PATHS

The common ingredient in all books is action, and I think it's in the kind of action preferred that readers initially diverge. What I see is that there are two basic kinds of action. There is interpersonal action, which usually involves solving personal problems, and learning about life. Then there is good versus evil action, which usually involves fighting something or someone outside an immediate circle of friends and family—such as wars, monsters, killers. This kind of action is adventure-type action rather than interpersonal action. Kids, and maybe adults, seem to have a lasting preference for one of these two types of action.

What I've found is that books can be divided mostly into three categories: books that get most of their action from interpersonal conflicts, and from characters learning to cope with life's ordinary events; books that get most of their action from outside, from events or opponents that their characters need to overcome; and books that seem to have significant amounts of both types of action. I think, especially, that large numbers of nonfiction books deal with both areas: interpersonal issues mixed with more global concerns.

In addition to the kind of action in books, books may have other elements that certain readers find especially appealing. A child who loves comedy, for example, will love most comic books whether they are good versus evil, or relationship oriented. I call these special qualities "hooks"; many such hooks are so strong that they overpower almost any other aspect of a book in the mind of a reader. So after I talk about the different action paths of books, I'll describe what I see as the most powerful hooks. In addition to these hooks, there are well-established genres such as mystery and science fiction. I'll also describe these. In the next chapter, I'll take up the question of which paths or hooks or genres to try with individual children.

So, first, what books are primarily concerned with interpersonal action?

## 1. Interpersonal Action

The classic kind of interpersonal-action book is a growing-up or coming-of-age book. A lot happens in this kind of book, but most of the happenings deal with characters getting along with each other, or dealing with everyday growing-up events. Many, many of my students fondly remember the Berenstain Bears books. These are books in which bear children learn to clean up their rooms, go to the dentist, deal with money—all of the everyday traumas that all kids go through. The Baby-sitters Club books, by Ann Martin, are also classics of this genre, only here the emphasis is more on friend problems than family problems. They are geared to a slightly older reader. Slightly overlapping the Baby-sitters Club in terms of age, but going on to deal with high school and dating problems, are the Sweet Valley High books, by Francine Pascal. In these books the main characters deal with jealousy, bad grades, dating problems, peer group problems—all problems teenagers routinely experience during their growing-up years. In the Sweet Valley series, as in the Baby-sitters Club series, these growing-up traumas occur at breakneck speed. Someone is always getting teased, or feeling left out, or getting in trouble with parents. Every few pages there's a new crisis. This is typical of series interpersonal books.

When kids start reading, they read so slowly that events have to happen quickly to keep their interest. It might take them a couple of hours to read fifteen pages, so lots had better happen in those fifteen pages. As kids get older, and start to read better, the action can slow down a little, and the events can be better developed. If your daughter falls in love with reading through the Baby-sitters Club books, for example, she may move on to the Little House books, by Laura Ingalls Wilder. There are also many interpersonal crises in those books, but they're a bit more realistic and they're more spread out. Moreover, some of the action doesn't revolve solely around interpersonal problems; natural disasters come into play also. Later on, your daughter may like the Betsy-Tacy books, by Maud Hart Lovelace. There are interpersonal crises here, but they are not painted in the same vivid colors as the action in the Baby-sitters Club books. The girls deal with more ordinary, everyday events: making paper dolls, climbing their favorite hill, going on picnics. The action isn't as riveting, but is more realistic and satisfying, for more advanced readers. Probably the most advanced children's books that rely on interpersonal relationships for the action are the Anne of Green Gables series by L. M. Montgomery. The style is kind of old-fashioned and leisurely. The things Anne worries about—having puffed sleeves, talking too much—seem kind of boring to a new reader who still needs all the trauma of a Sweet Valley–type book to pull her through. But an accomplished reader will probably find the Anne books much more satisfying because the situations and emotions are so much more fully developed and believable.

A teenager who likes interpersonal relationship books, but hasn't yet done much reading, may initially enjoy such adult authors as V. C. Andrews, Danielle Steel, and Terry McMillan. Like Ann Martin and Francine Pascal, these authors write books filled with interpersonal trauma; major events, such as incest and divorce, happen every few pages. More adept readers, however, will go on and be able to enjoy some fairly sophisticated adult authors who deal with interpersonal relationships, such as Barbara Kingsolver, Jane Smiley, and Anne Tyler. The action in their books also involves characters working out personal problems, but the problems are of a more realistic and everyday sort, the characters are more aware and believable, and the events are described in much more detail and depth.

When these readers are ready for more complex books, keep in mind that the books should still deal with interpersonal relationships. You might put *Pride and Prejudice* by Jane Austen into the path of a sophisticated relationship reader, or *Jane Eyre* by Charlotte Brontë. A student who is a very fast reader and likes long books will probably enjoy *Vanity Fair* by William Makepeace Thackeray. I get the occasional student—always a very good reader—who loves watching the machinations of Becky Sharp. These are the readers who will probably like F. Scott Fitzgerald—especially *The Great Gatsby*. They will like the short stories by Kate Chopin, as well as her novel *The Awakening*. If they are very good readers they'll love Virginia Woolf, especially *Mrs. Dalloway*. They might like D. H. Lawrence, and they'll love Kaye Gibbons's book *Ellen Foster*. Faulkner is a writer they'll like—remember, we're talking about very good readers now—as is Tennessee Williams. For a truly exceptional reader, you might consider Anthony Trollope. His Victorian novels are full of action too; it's just that his action often involves nuances of manners and social customs. For a fast reader who can understand these intricacies, the books are fascinating. For a slower reader who doesn't have the background of interest to care about nineteenth-century drawing-room repartee, reading a Trollope book is like watching grass grow. But he's an author your interpersonal-relationship reader may well grow into.

As far as nonfiction goes, readers of interpersonal books enjoy—no surprise—books about how and why people behave as they do. Psychology is a real interest for this type of reader. They love the Torey Hayden books about handicapped children, such as *One Child* and *Murphy's Boy*. They'll read self-help books, such as *Toxic Parents* by Susan Forward. As they get older, they'll start enjoying biographies, especially biographies that deal with everyday lives.

If you have children who like relationship books, you can probably count on this reading preference being long-lasting—at least until they're out of their teens. Just be aware that there are many different kinds of relationship books, and many different levels of sophistication in the writing. You'll want to find the types of books that have the strongest pull for your children.

## 2. Good Versus Evil/Adventure Books

Although these books certainly have characters, and have a certain amount of character development, the main focus of these books is usually on some outside, often cataclysmic events. Superhero comics fall into this category, for example. While we may occasionally see a human side of Superman and Batman and the Punisher, mainly we watch them overcome evil foes. In the Choose Your Own Adventure books, the main character, who is the reader, is continually making life-and-death-type choices that usually involve facing or overcoming some evil. Some mysteries—the ones that rely less on interpersonal relationships than on overcoming evil—fall into this category.

Currently the most popular children's books that fall into this category are the R. L. Stine Goosebumps and Fear Street series. While Stine does have a bit of interpersonal-relationship action in his novels, the emphasis is clearly on overcoming evil. In one of his most popular books, *Monster Blood*, the young hero does make an alliance with a girl in the neighborhood, but the heart of the story is about their joint fight against this monster blood that bursts out of its bottle and chases people, sucking them into its whirlwind.

An aside: Stine's Goosebumps books remind me a bit of Sesame Street, with their humor that is often humor only an adult would get. On the cover of *Monster Blood*, for example, we see green monster blood moving down some stairs and, in small white letters, the comment, "It's a monster blood drive!" I giggled, but I understand these books are serious reading for eight-year-olds who read half the night with flashlights under their covers.

Other than comics, choose-your-own-adventure books, and some horror and mysteries, there aren't many of these easy action/adventure books for children—although the popularity of the Stine books is so tremendous that, like his monster blood, they seem to be rapidly expanding and taking over bookstore shelves. (Which I think is wonderful. He's getting kids reading.) The other category of readers—those liking lots of interpersonal issues in their stories—have all of the growing-up and teen series to choose from, but readers who prefer good-and-evil conflicts had a much more limited choice until Stine came along. He's changing the landscape a bit. And now it may be easier to get boys reading— since boys are the primary readers of these types of books.

Once your child has read through some of these early, easier books, do try him with the books of Jane Yolen, Susan Cooper, Lloyd Alexander, Madeleine L'Engle, and Ursula Le Guin. They are fantasy writers for children with strong good-versus-evil themes. A few children's classics are also very strong in good-versus-evil action—*Treasure Island*, for example, or *Kidnapped*— but kids need pretty strong reading skills to enjoy them.

I find that readers of this type of book usually move to adult titles by the age of eleven or twelve. And in the adult section of a library or bookstore they can find many, many books with plenty of riveting action and adventure. Most fantasy series are essentially good-versus-evil battles (look for a complete list in my other book), as are many war/espionage novels such as those by Robert Ludlum and Tom Clancy. Their books are filled with evil characters and a wealth of technical detail that readers who prefer relationship books find offputting and tedious. But sophisticated readers of these action books follow all the details and find them fascinating. There are also the Clive Cussler books, the Brotherhood of War books by W. E. B. Griffin, and the cluster of military flying books, such as *The Flight of the Intruder* by Stephen Coonts, that are getting very popular, not to mention the "psycho killer" books such as the *Prey* series by John Sandford.

It's interesting that with all of this popular fiction around, there is very little classic or multicultural reading in the schools that is geared to the action-adventure reader. Maybe this is one reason boys tend not to shine in most English classes. As I'll point out in my chapter on school problems, most of the excellent readers who don't do well in high school are boys.

But there are some classics that appeal to these readers. The *Iliad* and the *Odyssey* are full of battles and have a satisfyingly high body count, as do many of Shakespeare's plays. Hamlet, for all his moaning around, does get it together in the end, and our last view of the play is a stage littered with corpses. My high school action readers, who are good readers, still love the short stories of Edgar Allan Poe, as well as *Huckleberry Finn* and *Tom Sawyer* by Mark Twain. The novels of Robert Louis Stevenson, such as *Treasure Island*, are usually enjoyed by these readers, as are the novels of H. G. Wells, especially *The Time Machine* and *The War of the Worlds*. They enjoy *Brave New World* by Aldous Huxley, and especially like *1984* and *Animal Farm* by George Orwell. *The Lord of the Flies* by William Golding, *Black Boy* by Richard Wright, and *All Quiet on the Western Front* by Erich Maria Remarque are modern "classics" that most action/adventure readers love.

Some authors, however, *seem* to have a lot of adventure but bury it in material that won't interest many kids. Dickens, even when he's portraying the depth of the very bloody French Revolution (*A Tale of Two Cities*), has to have one of his too-good heroines around to sentimentalize everything. Some of Hemingway's "grace under pressure" heroes do get involved in a bit of action—bullfighting comes to mind—but we spend much more time seeing them bear their troubles nobly than watching them actually engage an enemy. The "noble savage" tales by James Fenimore Cooper, such as *The Last of the Mohicans*, are full of action, but the unbelievability of some of the characters, as well as the turgid style, just about sinks the books for most modern-day teenagers. Some of Herman Melville's books may appeal to a very good reader in this category, but they probably won't be his two most famous: *Moby-Dick* or *Billy Budd*. I'd try some of his earlier novels, such as *White-Jacket*—they have more action and less philosophy.

The good news, with regard to school reading, is that all of their early fantasy, science-fiction, and espionage reading has given readers of action/adventure books an understanding and liking for history and political science. By high school age, many of these readers are doing a good deal of nonfiction history reading. After keeping armies of elves and orcs and wizards straight, they have no problem following the intricacies of who's on whose side during the world wars. They understand intrigue and power manipulation. They're interested in monarchies. And, most important, they're very good at remembering and making sense of the kind of detail necessary to any serious study of history.

I had a student a couple of years ago who was an avid reader of fantasy. (In fact, the excellent fantasy reading lists in my first book are due mainly to him.) By the time he came to my class, he was extensively reading history as well as fantasy—and helped explain the Napoleonic background of *War and Peace* to me and to a fellow student who was reading it for an independent study course. (We invited him to read *War and Peace* with us, but, it turned out, he'd already read it on his own—and got more out of it, I think, than this other student and I were getting out of it reading it together.)

So, when your eight-year-old is up at all hours of the night reading *Monster Blood II*, or neglecting his homework to hunch over X-Men comics, realize that he's just engaged in the first stage of a reading path that may well take him to great novelists or great historians.

## Books that combine interpersonal relationship action with adventure and action are loved by almost all readers.

I mentioned earlier that there are some books that almost all kids love. Probably the two writers with the most universal appeal for children are Roald Dahl and Dr. Seuss. When we look closely at their books, it's easy to see why. They are filled with fascinating characters who are always engaged in attempts to get along with each other. But they are also engaged in fascinating adventures with giant peaches and candy factories, and Loraxes and Thing One and Thing Two. In addition, these books have what I'm finding to be one of the strongest "hooks" for children, which is a comic handling of the characters and action.

The first four S. E. Hinton books—especially the first two, *The Outsiders* and *That Was Then, This Is Now*—also combine interpersonal drama with adventure. In *The Outsiders*, Ponyboy is trying to get along with his older brothers after his parents' death—but he's also involved in gang fights, stabbings, and rescuing children from burning buildings. *To Kill a Mockingbird*, by Harper Lee, is a young girl's coming-of-age story after the death of her mother—but it also has all of the turmoil and action of a Southern town in the early part of the century engaged in a racist trial.

R. L. Stine's books seem to me now to be principally good-versus-evil books, but he is making some effort at character development and interpersonal drama. *Monster Blood*, for example, has a couple of bullies who go after the main character, and bullies are a main staple of coming-of-age books. (His bullies get punished by getting sucked up in the monster blood—not your usual coming-of-age ending.) I think that's why he gets some crossover readers from the interpersonal-relationship side.

John Grisham is interesting because he too, especially in his first book, *A Time to Kill*, combines these types of action. In *A Time to Kill* he really develops a relationship between a couple of lawyers, as well as wrenching our hearts with his description of the rape of a young girl, and its subsequent effect on her and her family. But the book is also full of lynchings and terror and unruly mobs. *The Firm* isn't quite so good with the interpersonal-relationship pull—although it's certainly there—but is wonderful on the adventure/action side. I was interested to see that in *The Client* he made a real attempt to more completely develop his characters and their problems—to the point where the book is almost completely a relationship book. In fact, for me the characters were more appealing than the action, which seemed to have become predictable. And both *The Chamber* and *The Rainmaker* are almost completely interpersonal-relationship books.

Fantasy writers are less likely to get a crossover audience of readers interested in interpersonal drama, but a couple have managed. Piers Anthony, in his Xanth series, has a series of young people very much involved in growing up and making sense of their world—while fighting "tangle trees" and "gap monsters" and "Night Mares." This confused me at first because when kids would fall in love with his books I'd assume they were fantasy readers, and try to steer them to Terry Brooks and David Eddings and all of the other wonderful fantasy writers available today. And some kids would move right on and love those authors—but some wouldn't. What was going on? I finally realized these other readers were really interpersonal-action readers—usually the ones who loved stories of magic—and would only like fantasy that had a significant amount of this degree of action in it.

There is one children's fantasy writer whose work I'm not personally familiar with, but who, kids assure me, fits into this wonderful-on-all-fronts type of writing, and that's Brian Jacques. His Redwall books seem to be universally loved—although, again, they require a fairly accomplished reader. And J. R. R. Tolkien's fantasy books are really interesting because his first one, *The Hobbit*, combines the two threads of adventure/action and interpersonal relationships—Bilbo and the dwarves are funny and touching together, but the book is also full of dragons and goblins—his Ring Trilogy, however, is almost all action/adventure. So *The Hobbit* has a wider readership, but is looked down on as not serious fantasy by real devotees of the genre—as, actually, is Piers Anthony's Xanth series.

I've always thought that some mystery writers managed to get the best of both worlds, so to speak, in their books. Agatha Christie's books are full of murder and mayhem, but also have many really interesting characters who relate to each other in believable ways. Maybe that's the reason for the public's enduring love of her stories. Some of her books go more the one way, and some the other. For your lovers of "people books," try *Endless*

*Night*. For your action/adventure readers, try *And Then There Were None*.

A more modern suspense writer, Mary Higgins Clark, also has strong elements of both action and character development in her novels. Typically she has characters with traumatic pasts being caught up in the same type of trauma in their later lives. Stalkers and sexual molesters abound in her books. The Spenser novels by Robert Parker have both elements with a strong comic tone added. His detective, Spenser, who is exceptionally literate and well read, is always rescuing lost or runaway kids—the human element—but also fighting against some lovely, vivid villains. And these books are very easy to read.

On the espionage front, I think John le Carré is best at combining people interest and good versus evil action. The British agent who travels through most of his Cold War books, George Smiley, is so wrenchingly real and so saddened by the tragedies around him that the reader can't gleefully cheer when he finally gets Karla, his main Russian antagonist, in *Smiley's People*. In fact, le Carré develops his characters and their relationships so completely that purists of the espionage genre get impatient with him. His style is so complex—since he's trying to capture complicated situations in real depth—that only very accomplished readers can enjoyably read him.

It's hard to find classics that cover both bases, but your best bet is probably the books of John Steinbeck, especially *East of Eden*. It has wonderful coming-of-age characters such as Cal, but also great good-versus-evil drama. One of the characters, Cathy Ames, Steinbeck calls a monster and almost demonizes, having her do incredibly wicked things like shooting her husband and deserting her newborn twin sons. Almost all of my students with adequate reading skills love *East of Eden*. Unfortunately, most schools assign students to read some of Steinbeck's less appealing books, *The Pearl* and *The Red Pony* in particular, and many students never get past them.

*All Quiet on the Western Front*, by Erich Maria Remarque, is another classic that appeals to almost all excellent readers who are willing to give it a chance. It's a story of the World War I trench warfare in France, told from the viewpoint of a German soldier. The character development, which is rich and poignant, almost overshadows the war action, but there is enough battle description to pull through most action-oriented readers.

It would be ideal, I should think, if the books that were required school reading—since schools seem hell-bent on requiring everyone to read the same books—were books that appealed both to readers who were interested in relationships *and* to readers interested in good-versus-evil action. But they're hard to find, and it's *especially* hard to find such books that are inoffensive enough to get by all of the school censors. I find this whole topic incredibly frustrating because the obvious answer—having students choose most of their own reading—is viewed as highly radical, and is never seriously considered by any curriculum developers of high school or college courses. But that's another book!

## READING HOOKS

I got the concept of "reading hooks" from a former student of mine who had gone on to Harvard a few months earlier. When she came home for Christmas vacation, she told me she liked Harvard and found the other students very interesting.

"Of course," she commented, "I don't really fit in."

"What do you mean?" I asked, confused. This was a wonderful student—gifted, intelligent, an avid reader.

"Well," she said, "during orientation everyone went around saying, 'What's your hook?' I don't have a hook."

"A hook?" Now I was really confused.

"Yeah, like are you an Indian, or a chess player, or a basketball star? Something like that. I'm one of the few students that doesn't have a hook."

I don't remember how I consoled her—I guess I told her she must really be wonderful to get accepted without a "hook"—but I've recounted this incident for a couple of reasons.

The first reason has to do with what it says about Ivy League admissions. If your son is living and dying to get into Harvard, maybe it is okay if he lets his grades slide just a little so he can publish his own newsletter of stock-market trends. He might be only third or fourth in his high school graduating class instead of first—but at least he'll have a hook.

The other reason is that I became fascinated with the idea of hooks. I've found it's a way to figure out which kids might like which books. You try to assess what the hooks for various books are, and then try to figure out which hooks might pull in your child.

Just as the hooks these Harvard students had represented only a small part of their entire personalities, the hook that draws your child to a certain book will be only a small part of that book. And books, like kids, can have many hooks. As your kids' reading widens, more and more hooks will appeal to them.

Hooks are critical to keep in mind with older reluctant readers. That high school sophomore who hates reading can probably only be reached with a book that hooks into a strong interest of his— rock stars, for example, or sports. And the interesting aspect of hooks is that they cut across all kinds of action and all kinds of genre reading. A comic tone, for example, can be found in fantasies, mysteries, and even romances. There is often much comedy in action/adventure books as well as in interpersonal-relationship books. So another value of hooks is that they can often entice kids to try a new genre of type of fiction. It's really important, when looking for books for your kids, to be aware of hooks.

So, to start with, what is the most common hook?

### 1. Look for books your child can identify with.

I think this is the universal hook. If we can find books that seem to capture and illuminate the individual experiences of our children, they will be pulled forever into reading as a way of understanding their world.

The problem with this hook, as I explained in the section in chapter 2 on multicultural literature, is that we interfering adults seem to think that if it's valuable for a girl from a Chinese-American background to read *The Joy Luck Club* by Amy Tan, it's valuable for *all* kids to read this book, since it will sensitize them to the problems of Chinese Americans. Well, if non-Chinese-American students have read enough to be able to see similarities and appreciate differences, that's fine. Reading *The Joy Luck Club* will be a good experience for them—although probably not the intense experience it is for a kid who really *identifies* with the story. But if kids are not ready—if they haven't yet had enough experiences reading books that they *can* identify with—they'll think Chinese Americans have the most boring, obscure culture imaginable. Reading the book will have been a bad experience for them—on all fronts. Not only will they have failed to gain an appreciation of another culture, but they'll be further turned off to reading—and so less likely *ever* to gain that appreciation.

The key is to find books that your individual child can identify with.

What books? An obvious kind of book to try first is one that describes young people from a culture the same as your child's. Sometimes it's not easy to find such books, if you're of African-American, Asian, Native American, or Hispanic descent. I know I haven't been very successful in finding very many authors that the minority kids in my classes can immediately identify with and love. You might try the Ludell books by Brenda Wilkinson, which are about a Southern African-American girl who moves to New York. The Terry McMillan books *(Mamma, Disappearing Acts,* and *Waiting to Exhale)* describe the trouble young African-American women have in finding responsible, loving men. My teenage girls *love* these books. James Patterson has a thriller titled *Along Came a Spider* that features a black detective. But on the whole, the number of these books is limited. For example, almost half of all paperbacks sold are romance novels, but according to a September 1994 article in *The Wall Street Journal,* of the approximately 1,800 romance titles published yearly, as late as 1993 only thirty-one of the titles featured African, Caribbean, or African-American characters.

Publishers are starting to pay attention to this market, and are adding romance lines that have ethnic heroes and heroines. And it's interesting to note that the publishers are not being altruistic or "politically correct." The *Journal* article refers to a newsletter called *Target Market News*, which estimates that black Americans spent an estimated $178 million on books in 1993. And while purchases of books among white Americans fell 3 percent between 1988 and 1991, they rose 26 percent in black households.

In the summer of 1994, Pinnacle Books launched a romance line called Arabesque, featuring African Americans; the paperback divisions of Random House, Bantam, and Dell are launching similar lines. I bought copies of four Pinnacle titles and offered them to some of my African-American girls. At first they said, "We don't read those trashy romances!" But then one girl tried one . . . and another girl tried another . . . and now everyone is reading them. They're quick to tell me that they're not as good as Terry McMillan's books, but they are good.

And recently I noticed an article in *The Boston Globe* describing a Stamford, Connecticut, company called Black Books Galore. The company doesn't sell books directly, but arranges book fairs that feature "hundreds" of books about children from a number of different minority cultures. Black Books Galore can be reached at (203) 359-6925.

So cultural background is certainly one place to look for books your child can identify with. But, because people are more than just their cultural background, you might look in other places too. Keep an open mind. I just happened once to hand *Early Autumn*, by Robert Parker, to a kid whose parents—I later found out—were waging a bitter custody fight over him. The book is about a detective who is hired to return a boy who has been snatched by the noncustodial parent. Well, this student, who had formerly hated reading, *loved* this book. He had to go on and read all of the Parker books, many of which are about troubled teenagers.

So books that help illuminate a crisis in your children's lives might be books they can identify with. I think that's why Judy Blume's books are so popular; they are constructed on the stuff of common childhood and teenage traumas—being too heavy, going through their parents' divorce, losing a first love. It's very comforting for children, or for anyone, to see that other people have similar problems. This is the principle behind the huge success of the whole support-group movement. So let your children get at least some of their support from books. Then they'll be readers too!

And there are other ways a child can identify with books. A parent once asked me if she should allow her timid son to read horror books. "It's all he wants to read," she told me, "and I'm afraid to let him."

I couldn't figure out why a fearful child would want to read horror books, until my older daughter laughed and remarked, "He identifies with the main character. They're both scared!"

Of course. And the great thing about horror books—and certainly about the children's books such as those by R. L. Stine—is that this scared child can see the hero of the book overcoming the monster and so conquering the thing he feared. Adults may look at horror books as depressing, but a scared child will see them as optimistic. Children *can* win over things that go bump in the night. And, as my sister Nancy remarked, a child can control the fear in a book. He can always stop reading if he wants to. Or he can skip especially scary parts. And the more control children have in their lives—on any front—the more likely it is that they will grow up to be confident, independent adults.

So books that feature the *kind* of child you have—fearful, gregarious, foolhardy, whatever—will often be a book your child can identify with. I think that may be the secret of the Ramona books by Beverly Cleary. Ramona is always getting into minor trouble, but the reader sees that she isn't a troublemaker. She never *means* to do bad things. Stuff somehow just always happens. Things go wrong. I think there are many kids who can identify with Ramona.

The Anne of Green Gables books feature the same kind of heroine. Anne didn't *mean* to get Diana drunk. She loved Diana. And now Diana's mother won't let Anne play with her or see her. To Anne it's a real tragedy, and the reader agonizes with her. Why are adults so stupid and judgmental?

I sometimes think that the most unlikely books are the ones kids end up identifying with. The most reliable sign to look for is a book your child reads again and again. Whatever kind of book that is, you want to get more of them.

This might not, however, be a book in which your child identifies with the main character. There is another hook that is almost as strong as a book that features someone similar to themselves—and maybe, for some kids, it's an even stronger one.

## 2. Look for "wish" books.

Many people speak very disparagingly about what they call escapist fiction. Maybe it's our puritanical background, but we seem to think that books need to send useful messages. We think that books that kids can identify with are okay, since they can help kids to handle the problems in their own lives, or to appreciate their own culture, or to see that they're not alone in their trouble. But escape fiction? What good can it possibly do?

Well, if it gets a kid reading, it accomplishes a *major* goal. But I think wish fiction accomplishes other goals as well. Surely it's not so bad for a kid to dream a little. Wishing to be an astronaut or a military test pilot—or a brave warrior who can slay dragons—might help children to raise their sights in life. Whom do they see on television to inspire them? Roseanne? Bart Simpson? Al Bundy?

And there are all kinds of wish books. The good-versus-evil reading path is almost, by definition, a path of heroes and heroines. Both science fiction and fantasy are full of brave young men and women overcoming all kinds of disasters. Mysteries feature brilliant detectives who can outwit the most cunning criminals. It's very satisfying for young readers to identify with these larger-than-life characters—to dream that one day, like these heroes, they will be able to do great deeds.

But the interesting thing is that I think these good-versus-evil books often operate as wish books on other levels also. In the Xanth books, by Piers Anthony, all of his characters, when they're not out taking on different kinds of evil, live in very happy, functional families. I realized this when I noticed that these books were especially appealing to kids, usually boys, who didn't live in such happy families. So I think that when kids read these books, not only can they dream of accomplishing great deeds, but they can dream of gentle, loving, and wise parents. Also, as one of my students pointed out, mere existence in Xanth is happy:

> In many ways, Xanth is an ideal place to grow up. One of the inherent properties of Xanth is that each person has a special magical talent. For children growing up, this means they know that they have something different and special, even if the talent is only conjuring up rotten fruit. There is no need for everyone to fit in, because everyone is different in his or her own way.
>
> In addition, Xanth is a free and exciting land. There are many things to explore, and life is never too dull with magical friends.
>
> Still, the children are not let in on all the secrets in Xanth. In particular, children are consistently curious as to where babies come from. They believe (rightly) that it has something to do with storks, but in the so-called Adult conspiracy, the children never find out until they grow up and become part of the conspiracy. Xanth is overall a truly magical land for children growing up.

Many of the books on the relationship path are also wish books, especially the easier-reading ones that children are apt to love first. I'm sure that a major attraction of the Baby-sitters Club books is the presence of the group of girls who remain friends through thick and thin. Social groups are so important for elementary-school-aged girls—and sometimes so difficult to navigate—that these books about true friends must really function as a wish series for many of the readers. The books of Danielle Steel are great wish books for older readers. Most of her heroines are rich and beautiful, and end up with wonderful, loving men. Naturally the heroines have to overcome great obstacles to achieve their happy endings, but that just makes the books even better as wish books.

Sometimes children enjoy fiction that presents worlds vastly different from their own. When I taught a large number of inner-city minority children in Norfolk, Virginia, I was bemused to see that the favorite reading matter for many of them were Richie Rich comics. Richie Rich is a blond, incredibly rich little white boy who lives in a world of mansions, butlers, and private planes. For kids struggling with basic necessities, his world must have been a welcome escape, and an occasion to dream.

Literary critics really scorn the idealized world of many wish books. I remember that when the Sweet Valley Twins series first came out, critics were beside themselves. The protagonists were beautiful girls with long blond hair, who lived in upper-middle-class homes in a town called, for heaven's sake, Sweet Valley. But many of my students told me that they loved these books precisely because they were about lives so different from their own. They wanted to have a beautiful identical twin; they wanted to live in wealthy surroundings; they wanted to live in an idealized family. Is that so bad? I think critics worry that reading about these "beautiful people" will make kids value their own heritage and families less. But kids aren't that naive. They like to read about idealized worlds, but they know, deep down, that they don't need incredible beauty and piles of money to be happy. They just like to dream a little. And when they go on from idealized fiction to more realistic books, as they will, they'll acquire a more complex sense, I think, of what happiness means. Look at it this way: They certainly won't get a realistic sense of happiness from television or watching the movies. Falling in love with books is a much more reliable path—no matter how unrealistic their early reading is.

The next group of books might be called wish books also, but their fascination for readers goes beyond that narrow category.

## 3. Look for special-interest reading.

Special-interest books are often the earliest, easiest hook to get kids reading. For older kids, the most reliably enticing reading material is a magazine about a special passion of theirs, such as sports or music. The reading of these magazines will often lead to book reading. And with some kids, younger ones especially, you can skip the magazines and go straight to the books. Special-interest reading is an incredibly effective way to build a love and a habit of reading.

*Sports.* For many turned-off high-school-aged kids, sports is *the* hook to get them going. I had a young man in class a year ago whom I had almost given up on. I had tried teenage novels, mysteries, horror books, *The Autobiography of Malcolm X* (he was African-American), but almost nothing had worked very well. Then he was assigned to my Writing Workshop class, in which I allow the kids to read magazines, if they wish, for credit. He started spending his lunch periods in the library reading the sports section of the newspaper, and then the current issue of *Sports Illustrated.* He loved basketball, and I heard about the NBA and college playoffs all spring. Then he told me that he had discovered he could look up his favorite NBA players in the back issues of *Sports Illustrated* and read about their college careers. So he started doing that too. By the end of the semester he was spending almost all of his free time reading in the library.

If you have a younger sports enthusiast, you might try the Matt Christopher books. These are stories for elementary-school-aged children that feature young kids playing different sports. I don't know of an equivalent series for older readers, but there is a fair amount of nonfiction that sports readers enjoy. How-to books are really popular with some kids, as are other nonfiction sports books, such as biographies of sports figures, and books that feature descriptions of famous teams or matches. Just be aware that sometimes not only does the nonfiction have to be about a particular sport, it has to be about a particular team or player.

I wish there were more sports books. Although we are getting more sports fiction for children, there is very little adult sports fiction. One would think the incredible popularity of movies like *The Natural* and *Bull Durham* would encourage publishers to bring out more sports fiction. But where are our football stories? Our soccer stories? Our tennis stories? It is odd, when you consider how many children and adults love sports, that there isn't a real diversity of sports books available, both fiction and nonfiction. The majority of sports books seem to be instructional books, rather than engrossing stories about sports or sports heroes. There are a good number of these books around—usually biographies—but they pale beside the numbers of mysteries and romance novels . . . and even horror books. For older kids there is very little sports fiction. And for girls, almost none.

Some of our best sports writing appears in books that are not sports books. Many mysteries, for example, revolve around a sport. *Mortal Stakes*, by Robert B. Parker, is the story of a Red Sox pitcher who is accused of throwing games. Mainstream novels can also feature a sport. I was surprised when *The World According to Garp*, by John Irving, was the favorite book of a very down-to-earth, no-nonsense kind of student. I wouldn't have picked him to enjoy Irving's fairly bizarre plots and characters. But then I realized he was a wrestler, as is Garp. Ah, yes. And he went on to read all of Irving's novels.

The good news is that newspapers and magazines have extensive sports articles. Part of this is probably because so much of the interest in sports focuses on how a team is doing right now. Did they win that game yesterday? Newspapers and magazines also usually carry interesting features and follow-up articles about specific players and teams.

So a love of sports can bring kids to a newspaper-and-magazine habit, which is certainly good. It's just too bad it's not a hook that is a major path into books for many kids. The numbers of students I've had over the years who have loved sports and hated reading are legion. Hello, publishers! How about some good thrillers set in the sports world?

*Horses.* It's odd that the kids who love horseback riding are far fewer than the kids who love other sports, and yet there is a rich treasury of horse books, ranging from such classics as *Black Beauty* and the Marguerite Henry Misty books to the simpler Saddle Club series. There are also the works of Walter Farley, as well as the adult mysteries by Dick Francis. In addition, there are books featuring animals in general, such as the James Herriot books, that also appeal to the horse lovers. There is even some fantasy: the Apprentice Adept series by Piers Anthony features unicorns and, reportedly, was written with the author's horse-loving daughter in mind. Jean M. Auel features horses in some of her prehistoric sagas (*Valley of the Horses*, for example), and one of the most exciting novelists today, Cormac McCarthy, has written a moving, coming-of-age story called *All the Pretty Horses*.

So you would expect a love of horses to be a good reading hook, and in fact it is. I've had a number students, over the years, who have come to a love of reading through their interest in horse books. With the right kid, it's a powerful hook.

*Fantasy.* Books that are set in ancient times, and peopled with dragons and wizards and elves and human heroes, are wonderful for getting a certain kind of kid reading. As I mentioned earlier, many fantasy books, certainly most of the easier-reading ones, also function as wish books, but as kids get older and move to more sophisticated authors, the lure of the fantasy world itself remains strong.

I really can't overemphasize the importance of this reading hook. Most of my top-reading boys, at one time or another, went through a fantasy stage—and perhaps as many as one third of my top-reading girls did as well. Most fantasy novels are good-versus-evil books—which accounts for the high percentage of male readers, I think—but many have well-developed characters as well. A good number of my students have told me that they became so caught up in the fantasy world that they spent large amounts of time playing Dungeons and Dragons—either with each other, or on their computers. And this didn't seem to interfere with their reading at all; actually, a number of kids explained to me that the manuals for Dungeons and Dragons are so elaborate and detailed, that they think the manuals really helped their reading skills.

If you have a boy, definitely think fantasy. And if you have a girl, I'd also give it a chance.

*Science Fiction.* While fantasy and science-fiction novels are usually shelved together in bookstores, they're very different. Science fiction deals with future worlds, very unlike the medieval world of fantasy. And while magic abounds in fantasy books, science-fiction novels often rely on amazing technology for excitement.

As with fantasy novels, the majority of science-fiction books focus on a good-versus-evil conflict, rather than on the development of an interpersonal conflict. Also, much science-fiction reading hinges on aspects of science that readers find fascinating in their own right, apart from the plot. A number of scientists have told me that science fiction first whetted their appetite for real science—and, indeed, a number of science-fiction writers are respected scientists.

As with fantasy, the vast majority of my top-reading boys report that at one time they loved science fiction. Fewer girls like this genre, and the ones who do are almost always action/adventure readers, rather than interpersonal readers.

*Magic.* I used to confuse books that had a magic hook with books in the regular fantasy genre. So I thought that if kids liked the Narnia books and the Piers Anthony Xanth books, the next logical author for them would be someone like David Eddings or Terry Brooks (two entry-level fantasy writers). But a number of my readers, mostly girls, decidedly didn't like most fantasy. Finally my daughter explained the difference to me. "I like books with magic," she said, "but not regular fantasy."

Some fantasy books emphasize magic—like the Narnia and Xanth books, for example—but most are more politically oriented, with a strong good-versus-evil theme. Magic readers don't care for these as much. It's typically relationship readers who really like magic books, and they prefer books that develop characters and their interactions, rather than watching characters war with evil.

Once I understood the difference between magic books and most mainstream fantasy writing, the reading path of a number of my top readers really came into focus for me. They tend to like doll books when they're little, because books where dolls "come alive" are magic. They love the Indian in the Cupboard series by Lynn Reid Banks—books in which toys come alive. They love Roald Dahl's books, and many enjoy the whimsical Mrs. Piggle-Wiggle books (she lives in an upside-down house). They like books about witches, since witches do magic. Many go through a V. C. Andrews phase, since many of her books have an element of the mysterious about them. As teenagers, they love Anne Rice, or any books on the occult that they can find.

*Psycho-Killer.* My students use this term to describe a growing subset of books that feature deranged serial killers. Thomas Harris's *The Silence of the Lambs* is a big favorite, as is its predecessor, *Red Dragon.* Then there's a whole series by John Sandford called Prey. *Rules of Prey* is the first, and it is truly creepy. Actually, psycho-killer books are a personal favorite of mine, and I've just discovered a new one titled *Within the Bounds*, by Mark Lodge, that almost made my skin crawl. I can't wait to try it with some of my students. Some of Robert Tannenbaum's lawyer books are really psycho-killer books (such as *Immoral Certainty*), and Robert B. Parker's Spenser series even has a psycho-killer title, *Crimson Joy*—which most of my students assure me is the best Spenser book. There are also a large number of nonfiction books about serial killers.

A couple of years ago I had a high school senior in my class who hated to read, but who discovered in the library the true story of a psycho-killer. I can't remember the book's title, or which particular killer it highlighted, but this young man loved this book. He read very slowly—I think it took him almost the whole quarter to read this long book—but he lovingly updated us every week on the newest gruesome details. He passed it around to his friends, pointing out favorite passages. I think it was the only book he finished all semester.

Although you would think a psycho-killer book would function as a good-versus-evil book, I find that relationship readers seem to like them the best. They enjoy the psychological view of evil, which is more personalized than a sweeping, political view. But they are also books that I can usually get almost any student to try.

*Horror.* Horror books are an interesting cross between suspense and science fiction. They are set in modern rather than future time, but have some supernatural or occult element. R. L. Stine, with his Goosebumps books, is bringing this genre to eight-year-olds—for the first time, as far as I know. His books are so popular that it will be fascinating to see where his legions of young readers go after they tire of juvenile horror. It's too early to tell yet. They may go on to read such adult horror authors as Stephen King, but I'll bet many of them move into science fiction and fantasy.

In any case, horror is a powerful hook for kids, as every children's publisher has discovered in the last few years.

**War.** I think Tom Clancy started, or at least reignited, the current love of military books that I see with my students. His *Hunt for Red October* was the first of a series of high-tech military thrillers that many of my students devour. They love Tom Clancy and also writers like Mark Berent *(Steel Tiger* and *Rolling Thunder)*, and W. E. B. Griffin, who wrote a long series called the Brotherhood of War. Some kids are so specific in their tastes that they only want to read aircraft books, like *The Flight of the Intruder,* by Stephen Coonts. A good number of these have been published. Look for book covers with blue sky and sophisticated planes that look more like rockets than regular airplanes. Often you see an aircraft carrier on the cover somewhere too.

My husband, a retired navy captain, enjoys these books, and gives them to me to take to school, so I have a pretty good selection. They're my secret weapon with a lot of boys. I can remember one mother who ruefully told me of her effort to find books for her son and then said, "I don't know why, but he only seems to find books he likes in your room." I laughed. Military airplane books. That's what he liked.

**Lawyers and Trials.** *Presumed Innocent,* by Scott Turow, was one of the first lawyer books to really catch on with my kids. Then came the mega lawyer book of them all, *The Firm,* by John Grisham. This book has swept my classes, as well as the country, and paved the way for many more writers of lawyer books. *Cruel and Unusual* by Patricia Cornwell is popular with kids, as are books by Steve Martini and William Coughlin. Except for Grisham's books, which are easy, fast reading for most readers, the other lawyer books usually demand a more sophisticated reader— someone who is willing to follow complicated legal reasoning. They are often the perfect books for kids who are bright, interested in history, and good students, but don't do much leisure reading. I've found that these books will sometimes hook this kind of kid.

*Romance.* This is a tricky category for kids, because even though many students—usually girls—enjoy romances, they're often embarrassed to admit it. For some reason, teenage romances like the Sweet Valley books are more acceptable to them than adult romances, perhaps because the teen ones are more widely read among their friends. But I see very few high school students reading Harlequin romances, or even the works of such writers as Rosemary Rogers or Kathleen E. Woodiwiss.

I think a big problem is the packaging of romances, and I have a bit of advice for romance publishers. Stop making the covers—and the titles—so *goopy.* High school girls are really embarrassed to pick up something with a title like *Passion's Promise* and a cover that's full of naked bosom and flowers. Put out a line of books that are basically romances, but that don't scream at the readers. Make them look classier. *The Bridges of Madison County* is essentially a romance, but without the formula-fiction trappings it has sold millions of copies. Learn from that.

My own theory is that certain mystery lines owe their popularity to the low-key romance that runs through them. That was always the attraction for me of the Lord Peter Wimsey mysteries by Dorothy L. Sayers, and I see the same thing in many of the current series, such as the Spenser mysteries by Robert Parker. I think this may be one reason why mysteries are often most popular with relationship readers.

*Mysteries.* I teach a sophomore elective course titled "Mysteries," which is always very popular. I find, though, that most teenagers don't enjoy the classic puzzle mysteries. Except for very accomplished readers, they prefer suspense, horror, and espionage (all of which I agree to define loosely as mysteries, so they can read them for class). Traditional mysteries usually work only with excellent relationship readers who enjoy the leisurely descriptions of characters and motives.

*Science.* Michael Crichton is the big name here. His *Jurassic Park* is almost as popular as *The Firm* with my students. And kids then go on and read his other books, such as *Congo* or *The Andromeda Strain*, which also have scientific themes. The books of Clive Cussler fit into this group also, although his have a stronger adventure/good-versus-evil component. Robin Cook writes thrillers that rely on sophisticated medical technology, and are fascinating to kids interested in science. All of these writers are good lures for any science-oriented child.

*Local Setting.* Most people enjoy reading about familiar places, and I think this is especially true of kids. We're lucky in Concord, Massachusetts, because so many books are set in this area. My students are always amazed when they first read a Robert Parker Spenser novel, and find that his characters drive up and down Route 128, eat in restaurants in Lexington, and go to the Red Sox games at Fenway Park. "I've *been* to that restaurant!" they tell me excitedly. "I've sat in the skyview seats at Fenway." They feel he's writing about their lives somehow.

So setting is certainly something to keep in mind when choosing books. Regional mysteries are very popular now, and you can probably find a series set somewhere close to where you live. Ask your bookseller or, better yet, go to a specialty mystery bookstore. A good deal of historical fiction is very descriptive of real towns and cities also. When we moved around with the navy, I found I especially enjoyed authors who wrote about the new areas we moved to. John Steinbeck became my passion in Monterey, California, and I loved James Michener's *Hawaii* when we lived in Honolulu. And I see the same thing with my students.

I know I haven't covered all of the many possible special-interest hooks. Just be alert to any passionate interest of your child, and look for any reading that is about that interest. And now I have one more hook, maybe the most powerful one of all.

## 4. Look for books that are comic.

Comedy is really a universal hook. I think all children love funny stories, probably because funny stories are usually happy stories. Certainly most of the authors that come up again and again as all-time favorites (Roald Dahl, Dr. Seuss, Beverly Cleary, Piers

Anthony, Robert Parker, etc.) write stories that are fundamentally comic in tone.

I find that it is often a comic novel that finally pulls in that kid I thought I was never going to get reading. I've had that experience quite a few times with Robert Asprin's Myth series, with Robert Parker's Spenser series, and with Pier Anthony's Xanth series. The first time I see a kid smile when he's reading, I know I've won.

There are plenty of comic picture books for young children. Richard Scarry is a funny author whom my own kids especially loved. *Mad Magazine* is incredibly popular with the preadolescent crowd, particularly the boys. Garfield and Calvin and Hobbes remain popular right up through high school.

The one thing you have to watch with comic novels is that sometimes kids get tired reading them because, they'll tell me, it gets to be like reading a joke book—good for just a short time. Douglas Adams's Hitchhiker's Guide to the Galaxy series affects a lot of kids this way. They love the first two or three books in the series, and then they get saturated with the humor. Be alert to this happening, and stand by ready to slip in another fantasy novel, maybe one by David Eddings. I think that perhaps for a child to experience the really deep pull of reading, he has to find books that move him on a more fundamental level than just his sense of the comic or the absurd.

But for kids who have been traumatized by their reading experiences—who have learned to fear and hate reading—I think humor is initially the best thing to try. A funny book doesn't demand an emotional commitment. You can read an amusing book and still keep your distance. Perhaps that's why they're successful. Or perhaps poor readers initially need a book that makes them laugh to help them see that reading—that hated chore—can actually be a happy experience.

Whatever the reason, when all else fails—or *before* all else fails—try humor.

Now that you have a general idea of the kinds of reading paths and hooks that appeal to kids, read the next chapter to get an idea of which kids read which books, and how typical readers progress along these paths.

# 7

## *Finding Your Child's Path*

• • • • • • • • • • • • • • • • • • • • • • • • • • • • • • • • • •

In chapter 6 I've described what I see as common reading paths for children and teenagers. I've explained that most kids seem to have a basic preference either for books about relationships or for books containing primarily action and adventure. In addition, I've described a number of "hooks" or special interests that pull children into reading.

In this chapter I'll give you suggestions for finding the right paths for individual children. Keep in mind that children are always surprising us, and that it's often very hard to assess what will interest an individual child. These are just suggestions. As a parent, you must simply do whatever it takes to get your children reading. If these suggestions help, fine. If not, ignore them completely.

So how do you figure out which books will spark your child's enthusiasm?

## Step 1. Figure out whether your child is a relationship or an action/adventure reader.

Early preferences in play activities are helpful here. For example, my younger daughter grew up in a neighborhood full of boys. A neighbor, almost convulsed with laughter, explained to me how her son Josh and my daughter Molly played with his collection of little cars and trucks. Josh raced them, and had them crashing into each other; Molly, essentially, had the cars playing house. "Okay," one car would say, "now it's time for dinner, and . . ."

It was pretty clear even then that one would be a relationship reader, and that the other would prefer books with more adventure and conflict.

Also notice the picture books that young children like. Budding relationship readers like picture books about characters learning about life, and how to get along with each other, such as the Berenstain Bears. The adventure readers, who basically seem more interested in how things work, prefer books like those of Richard Scarry. These readers are always busy working on little projects, like seeing what happens when you slide pennies into the steam vents of the dishwasher (my son's project when he was four). It's no surprise that, years later—if they, and everyone else, have survived their childhood—they are avidly following the wealth of technical detail that a military action writer like Tom Clancy weaves into his stories.

So notice this basic preference about each of your children. If you have a son who's always playing cowboy games, he's going to enjoy books with much adventure and action. A daughter who collects Barbie dolls, and loves to dress them and pretend they're going on dates, is going to be a relationship reader. Earlier I described the elaborate war game my two older children organized for the neighborhood. They both turned out to be primarily action/adventure readers.

I think it's important to note here that it doesn't matter which kind of child you have—people oriented or action oriented. Kids who like gentle role-playing, and starting social clubs and playing with dolls, will also become a bit interested in more action-related activities as they get older—especially if they become wide readers. And kids who only want to climb trees and pretend they're spacemen will eventually grow into more socialized human beings—again, especially if they become wide readers. Don't view books as medicine to change your children; instead let them happily read whatever books have that strong emotional pull for them, and they'll branch out a bit later by themselves. By high school age, *all* of the avid readers I interviewed were lovely, gentle human beings who had acquired wide frameworks of knowledge. And they did this happily reading the books that appealed to them over the years. My motto: Love and enjoy your children for whatever they are, *and use their basic interests to get them reading.*

## Step 2. Look at the degree of realism your child enjoys.

Not all relationship or action/adventure readers are the same. Within each category, some kids seem to enjoy more imaginative, fanciful games, and others are more down-to-earth and like their play, and reading, to be a bit more realistic.

This translates to reading preferences. Readers who have a real passion for seeing exactly how things work are probably going to like realistic adventure books, while kids who aren't so tied down to reality will enjoy such genres as fantasy and science fiction. Relationship readers who are more down to earth will like books with realistic settings either in the past, like the Little House books by Laura Ingalls Wilder, or in the present, like the Baby-sitters Club books by Ann Martin. Relationship readers who are more imaginative seem to like books that have a magic or unrealistic element.

These preferences can be very strong, especially in the case of teenagers who are coming fairly late to reading. I tried once to get everyone in a class to read *A Spell for Chameleon* by Piers Anthony. It's a wonderful fantasy book that has brought many of my students to a love of reading, and since it is strong both in interpersonal relationships and good-versus-evil conflicts, I thought everyone would like it.

I was wrong. About a third of the class couldn't get past the Gap Dragon and the tangle trees and the magicians. "It's *dumb*," they insisted. When I finally let them quit reading it and pick up an espionage author instead (Robert Ludlum and Tom Clancy were the two big ones with this group, as I remember), they immediately became happy again. *Clear and Present Danger*, by Tom Clancy, was, to them, a *good* book that wasn't filled with dumb things like magic trees and spells.

So be aware of this preference too. Some kids go back and forth happily between realistic and unrealistic stories, but other children are not so flexible. Don't worry about your child's preference; just respect it. Fanciful kids have to deal with reality sooner or later, and realistic, practical children will become more open to whimsy and new worlds as they read more.

## Step 3. Consider which of the following four paths best suits your child.

I haven't done any formal research on which kids, exactly, prefer which kinds of reading, but I have taught for twenty-five years and paid attention to my students' choices of books. I always allow students to choose books as part of my courses, and I'm always asking my students what they read as children. In addition, while on sabbatical last spring I was able to survey students from two different regions, Massachusetts and Wisconsin, about their reading preferences. What I've found is that my students, and the students I surveyed, seem to divide loosely into four major reading paths, dependent on the kind of action they like and the degree of realism they prefer. The various reading hooks are scattered throughout all of the paths, with some hooks being much more common in one path than in another.

Again, this is far from being a scientific study—it's just what I've observed—but it might help bring your child's reading preferences more into focus for you. If none of these paths seem to fit the kind of reading your child is doing, that's fine too. The crucial thing, as always, is to get your child reading. If you have a more helpful way of organizing your child's reading in your mind—so that you can anticipate the next books to have available—that's terrific, and I'd love to hear from you.

If you want to know more about these reading paths, see the appendix at the end of this book, which includes excerpts from interviews with many of my top readers. Not only will you see the kind of reading each student did, but I think you'll get a sense of the personality of each student, so you'll have some sense of what kinds of kids read what kinds of books. You'll also notice in these interviews that readers don't always stick closely to their reading paths. As students become more adept readers, they are much more likely to enjoy a wider variety of books. These paths are just a starting point.

You should also keep in mind that kids stray from reading paths for a number of other reasons: Some are born with eclectic tastes; some diverge to read what their friends are reading; some can't find any books they really love, and read for a while in a new category or genre. And I've found that most children are strongly influenced by the books their parents read.

Keeping all of that in mind, you might find these paths helpful.

## Path 1. Relationship Reading with Magical Elements

This is a path that a great many of my top-reading girls seem to follow. Generally these girls aren't adverse to realistic fiction, but the danger is that they'll find it boring.

Magic is a strong hook for these readers, and I think many of their books also function as wish books. When they're little, they love books about witches, such as the Dorrie books by Patricia Coombs, or other books that have magic elements, such as the E. Nesbit books (*The Carpet* and *The Phoenix*), or the Narnia books by C. S. Lewis. Many of these readers enjoy mythology too, as well as books of fairy tales. There's a fairy-tale series that young readers rave to me about, edited by Andrew Lang, each of which has a different color as part of its title: *The Red Book of Fairy Tales, The Green Book of Fairy Tales*, and so on. Doll books and magazines are very popular, as are books in which animals act like people, such as the Redwall books, or *Charlotte's Web*. All of these categories involve magic somehow, as well as describing worlds these children wish they could inhabit. Many of my students in this group remember being read *The Hobbit*, and loving it, and almost all of them loved Roald Dahl, especially his *James and the Giant Peach*.

Comedy also is a strong hook for this group of readers—which is probably why such a writer as Roald Dahl, who combines magic, comedy, and interpersonal relations, is so popular—and these readers especially like books with a warm, comic tone. I think the Fudge books by Judy Blume are loved for this reason, as are the Betsy-Tacy books, by Maud Hart Lovelace. An interesting aspect of the Betsy-Tacy books is that, while they are not set in a magic world, the main characters are always doing imaginative things, like pretending they can fly, or that they live in a mirrored, upside-down house.

There is such a rich supply of children's books with magical or comic elements that these girls often become very accomplished readers quite quickly. Many of them also branch out fairly early, reading such essentially realistic books as the Baby-sitters Club and Nancy Drew series.

As they head toward junior high school, they usually avoid—and often actually dislike—most teenage novels (except for those of Lois Lowry, who writes books with supernatural elements, and S. E. Hinton, who is universally loved). Teenage novels tend to be realistic, as well as fairly simple in plot structure, and by junior high school age, most girls find them boring and depressing. Instead they read such authors as V. C. Andrews, who has rich, complicated plots full of vivid, psychotic characters, or Jean Auel, who sweeps the reader back to an exciting prehistoric time that is largely imaginative. Many continue their animal reading, discovering such authors as James Herriot, with his All Creatures Great and Small series, or, if they're really avid horse lovers, the Dick Francis mysteries. *Watership Down*, by Richard Adams, a "magic" book with animal characters, is another book many junior high school girls love. Although it would seem that these readers would love Stephen King, with his supernatural horror, for some reason I haven't found that to be the case. It may just be that the girls never happened to pick him up. Whatever the case, not many of these unrealistic relationship readers seem to be charmed by him. Perhaps that's because his characters are so realistic, and—if you ignore the horror element—the plots are quite realistic too. There isn't any softening or magic glow thrown over what happens to the people in his books.

But Anne Rice's books *are* loved by this group. Again, she has the rich, complex details and plots that these excellent readers appreciate, plus magic elements. Maybe the difference is that the horror elements in a Stephen King novel (ability to start fires, graveyards that can raise corpses from the dead) are usually portrayed as causing nothing but grief and havoc, whereas the supernatural characters of Anne Rice—vampires and witches—lead rich, passion-filled lives. The reader likes Rowan Mayfair all the better for being a witch, and even the vampire Lestat, for all his evil doings, is pretty thrilling and to some degree admirable.

As high school students these girls also continue to like books with warm, comic elements. I think perhaps that's why they tend to like Agatha Christie mysteries better than some of the newer, more hard-boiled women detective mysteries. Agatha Christie has gently comic characters who live in a world that is almost as idealized as the doll world these readers liked as children. Maeve Binchy creates the same warm, comic world, and I see my students reading her books more and more. Anne Tyler has quirky, lovable characters that many girls like, as does Barbara Kingsolver.

Most of these girls are excellent students in high school, and so tend to be in the top English classes, and assigned to read many classics. They like such classics as *Pride and Prejudice* because of their comic element, and *Jane Eyre* because of the mystery content. They are usually such good readers by high school that they can appreciate F. Scott Fitzgerald for his dazzling, image-filled style, while not particularly liking his characters or plot. Shakespeare's plays are the same; the language is wonderful, even though most of the plots of the ones read in high school are good versus evil. A few comedies, such as *A Midsummer Night's Dream*, are the happy exception to this rule. They won't like Joseph

Conrad's novels—depressing, dark, good-versus-evil plots—or *Ethan Frome*. Hemingway's language may carry them through, but they'll probably find his plots too simple and realistic. Virginia Woolf is a writer they may really love, especially novels like *To the Lighthouse* and *Mrs. Dalloway*.

I only get to track these girls through high school, and by then I don't see very many of them turning to nonfiction. They may be doing magazine reading, but the vast majority of their book-length reading continues to be fiction. I have seen an occasional girl discover an essay writer like Annie Dillard, and really enjoy her work. Dillard is certainly a nonfiction writer, but her gentle, warm sense of humor so pervades her work that reading it is almost more like reading fiction.

Besides being excellent readers, many of these young women end up being wonderful writers. The whimsy, the rich imagery and metaphors, the unexpected, complicated plot turns that they love in their reading, they often manage to duplicate in their writing. Most of the good high school poets I see come from the ranks of these unrealistic relationship readers, as well as many of the most exciting fiction writers.

So, if you have a daughter who loves to pretend, who laughs easily, and who is very interested in social interactions, you should have a fairly easy time getting her reading. This is a wonderful path because so many of the great children's books fit so neatly into it. The older girls have a bit more of a difficult time, as I explain in chapter 8, because there are relatively few relationship books for adults that aren't formula driven (like romances). But these readers are usually so adept by their teenage years that they can enjoyably read almost anything. And with new writers like Barbara Kingsolver gaining prominence, the problem should resolve itself soon.

## Path 2. Relationship Reading with Realistic Elements

There are readers—almost always girls—who really love fairly realistic descriptions of how people get along with each other.

As young girls they like the series books, especially the newer ones like Baby-sitters Club or Sweet Valley. Many of these girls tell me that they prefer the new Nancy Drew books, but some of the really avid readers prefer the old ones because, they tell me, they're more complicated. This group tends to like "problem" writers, such as Judy Blume and Paula Danziger, and they tend to be the group most likely to enjoy teenage novels, which the good readers read in late elementary school and junior high. On the whole, when looking for books for this group, look for writers who have characters they can identify with. That seems to be this group's strongest hook.

This group of readers is also much more likely to read nonfiction, or specialized fiction, such as horse books, or books about disturbed children. Torey Hayden's books about her experiences as a special-education teacher are very popular, as are nonfiction books about growing-up issues. These girls love teenage magazines, and magazines about fashion and health.

I find that, as a group, Path 2 readers come to reading a little later than the first group I described. I think the reason is that there simply aren't as many realistic books for young children. But as soon as they can start with some of the series, they're in good shape. I'm starting to get students now who tell me that they like teenage horror writers like Christopher Pike and R. L. Stine (his Fear Street series). My guess is that the Goosebumps readers who like relationships will end up in this reading path—although some of the whimsy I see in some Goosebumps books may attract Path 1 readers as well. With the recent overwhelming popularity of the Goosebumps series, we may be getting readers onto this path much earlier.

When this group moves to adult authors, they like Danielle Steel, Sidney Sheldon, Rosamunde Pilcher, Kaye Gibbons, Terry McMillan, Alice Walker, and some adult horror writers like Clive Barker and Stephen King. They enjoy the realistic relationships in the horror books, and the horror elements keep the plot exciting. Also, the very realism of the characters and setting is what makes a horror novel so scary. If a horrible thing could happen to those ordinary people, it could happen to anyone! So horror novels have to be very realistic. V. C. Andrews is a writer who is a big draw for these readers, as well as Path 1 readers. My guess is that these readers enjoy the realistic nature of the problems that enmesh her characters.

Realistic problems also make Mary Higgins Clark very exciting for this group of readers. She's a suspense writer, but many of her heroines are victims of abuse of one kind or another. I find this group of readers most open to the new gun-toting female detectives like the heroines of Sue Grafton and Sara Paretsky, and they like mysteries that teach them things. In the Jonathan Kellerman mysteries, for example, they like learning a bit about psychology. Some like the psycho-killer books for the same reason. They read Robin Cook thrillers to learn about the medical world, or Tony Hillerman mysteries to learn about the Southwest and the culture of the Navajo people.

Very good readers from this group will enjoy some of the classics, especially writers like D. H. Lawrence. Along with Path 1 readers, they'll probably like *Pride and Prejudice*, *The Awakening*, *My Ántonia*, *To Kill a Mockingbird*, and *Romeo and Juliet*. But they continue to enjoy realism. I thought one student summed up this mindset in the survey I gave. She listed as "good books" *Go Ask Alice*; *Animal Farm*; *Seventh Heaven*, by Alice Hoffman; *The Things They Carried*, by Tim O'Brien; *Wuthering Heights*; *The Scarlet Letter*; *Song of Solomon* and *The Bluest Eye*, both by Toni Morrison; and *The Crucible*, by Arthur Miller. Then she commented, "The books that I liked were usually stories that could've happened to someone I knew. Real-life stories are enjoyable to read, especially when written in a very simple fashion. The reading that I did sophomore year was not enjoyable at all." Sophomore year, she went on to say, she had read *The Hobbit* and the *Odyssey*, both imaginative, unrealistic stories.

I have also gotten some excellent writers out of this group, writers who are particularly adept at understanding *exactly* what a book or poem is about. They aren't tempted to veer off into imaginative byways. Their writing, and thinking, tends to be realistic, down-to-earth, and very insightful. Like Path 1 readers, these young women tend to be excellent students, often excelling in science and history as well as English.

This story may illustrate the particular strengths of Path 2 students. A few years ago, when we were reading "The Wife of Bath's Prologue" in *The Canterbury Tales*, I was laughing about the Wife's outrageous opinions, and commenting that Chaucer had wonderful, vivid women characters (I tend to be a Path 1 reader). One of my students brought me up short. "Yeah," she said, "but all of his women are either promiscuous or bitchy." She was right. And, like a true Path 2 reader, she went right to the heart of the matter.

By the time these young women are leaving high school, usually laden with academic honors, I find them enjoying such sophisticated authors as Amy Tan, Margaret Atwood, John Irving, Jane Smiley, Anne Rivers Siddons, Milan Kundera, and Toni Morrison. I see them going into all kinds of professional fields, such as medicine, science, law, and history.

See where an early love of Baby-sitters Club books and Stephen King novels may lead?

## Path 3. Action/Adventure Reading with Fantastic Elements

The majority of readers in this path are boys, but there are significant numbers of girls also, although some of the girls tell me that they like a "humanistic element"—as one girl phrased it—in their reading, as well as the action-filled conflict.

Probably the easiest entry onto this path is comic books, usually superhero comics for the boys, and almost any other kind for the girls. One girl, in fact, who was bilingual, with Danish parents, told me she had read Danish comics as a child. My older daughter, who reads primarily in this path, read Richie Rich comics. Some students tell me they didn't read regular comics, but loved collections of comic strips, Garfield especially. But the majority of comic-book readers tell me they read X-Men, The Punisher, The Amazing Spider-Man, The Avengers, Batman, Cyberforce, and Elfquest—along with many others. Kids can start reading these by the time they're seven or eight. The value of comic-book reading is that it gives this group of readers a jump-start on reading skills, which they'll need, because most of the reading in this field is pretty sophisticated.

But many readers—the majority, I think—come to this field through children's books rather than comics. They read the easy science-fiction ones, like *My Teacher Is an Alien*, and *Danny and the Dinosaur*. Many take a brief detour into mystery, and read the Hardy Boys; virtually all read the Chronicles of Narnia.

As they become more proficient, they read *The Hobbit* and then the Ring Trilogy. The Redwall books are really loved by this group (you can see the overlap with Path 1 readers), as are the Lloyd Alexander fantasy novels. Some of these readers—often the girls—love the novels of Madeleine L'Engle, Ursula Le Guin, and Susan Cooper.

The DragonLance books usually come in by junior high, as does the Forgotten Realm series. David Eddings is popular around this time, as are Terry Brooks and Piers Anthony. Notice that even if the early reading is basically comics, which are usually science fiction, most readers then switch to fantasy, and spend a good deal of time reading in the fantasy genre. Some do start reading the more fantastic, or adventurous, science-fiction authors here, usually Robert Heinlein, and sometimes Frank Herbert (*Dune*). *Star Trek* novels are often wildly popular in junior high school as well.

By high school these readers have become more sophisticated. Their fantasy tastes are starting to lean toward complicated authors like Robert Jordan, and many read extensively such sophisticated writers as Isaac Asimov and Arthur C. Clarke. In addition, I start to see much crossover reading to Path 4, the real-istic action/adventure path. Many of these Path 3 readers start reading espionage and military books. The novels of Tom Clancy become favorites. Like the Path 1 readers, these readers seem to have acquired a taste for rich, complex story lines with many sub-plots, which may be why an author like Tom Clancy appeals to them.

This group does well with classics that have plenty of action and deal with global issues. They enjoy the political and social commentary in Dickens, in Steinbeck's *East of Eden* and *Grapes of Wrath*, and in Dostoevsky's involved stories. I've had a couple go on to read *War and Peace* and really enjoy it. They like the humor, satire, and complicated plot of *Catch-22*, by Joseph Heller. I used to teach *Catch-22* as a class book until it became apparent to me that many students either couldn't read it or didn't like it. (Path 2 readers especially didn't like it.) But this group loved it, and one day while I was riding my bike to the store, a young man jogged by me. We turned back to each other at the same time, realizing he had been in my class a number of years ago. He had one comment for me, which he shouted out, "Keep teaching *Catch-22*!" A Path 3 reader!

Some of the readers in this path go on to be truly amazing English students. Most of them read very well, for one thing, since this path easily develops avid readers. There are just so many fantasy and science-fiction writers, and if, in addition, they get involved in Dungeons and Dragons (as many do), they've also read a large amount of complicated nonfiction. So they do very well with Shakespeare, as well as with many of our great poets, such as the Renaissance, Romantic, and Victorian poets in England, and the twentieth-century poets from both England and America.

This group is strong in many areas of writing. Some become sly, funny satirists, while others write really stunning, imaginative poetry and fiction. Like Path 1, this path seems to develop iconoclastic thinkers, and a deep vein of humor runs through much of their work.

One aspect of the students in this group, however, is that of the group of very bright, competent, well-read students, they seem to be the ones most vulnerable to being bored and turned off in school. I'm not sure why this is, but I've seen it again and again. Most students who dislike school are kids who don't read well, and find the work very difficult. These students, however, read *very* well, but often refuse to do the work, which they see as boring and meaningless. I discuss this problem at much greater length in chapter 9, but you should be aware of it now.

The good news about these readers, as students, is that they often go on to read extensively in different areas of nonfiction. I see some of them reading extensively in history, computer science, politics, or even drama. These kids seem to drop out of the academic game in junior high or early high school (they don't actually drop out of school; they just go underground and do the minimum required to get by), but often reenter in full force in later high school years, or in college. I've been able to chat with many of these students a few years after graduation, and almost all seem to be doing very well.

So try not to worry when your son seems to be spending much more time reading fantasy authors you've never even heard of than memorizing details for his next history test. The chances are that, by the time he's twenty-five or so, he'll have a much more solid academic record than his more studious high school peers, *and* he'll be a reader.

### Path 4. Action/Adventure Reading with Realistic Elements

I think the kids who prefer this reading path—almost always boys—are at the highest risk for getting turned off to reading in elementary school. Most children's books that win awards and are featured in elementary school curricula and libraries have a fanciful element and/or are about a relationship. When you think of classic, "good" children's books, don't you think of books like *Charlotte's Web*, *James and the Giant Peach*, the Little House books, or the Narnia books? And while many children love these books, there is a fairly large group of readers who don't see much sense in them.

I get very few kids in this group who have been avidly reading since elementary school. The ones I do see are usually the boys who have discovered nonfiction—often magazines—and read extensively in an area of interest for them. Special-interest "hooks" are most important for this group, and the two most common hooks are probably sports and military themes. I mentioned the relative paucity of sports books in the preceding chapter, but there still is a good deal of sports writing available for boys if you're diligent about looking for it. Definitely encourage your sports enthusiast to collect sports cards. It's a very easy entrance into reading, and it opens up a world of magazine reading for him as well, from the Beckett magazines, which are specifically about sports-card collecting, to other sports magazines that specialize in the major sports. From his card collecting he'll be up on all the major players, and so be more interested in reading about them. How-to books are very important for this kind of reader, also, because he'll see a purpose to reading them. Books about dragons may be dumb, but a book describing how to field a low grounder to second base—now, *that's* worth reading.

A girl who loves sports isn't as easy to get reading, because few books feature girls as athletic heroines. Nor do we have sports cards with women as featured players. I got my own athletic daughter reading with Richie Rich comics, but that was just happenstance. I then went on and tried to get her reading all of the books I'd loved, like Nancy Drew and Betsy-Tacy. She was supremely uninterested in any of them, and it's only now, years later, that I understand why. She's primarily a good-versus-evil reader, and the books I kept getting her were relationship books. I find that most sports lovers are good-versus-evil readers, and when you think about it, that makes sense. An athletic event is a game in which one side tries to overcome the other. She eventually started reading fantasy novels—Piers Anthony and Robert Asprin were two early favorites—and she now goes between historical fiction (wars, political trends), science fiction, and nonfiction. Orson Scott Card is a current favorite. She really reads a mixture of Path 3 and Path 4 reading.

While I think few athletic girls are pure Path 4 readers, it's a good place to start. Girls who are avid sports enthusiasts but not avid readers will generally be very uninterested in typical relationship books. With a girl like this, I'd start with nonfiction books and magazines about her particular sport. Unfortunately, you'll find relatively little writing that features women, but find what you can. She may also be open to books featuring male athletes, as long as they are playing her sport. It's really too bad that we have so few books for young girl athletes. We have the Saddle Club series for young horseback riders, but no "Soccer Club" books—or books about girls who love tennis, swimming, softball, or basketball.

Recently I was given the opportunity of interviewing some young women who were part of a university women's soccer team. These were excellent athletes, some of the top soccer players in the country, and I was curious to see what kinds of readers they were. Most reported to me that, although they were good students who took pride in their academic achievements, they did little or no independent reading. In fact, most of these women told me that they didn't even do very much of the required reading— and these players had been in honors and advanced placement classes in high school. They read the Cliffs Notes, or part of the books, or got by on class discussion. A few, now that they're in college, are starting to read for pleasure, and all of them told me that they thought if they had had reading available about girls or women playing their sport, they would have read much more. Interestingly, many also mentioned that if they had had more choice in high school reading, they would have read more.

The athletes who did read came to it by non-sports means— since they couldn't find any sports reading for girls. On the whole, they seemed to be Path 2, Path 3, or Path 4 readers—but I didn't really find enough readers in the group to form many conclusions. Some were interested in relationships, but they also liked practical information. They read a good deal of nonfiction, and especially liked magazines and newspapers.

After sports, military reading seems to be the next most popular special-interest hook. There are many readers of military matters, and they like a rich variety of books featuring such different aspects as naval aviation, World War II battles, and ground combat in Vietnam. I find it interesting that there are many picture books featuring planes and trains and ships, but very little children's fiction or nonfiction after that. Most children's war books are really relationship books, like *The Diary of Anne Frank*. Maybe this is political correctness, or maybe it's just happenstance, but with a son whose interests run this way, you're really going to have to look. Try adult nonfiction books with plenty of pictures that describe things like the battles or ships of World War II. There are a great number of these, but they're usually very expensive. A library card is the key here. And haunt the magazine stands to see what's available. The trick is to keep your son reading enough through those early elementary school years to make it possible for him to jump into adult authors by fifth or sixth grade. When he's ready for adult fiction, there is a wealth of writers for him, ranging from Tom Clancy to Mark Berent, and from Jack Higgins to Robert Ludlum.

I often used to see that some Path 4 readers were big readers of electronic and auto mechanics magazines and books. They still are, but the lure of computers is now outdistancing interest in most other technological fields. The danger of a child getting hooked on computers is that he may only want to play computer games, and actually end up doing very little reading. You can help make his computer interest also a reading interest by buying lots of computer magazines, looking for computer games with extensive manuals (really—he *will* read them!), and, if he's a bit older—junior high age, at least—showing him some of the cyberpunk science fiction, which is about alternative computer worlds.

But do make an all-out effort to keep your computer expert reading. It's not knowledge of computers that's going to be the main ability necessary to function in our new, information-intensive computer world, but the ability to absorb and make sense of all the information a computer can retrieve for us. Avid reading develops that ability.

Other kids with a practical bent, and an interest in how things work, might like some of the children's books about science or nature. There's a pretty good supply of these—again, you'll really want to check out your library in this area—and reading them often develops a lifelong interest in science. Kids who have done this kind of reading also told me that they really enjoyed some television science programs, particularly shows like "Nova," and National Geographic specials. These shows can develop an interest that you can feed with reading material.

I'm hoping, as I write this, that the explosion of R. L. Stine's Goosebumps books is scooping up Path 4 readers, along with everyone else. They're full of action and adventure, and if you lay aside the unrealistic element in each one, they are very realistic in their other aspects. I know that this type of reader will often like Stephen King by high school, so if you have a young reader with this bent, you should certainly try R. L. Stine. If I'm right about this group liking juvenile horror books, this path might start producing as many top readers as Path 3.

As these kids get older, it becomes much easier to find books for them, not just military books, as I've already noted, but almost any kind. Some start reading biographies of notable people in their field of interest. Sports and music biographies are the two biggest areas I see, although I had a student last year who loved comedians, and read biographies of every comedian he could find.

The students in this path who started reading early often do very well in high school. They have extensive frameworks of knowledge, even if they've read mostly in one area. If the area was baseball, for example, they've picked up a good deal of American history by reading about baseball during the Depression, during World War II, and during the eras of Mickey Mantle and Babe Ruth. Their interest in batting averages and RBIs gives them a good framework for math. Most important, they're used to looking carefully at specific facts, and they're used to seeing how authors bring information together in persuasive articles or books, which is great preparation for doing research in any area.

But, as I noted earlier, many potential Path 4 readers enter high school having read very little. The good news is that there is so much interesting nonfiction and realistic fiction available for adults that, if the teacher opens up her curriculum, it's easy to get these kids reading. Once they find out that there are whole books about Jim Morrison and Kurt Cobain, in fact, it's hard to *stop* them from reading. The bad news is that few high schools encourage this kind of reading, instead giving these students books they are almost sure to dislike. A Path 4 reader who has read extensively before entering high school will probably have become sophisticated and open enough to enjoy a book like *Catcher in the Rye*. A very realistic, down-to-earth kid who has done very little reading will see no sense in Holden Caulfield at all. Why doesn't he just straighten up and get on with his life? There are very few realistic action/adventure books in a typical high school English curriculum, which is why early avid reading is so important for these readers. Reading widely early on will make it much more likely that they'll enjoy *The Old Man and the Sea*, *To Kill a Mockingbird*, and the other staples of high school curricula.

The classics that these readers can easily enjoy are pretty much out of favor now, books like *Treasure Island*, *Kidnapped*, and *All Quiet on the Western Front*. *Pride and Prejudice* will probably be pure torture for them to get through, and the complex, almost baroque style of writers like Charles Dickens will make these writers completely inaccessible for any but the most avid readers of this group.

I've found that these Path 4 readers will become very interested in writing if they're allowed to write about their areas of interest. One wonderful writer that I had from this group—who came to reading through sports—used to use sports metaphors in almost everything he wrote, even describing *Beowulf* in baseball imagery. He covered sports for the local paper while he was in high school, and went on to work in sports writing and public relations after college. I've also found a number of young men, adamant about reading only realistic action/adventure books, who loved poetry— and wrote wonderful poetry. For some, music is a real passion, and they write poetry to use as song lyrics. Many of these kids have bands, and some play professionally, even in high school.

In short, if your child is a realistic action/adventure reader, you are going to have to provide most of his reading material, perhaps even up through high school. Very little school reading will be to his liking. On the brighter side, these readers, with their curiosity and insatiable appetite to learn how things really work, have the potential to be wonderful students and real scholars—*if* you can keep them reading.

# 8

## *Tips and Strategies for Teenagers*

●●●●●●●●●●●●●●●●●●●●●●●●●●●●●●●●●●●●

There's no question that things become harder with junior high and high school students. Your ten-year-old who loved going out to lunch with you, and visiting bookstores and libraries to pick out books, has turned into a self-absorbed bundle of insecurities who spends hours hunched over a phone receiver, detailing daily traumas to other self-absorbed teenagers. Now, most teenagers are *nice* kids still—often wonderful, engaging, charming kids—but lunching with mother is no longer at the top of their hit parade. So you have to adjust.

What follows are not really tips for getting a completely turned-off reader reading. I went into considerable detail about how to do that in my first book. What I'll offer in this chapter are tips and strategies for how to keep average-to-excellent readers reading.

## ACQUIRING BOOKS

You would think that, by junior high or high school age, kids would take responsibility themselves for acquiring books. A few kids do, but many of my excellent readers don't. They report to me that they're still reading what they find around the house, or books they've been given as gifts. Usually, as they progress through high school—especially when they get their driver's licenses—excellent readers do take a more active role in acquiring reading material. But if you have a twelve- or thirteen-year-old, be prepared to be responsible for acquiring most of your child's reading material for a good many years still.

Here are a few tips culled from my years of teaching, and interviews with my excellent readers:

### 1. Encourage your young teen to read books by adult authors.

A crisis point in reading seems to come in the early teenage years. Some kids who enjoyed a variety of children's books fail to make the jump to adult authors. Girls seem especially vulnerable to this happening, perhaps because there are so many wonderful children's books for girls, but not as many adult authors who write the same kind of family interrelationship books. The girls who loved the Baby-sitters Club and Little House books, and the Anne of Green Gables books, have trouble finding a large number of adult authors who write the same kind of warm, happy, slightly old-fashioned kind of novels. Most of these girls don't care for romance novels, and even Danielle Steel's books are too formulaic and plot driven for them. Sometimes they'll discover Rosamunde Pilcher, and enjoy a few of her early ones until they find that those books are also very predictable. If they're fairly good readers, they'll probably go on to enjoy *September* and *The Shell Seekers*, but then have trouble finding other books like them. They may try various mainstream writers, such as Kaye Gibbons, Barbara Kingsolver, or Jane Smiley—or they may move over to another genre—mysteries, for example. Or they might stop reading for pleasure altogether. A number of my students report doing just that.

I think what happened was that when these early, wonderful readers got to junior high and high school, they realized they had to put in much more time on homework. They were used to doing very well in school, and didn't want to let that slip. In addition, they discovered all of the enticing extracurricular activities in high school. Their social lives became more demanding. Perhaps they were playing a sport. And, since there was not easily available to them a wide variety of books with the same emotional pull that many of their childhood favorites had, letting go of pleasure reading was the inevitable outcome.

The situation is slightly different for boys, especially boys who enjoy action/adventure books. While there aren't enough of them available for children, there are many popular adult authors writing those kinds of books. Look at any best-seller list, and you'll probably see titles by John Grisham, Michael Crichton, Stephen King, and Clive Cussler, as well as a sprinkling of fantasy or science-fiction writers. The women writers on the list are almost all romance writers like Danielle Steel or suspense writers like Mary Higgins Clark. If a teenage girl likes relationship books—but doesn't enjoy obvious romances—she has to really dig around to find books that she'll enjoy.

By junior high and high school, the opposite occurs, regarding easy accessibility of books. In elementary school it's much easier to find books for girls; by high school, it's easier to find books for boys. It's critical that you get boys reading adult authors early because these authors are writing the kinds of books they'll probably like. Most juvenile authors don't. It's also critical, however, to get girls reading adult authors, so they'll keep reading and maintain their excellent reading skills.

The ironic consequence of the dearth of these books is that although girls read better than boys in elementary school, they read less in high school, and their reading scores drop. I know that there are supposedly many sociological reasons for the drop in girls' scores—that's the case made in *Failing at Fairness: How America's Schools Cheat Girls*, by Myra and David Sadker (Scribners, 1994)—but what I see is that girls simply do less pleasure reading than boys in high school. And I'm convinced that a major reason is the absence of the adult equivalent of the kinds of books they enjoyed as younger children.

Be alert to this danger. I'm hoping that my observations about reading paths will point you to adult authors your daughter enjoys. Encourage her to continue her independent reading. Tell her that she doesn't have to get all A's; you'd rather see her curled up with a good book now and then.

## 2. Do a good deal of reading yourself, both of books you think your teen will enjoy, and books that you enjoy.

All but a handful of my excellent readers have at least one parent who is also an avid reader. I know the conventional wisdom is that kids imitate behavior they see, and so you should read so that your child sees that reading is a valuable activity.

But I think the more important reason to read is just to get great quantities of books into your house. Almost all of my avid readers reported borrowing books from their parents. By high school age, a parent's bookshelf was the main source of reading material for at least half of my avid readers—boys especially. If you've had a warm, book-friendly kind of relationship with your child all along, I think you'll find that by high school age your teen will be very receptive to your recommendations, and will see your enjoyment of a book as an incentive to try the books also. And if the book is sitting right there, on the bookshelf in the living room . . .

I find, as a teacher, that I need to read at least some of the work of each author my students particularly enjoy. Having my classroom filled with books isn't quite enough; my students want to know if I've read the authors. What's the best Danielle Steel? they want to know. What's the best Stephen King? If I've read a number of their books, I can tell them my favorites. I've also had the advantage of watching kids read these authors for years, and so can also tell them which titles students seem to best enjoy.

But making sure a large quantity of books is available is just one reason for reading a large quantity of books that you, and your teenagers, will enjoy. I think an even more important reason is that, by reading the authors your children like, you're validating their choices. The influence of the literary and educational establishments has been so destructive regarding book choice: I think it's impossible to overstate the harm done by the snobbish, holier-than-thou attitude of book reviewers and curriculum planners. You know their mantra: Everyone should read only "good" books. And their definition of "good" literature is narrow and depressing. You have to do everything you can to counteract this attitude, because it will kill your children's pleasure in reading. It makes your children feel stupid, and uncultured, for liking the books they like. The best way I've found to combat the literature snobs is to read the so-called trashy books myself, and tell my students how much I enjoyed them. You can point out the good features of the books that they might have missed—the strong women characters, the humor, the interesting themes. You do this so that your teenagers feel good about their reading choices, and keep reading.

So you're going to bring lots of books into your house for you to read—with the added agenda of recommending them to your teenagers. What else can you do?

### 3. Keep doing the things suggested in the previous chapters.

My students tell me that their parents give them books as gifts, take them on book-buying sprees, introduce them to the fun of poking around used-book stores, buy up collections at flea markets—all of the things I've recommended in the preceding chapters. Keep doing these things too. Also remember the importance of getting that next book in the series your son or daughter is enjoying.

I would especially emphasize dropping frequently into bookstores with teenagers. As I write this, I've just returned from Minnesota, where I visited the Mall of America, allegedly the largest mall in the United States. My Minnesota friends told me that visitors come from all over—even from Japan—just to stay in one of the nearby hotels and visit the mall.

But here's what troubled me: I went on a Saturday night, and the mall was full of teenagers. They were everywhere—everywhere except in the two bookstores I managed to ferret out. The record stores, the clothes stores, the food courts, the amusement park (yes, there's a whole amusement park in the middle of the mall) were packed with young people. But the bookstores were almost empty, except for a handful of adults. I found that really sad.

You might try taking your teenagers to one of the new book-stores with a café as part of it. Buy them a couple of magazines and a cup of cappuccino. Let them soak up the literary atmo-sphere. Offer to buy them a few books. Some of these large book-stores are wonderful for teenagers in that they have nonfiction books on every imaginable topic—and nonfiction and magazines can keep a teenager reading through the I-don't-have-time-to-read periods of high school. Then you also get to work on the book-and-food link with teenagers: connecting anything with food can only raise it in the estimation of most kids.

The crucial thing, when your children are teenagers, is just to keep that supply of reading material available. Remember that they're not independent yet about finding books. Help them.

## READING FRIENDS FOR TEENAGERS

By your children's teenage years, you're realizing that you have very little influence over their choice of friends. If anything, you seem to have a reverse influence: Just keep praising one of their friends as a lovely, sweet girl—and the girl will probably get ditched. Keep criticizing a friend as unkempt and rude and not worthy of your teen's regard—and the young man is a friend for life with your teenager.

But it's still important—more important than ever, really—that your child has friends who are book-loving people, friends who will keep recommending new authors, trading novels, and making your teen feel part of a literate culture. So here are a few suggestions:

### 1. Encourage your teen to join school activities that attract avid readers.

If your school has a literary magazine or a student newspaper, those are the two key activities to encourage. The yearbook is good too, but not as reliably staffed by avid readers as the literary magazine or newspaper. The additional advantage of these two activities is that they encourage writing also. Not only will your teenager be around kids who love reading, they will be around kids who write for pleasure.

The way you encourage participation is, first, by suggesting it. I can almost guarantee that your teen will be welcomed with open arms by a newspaper or magazine staff—first, because it's always hard to find students to do extra writing in school, and so these publications are always looking for more writers; and second, because the kids staffing these publications are almost always gentle and accepting—avid readers, remember? Often, too, the kids staffing these publications are not the cool, "in" crowd—and so are much kinder to newcomers.

To find out how to join, your teen can just go to the main office and ask. Someone there should know the meeting schedule—or at least the name of the faculty adviser. Tell your teen that these are not activities that cut kids—like sports teams do. If your daughter is willing to write, or to learn desktop publishing, she should be enthusiastically welcomed.

Your job, then, is to make sure your teenagers have rides to and from the meetings, to give them group refreshments to bring occasionally (remember the important food-and-literacy link!), and to admire, without reservation, the publication when it finally comes out.

It's important that you and your teenagers realize that usually these publications can be joined at any time during the school year. I know that during all the years when I was the newspaper adviser, we welcomed with open arms anyone who was willing to write, do layout, run around and get ads for us, or even just fold the finished product.

Even if your teenagers are playing on sports teams, with practice every day, they can usually join at least the newspaper. Such kids may not be able to stay for long meetings, but they can come for a few minutes before practice to negotiate a writing assignment, or to turn in an article. And during the off-season we see them all the time.

If your teenager has been cut from a team, it's even more important to get him quickly into other activities—and, again, a high school newspaper or literary magazine staff is usually warm and accepting of newcomers. These staffs are made up of many of the top readers in the school. The kids will end up talking about books, trading books, helping each other with writing—all the kinds of things that will help your child acquire sophisticated literary skills.

The other thing you can do as a parent, perhaps through your school parent group, is to make sure these wonderful activities are funded. With desktop publishing, these are very inexpensive activities for schools to support, and yet it is often funding for these activities that is cut first—long before sports money is cut. So go to meetings. Raise a little hell. Point out that the cost of the student newspaper—adviser's salary, paper, film, and use of the computer lab and copying machine—is *nothing* compared to the cost of a football team (many coaches and a trainer, bus trips for away games, uniforms, sports equipment, field upkeep, etc.). Just the cost of buying helmets for the football team could probably keep the literary magazine solvent for years.

## 2. Have lots of sports reading material around for your athletes.

You want to do this anyway—just so your teenagers read. But, again, it's great if your kids have reading friends, and since members of an athletic team tend to stick together socially, you should see what you can do to get everyone reading. On the whole, avid athletes are not avid readers. Athletes tend to be really nice, really conscientious kids—but they are not usually great readers.

A few suggestions: If your son's or daughter's team has a booster club—which is becoming more common as money gets scarcer—see if the club will donate some magazine subscriptions to the team—*Soccer America* if it's a soccer team, or a basketball or football magazine for those teams. There are magazines for every sport. In addition, ask the club to donate a subscription to *Sports Illustrated* to all of the teams, and subscriptions to all of the local newspapers. The magazines and newspapers could be around the locker rooms, or on the buses for the long bus rides to away games. Once the coach sees how a pile of fascinating reading material quiets down a bunch of teenagers, he may welcome them on the buses and in the locker rooms.

I find that most coaches are very interested in anything that will improve the academic performance of their teams. Coaches are great allies in getting kids motivated and working. So you might approach the coach and ask if he would like a team library started. Explain that you'll enlist other parents and provide the reading material. There are sports biographies for players of almost all sports, and I think team copies of the books really would get passed around and read. For some sports—baseball comes to mind—there is an incredible wealth of wonderful fiction and nonfiction books. If you explain to the coach that any reading that kids do will help college board scores, you should have a firm supporter. Many promising high school athletes have decent enough grades but college board scores that are too low to enable them to play on a college level. Coaches are very aware of this problem.

Another suggestion is just to have lots of sports reading material around your house, and to lend it out willingly. Don't have a television near the food—the first place in a house that athletes congregate—instead have current sports magazines and newspapers. You also might start talking to your own kids and their friends about sports articles you've seen and read. What did they think about that newspaper column on your town's quarterback? Do they think their team is getting enough coverage in your local paper? If not, encourage one of them to contact the editor and offer to supply some write-ups. What you're trying to do is start to gently nudge your teenager's sports friends in the direction of print material for their daily fix of sports information.

### 3. Most after-school activities help kids make reading friends.

Although music and drama, for example, don't attract especially literate kids to start with, an interest in those fields often leads to an interest in reading. The members of the drama club at our school are always reading through plays to find ones they want to perform. The kids who take part in the model United Nations are scouring the library for information on the countries they're representing. Kids in debating clubs are always reading. I think even kids interested in music often become interested in the lives of composers, as well as in the scores of musicals and operas. Science clubs are great for branching kids out in their science reading.

What all of these activities do is develop specialized interests in kids, and these interests, I think, almost always lead to more reading. Or at least they can lead to more reading with just a little help from you.

## 4. Realize that reading friends will often turn up in unlikely places.

You might think that if your daughter chooses most of her friends from other students in her honors classes—lovely, polite, conscientious kids who do well in school—she'll have plenty of reading friends. But that isn't necessarily so. Often kids who do well in school don't take time to read. This usually starts to catch up with them by the last couple of years of high school, but in the early teenage years these no-time-to-read kids can do pretty well. What your daughter might be learning from them, unfortunately, is that pleasure reading is a waste of valuable time.

You can't do anything about this—it's impossible to choose high school friends for your daughter—but just be aware of the problem. Your daughter will undoubtedly reap other wonderful benefits from associating with such a nice group of young women—but avid reading may not be one of them.

On the other hand, your daughter may come home with a friend you have severe qualms about—a counterculture kind of girl who wears long skirts, boots, and about eight different earrings at the same time. She might even have pink hair. You're a little taken aback. Do you really want this young woman as a friend for your daughter?

Well, again you essentially have no choice. But at least know that there's a good chance that this quirky, gypsy-type girl is more involved in serious reading than are the girls who are getting all

A's in honor classes. I've known kids like this who read widely, write wonderful poetry, and, although often emotionally fragile, are very gentle, loving people. I think too many adults associate this mode of dress with the hippies of the sixties, and worry about drug use. Drug use is always a worry with high school students, but you can't tell a drug user by dress. I see as many preppie drug users as counterculture ones.

So receive your teen's friends with an open mind. Engage them in reading discussions. You might be pleasantly surprised. Remember that avid-reading teen friends can be a strong influence in keeping your son or daughter reading.

## ENCOURAGING CRITICAL THINKING ABOUT READING

Critical thinking: the "in" skill! Helping your children to read with a critical eye becomes more important as your children turn into teenagers. While simply a love and habit of reading will turn out a very good reader, the kids who are always asking me the uncomfortable questions—and making the astute, uncomfortable observations—are the ones making the top scores on the SATs. How do you foster this habit of mind in your teenager?

### 1. Realize that kids who think critically about one thing will think critically about everything.

When it comes to developing critical thinking skills, as parents, and especially as teachers, we seem determined to have our cake and eat it too. We want our kids to think critically about MTV (trashy, violence laden) but not about their great-aunt (preachy, boring, smelly). When it comes to great-aunts, we want to teach compassion and understanding as well—but we can't deny our children their critical insights.

I'm a firm believer that a habit of critical thinking in one area will carry over to other areas. When our teen explains to us that the way we have the kitchen set up is inefficient—dishes should be in the cupboards right above the dishwasher, not in the pantry—I think we have to respect the insight, instead of getting defensive and shouting, "Fine! You run this kitchen!"—an impulse that is almost irresistibly tempting.

Maybe it will help your discussions at home if I explain how I try to run classroom discussions. The idea is to encourage critical thinking, but to discourage personal attacks. I tell my students that I would like our classroom to be a free marketplace of ideas, but to do this we have to agree to maintain civility of discourse. This means, I explain, that any idea can be brought up. "For example," I tell them, standing up to show off my full height of five feet two inches, "I've always thought that short people were the smartest." I always get a few snickers, but everyone is paying attention. Then I tell them that, under the rules of civility of discourse, no one may shout out, "You're really dumb, Mrs. Leonhardt. How could you think that?" What students *can* say is something like, "Well, Mrs. Leonhardt, have you ever considered that Abraham Lincoln was over six feet tall?"

The students are usually more than happy to commit themselves to maintaining civility of discourse in order to be assured of a free marketplace of ideas. I tell them that I will agree to maintain civility of discourse also. If someone does poorly on a test, and comes to argue with me about the fairness of the test, I agree to say something like, "Okay, what exactly wasn't fair about the test?" rather than, "What's the matter? Didn't you study?" I pledge that I won't personally attack them.

I think this can also work in your home. No matter how immature your teenagers' insights are, you need to respect them, and discuss the insights on their merits. You realize that your teenagers probably think that *your* insights are dated and unrealistic, so a commitment to a free marketplace of ideas—with civility of discourse—might help to ensure that they actually start listening to you again too. We tend to listen to people who listen to us.

In the beginning you should try not to be hard on your teen's insights. Try to see some aspect of their argument that is valuable and that you can agree with. Get excited about their ideas. "Yes, I really agree that punishing you if you're not home at *exactly* twelve might encourage you to run a red light and get in an accident. I hadn't thought of that. How can we set things up so that

I'm not worried, and know where you are, and so that you aren't tempted to drive dangerously?"

Remember, it's impossible to teach someone to think critically only in selected, preapproved areas. And don't worry that if you encourage your teenagers to look at everything in a critical manner, they'll end up with no beliefs at all. My own theory is that any belief that can't be questioned is a belief not worth having. And in practical terms, when teenagers are told that certain beliefs are sacrosanct, those are the very beliefs they'll be *most* likely to question. So encourage their questions. You've raised good, compassionate, loving children: you won't lose them to a nihilistic lifestyle just because you encourage them to think critically.

Something else about critical thinking:

## 2. Try to move your teen from just thinking critically about personal experiences to thinking critically about less personal topics, such as sports and music.

After creating an atmosphere in your house that encourages your teenager to think and express ideas, gradually try to expand your topics of conversation to include more abstract topics. One of the biggest differences between my excellent readers and my mediocre readers is that my excellent readers get excited about ideas—while mediocre readers get bored with "all this analyzing." Mediocre readers are more than willing to talk about things of personal importance to them, such as curfews and class attendance policies. But abstract topics? Forget it.

So start with an area of interest for your teen. Who's the best pitcher, this year, for the Red Sox? What's the best rock group? Ask them to explain their opinions to you. Listen respectfully.

After they're comfortable expressing opinions, challenge them a bit. How can anyone respect rap, ask them, when so many songs denigrate women? Don't overpower them with your arguments, but do insist, gently, that they give reasons for their statements. If they can give you arguments—but you still think they are maintaining an outrageous position—tell them that you respect their opinion, because they've backed it up with facts, but you just don't agree with them on this point. If nothing else, your kids will learn the valuable lesson that reasonable people can peacefully disagree. After getting them used to talking about abstract subjects, move on to books.

## 3. Encourage your teenagers to discuss their reading critically with you.

There are all kinds of reasons for doing this. Kids who read with a critical eye always have the best comprehension. They start to see nuances of meaning. They read in an alert state of mind.

Start easy with this. Ask your teenagers about favorite authors, favorite books. Do active listening with them. "Oh, you like Stephen King because of the horror he throws in. Yeah, I can see that would be exciting." After you've done this for a while, push a little harder. "I wonder how Stephen King gets the reader to believe all of his horror. I mean, doesn't he run the risk that you'd just start laughing?"

Agree with whatever your son says here. Perhaps he'll tell you that Stephen King's books are really realistic. Realistic? You can't believe your bright son said that. But don't say anything negative. Look thoughtful. Venture a guess. "You mean his characters are realistic?" He'll probably agree with you. With more gentle prodding, you may get him to come up with the realization that Stephen King's novels are realistic in all of the detail—character, setting, tone—and it's that very realism that lulls us into trusting him, so when he throws in his horror part (animals and people rising from the dead in his *Pet Sematary*) we just keep right on believing him. If you can get your son to figure that out, he'll see Stephen King's books in a much more critical way. (I don't think I'd do this until he's already read most of King's novels. You don't want to ruin them for him.) What you've helped your son do is raise the curtain on King's sleight-of-hand trick in his books.

Once your teenagers get the knack of looking at books with this kind of critical intelligence, they'll be much better readers, and much better writers—since they'll have some idea of how authors create certain effects. And I think it's actually when kids start reading with this critical acumen that they tire of many of the early authors they once loved. When this happens, you can start suggesting other authors.

## Start gently pointing your accomplished readers in the direction of more complex authors.

I think everyone, no matter how great a reader, likes to relax with a page-turner now and then. But once your teenagers start reading in a critically sophisticated manner, it's time to start offering them some of the great writers of our past, as well as some of the most exciting writers of our present time.

### 1. Start by finding classic authors similar to the popular authors your teenagers enjoy.

As I mentioned in the chapters on reading paths, you should suggest your kids read the classic writers that write the same kind of novel as that of the popular writers they've already enjoyed. If your daughter loves the suspense novels of Mary Higgins Clark, she will probably not like the novels of Joseph Conrad—but she might love *Jane Eyre*. Just use your common sense.

### 2. Read some of the authors along with your teenagers.

You'll want to do this for a couple of reasons. One is that you can, in an unobtrusive way, help your kids with the more difficult parts of the book. But the more important reason is that they'll then have someone to talk with about the book. You're also validating their choice in authors by enjoying the book yourself.

### 3. Plan other enriching activities.

Trips to the part of this country, or overseas, where these authors came from are incredibly motivating and exciting for an avid reader. I know this is an outrageously expensive suggestion, but keep it in mind when planning vacations. And you can certainly do lesser things. See if your teenagers will go to drama productions with you, or visit historical museums, or watch some of the excellent videos out on classic works. If you do nothing else, rent the video of the 1993 movie *Much Ado About Nothing*, and you'll be dazzled at the power a Shakespeare play can still have today. *Henry V* and *Hamlet* (with Mel Gibson) are two other movie videos your children should enjoy.

## 4. Share your own classical loves with your teenagers.

I sometimes think that the most effective teaching technique— maybe the only effective teaching technique—is to share enthusiasms.

If you love Auden's poetry, or the lyrics of Cole Porter, don't be afraid to recite or sing for your teenagers. (As one of my children pointed out to me once, parents are *supposed* to be geeky. It's geeky if parents *aren't* geeky.) Insist that, sometimes in the car, the tape *you* want to hear is put in, rather than their rock tapes. You might even get the tape of a classic book you know they'd like, and play it on a long trip. If they're ready for this kind of reading—and listening—you should be successful.

## 5. Explore local summer enrichment programs.

In the Boston area, where I live, there are a number of enrichment programs offered for high school students in the summer. Some of these are presented through private schools, and some through colleges. If you can afford to do so, explore similar programs in your area. My students who have attended them usually give them positive reviews:

> I went to Milton Academy for the summer. It's college level stuff crammed into six weeks so it's very intense. The class sizes are small so there's a teacher or intern for fourteen students so there's a lot of personal interaction. The pace was quick and the emphasis was on reading and writing about reading. And taking what you learned and trying to do it yourself. A large part was writing, exploring other people's style and trying to develop your own.

Once teenagers start reading complex, difficult authors, I think you'll see a jump in their analytical ability as well as in their habit and love of reading. It's all connected somehow. The one important piece of the picture I haven't really discussed yet, in terms of teenagers, is writing.

## KEEP ENCOURAGING YOUR CHILD'S WRITING

One of the most effective ways to ensure that teenagers with better-than-average to excellent reading skills keep writing is to make sure they're in an excellent school system. Excellent school systems are more likely to have lower teacher-student ratios; the fewer students a teacher has, the more likely it is that she'll assign writing. If your son's English teacher has a hundred and fifty students, forget having him do much writing in school—or at least forget having the teacher pay much individual attention to his writing. With all kids it's important to encourage at-home writing, but it's especially important if your child is in an overcrowded school.

So what can you do? Here are a few suggestions:

### 1. Invest in a good computer, preferably one that is compatible with the kind your teenagers use in school.

By high school age all of my good writers use computers almost exclusively. Even kids who report to me that they used to dislike computers have all switched over by high school. The computer makes it much easier for them to rewrite, to save their writing and compile a portfolio, and to show off their writing to you and to their friends. They don't need a computer for their exclusive use, certainly, but they should have easy, generous access to one. And you certainly don't need to buy the most expensive one.

In my area of the country, there is a little magazine called *The Want Advertiser* that comes out every week and lists what people in the area have for sale. There are many nice personal computers listed in it for several hundred dollars, or less. I think you should be able to get a pretty good one for about the price of a new television set.

So you have your teenagers doing their homework writing assignments on a computer. How can you encourage them to do creative writing on their own?

### 2. Suggest to your children that they try to get some of their work published.

In many smaller towns the local newspapers are very open to publishing letters, and even columns, by local high school students. Some of my students, over the years, have even become salaried sportswriters for the town paper. They learn to adhere to professional writing standards, and to meet deadlines. Wonderful experience!

I mentioned in the chapter on elementary school writers that you might buy the *Market Guide for Young Writers*, which lists publishers and contests that accept work by young people. You can get this for your high school student as well, along with the adult *Writer's Marketplace*. There is also a *Songwriter's Marketplace*, and a *Poetry Marketplace*. These reference books can be found in most large bookstores, and they're full of ideas for kinds of writing.

### 3. Check out summer programs that offer enriching writing experiences for young people.

I mentioned similar programs in the above section on reading; you should be aware of the potential of summer programs for developing writers also. The good thing about this intense kind of experience is that it makes kids feel part of a literary community; it makes them feel like real writers. It also allows them to concentrate completely on their writing without having to stop and do some other work.

I know these summer programs are expensive—but so are summer sports camps, and they are a thriving business. If your teenager is willing, try to squeeze it out of the budget somehow.

## A FINAL WORD ON TEENAGERS

What if you have a teenager who, in spite of your best efforts, stops doing independent reading in high school? Let's assume it's your daughter, and let's assume that she loved reading in elementary school, but simply gave it up as too time-consuming in high school. Or she stopped finding books that she liked. This is a situation I often see. Usually these children are excellent students; often they're pretty good writers. But they just don't seem to make time for independent reading in high school.

You can do a couple of things. First, make sure your daughter is at least reading magazines and newspapers. Be sure to keep a good current supply of any she might be interested in. By doing this, you're helping to keep up her love and habit of reading. Then make sure you have some adult books around that are similar to the ones she liked as a child (see chapter 7). And, finally, try to schedule family activities—like long plane or train rides, a week in a cabin or on a beach—where she won't have schoolwork and she will have time to read. If you're subtle and persistent, it shouldn't be too hard to get her reading again. I think kids who once had a love of reading always come back to books, sooner or later.

But the other thing you have to pay attention to, with a teenager like this, is your attitude toward school. Are you actually making her afraid to spend time reading by your insistence on high grades?

In the next chapter we'll try to sort all of this out.

# Education Goals and Dealing with Homework

Before we can talk about how to deal with homework—and school issues in general—we need to talk about your goals for your child. What kind of eighteen-year-old do you want to have?

In my last book I talked about the impact of school problems on poor readers, and suggested, in essence, that a parent give any help asked for, and try everything to get the poor reader reading at home—because reading is everything. A poor reader is probably going to have a lousy school record anyway—so his time is better spent reading *Sports Illustrated* than struggling over some unreadable history handout. Read the handout to him, if he wants you to. And if he doesn't? Well, it's *crucial* that he become literate, and it's not crucial that he pass history—at least not at this moment in his life. After he becomes a competent, fluent reader he can worry about getting his academic credentials in order.

But what about the children who are average-to-excellent readers? What do you want them to get out of school, and what should your role be in helping them?

I would argue that the primary academic achievement we want for our children is that they develop an independent intellectual life. It's better to have children who have a wealth of intellectual curiosity—who are always reading books to find out answers to their questions, or watching documentaries on television, or stealing your copy of *The Wall Street Journal*—than to have children who get all A's in school.

But wait a minute, you say. Shouldn't a kid with curiosity and drive and excellent reading skills be getting all A's in school? Isn't that what school's all about?

It *should* be what school is all about, but unfortunately it's not. From my talks with parent groups, from the letters I receive, and from my own twenty-five years of experience in teaching, I can assure you that much of what your child will be asked to do, both in school and for homework, will be work that seems designed to make him hate learning. Some assignments will be boring and repetitious, some will be arcane and ridiculously difficult, and some will seem—and may be!—random and meaningless.

Of course, to take the teacher's part for a minute—since I *am* a teacher—it's hard to think of assignments that are exciting and worthwhile for every single one of your students. It's *impossible* to do this if a teacher buys into the accepted ways of teaching, and the traditional curriculum, in which all students do pretty much the same thing at the same time. If a whole class is assigned to read the same book—no matter what the book is—I can guarantee you that for at least some of the students, that will not be a good book to read, at this point in their life. I'm always telling teachers that they need to open up their curricula and individualize assignments, but this is a very difficult message for teachers to hear—especially teachers who are getting low pay, teaching far too many kids, and dealing with far too many administrators and curriculum specialists who are telling them to teach an inappropriate curriculum.

So your problem as a parent is that much of the work your child is asked to do is work that is not intrinsically motivating for him. It's work that makes him feel stupid, or bores him, or confuses him. What, as a parent, do you do?

Well, first you decide on your goals. I would suggest the following goals, which I've set up in the same kind of prioritized fashion as the reading goals outlined in chapter 2.

### First Goal: You want to raise a child who possesses courage, compassion, and integrity.

I think this should be the fundamental goal, the one that no other goal can be allowed to put in jeopardy.

Now, this is a goal that people usually think goes without saying. *Of course* we want our children to be good people, whether we view that concept in a religious sense or not. But I find that parents and teachers, without thinking the issue through properly, often send their children messages that can be easily misinterpreted.

For example, suppose your daughter has an important biology test tomorrow. Tonight her best friend calls her on the phone, crying. Her parents have announced they're divorcing. She needs to come over and talk. What do you urge your daughter to do? Should she really say, "I can't talk now, I have a huge biology test tomorrow?"

Or suppose your son is in a history class that demands recall of every trivial fact the teacher has ever mentioned. And suppose your son stumbles on an advance copy of the final exam. What should he do?

I pose these questions because I believe—and I hope you do too—that it's much more important for our children to acquire integrity, courage, and compassion than high grades. So we have to be very careful in the messages we communicate. If we put too much emphasis on grades, kids can easily misinterpret this to mean that getting high grades is the most important thing—more important than helping a friend in need, or refusing to cheat.

This issue comes up again and again in schools. Should your daughter write a paper that says what she truly thinks—or should she write the kind of paper she thinks the teacher wants? Should your son take time to help a friend learn a difficult aspect of math—or should he be studying all of the time for himself? A lot of the fury I hear from parents over heterogeneous grouping, which involves putting students of different academic abilities in the same classroom, revolves around this issue. Many parents don't want their children taking time out from learning to help other students. Personally, I think that's the wrong message to give children.

Here's why: Just as we can't pick and choose the issues we want our children to think critically about, we can't pick and choose the times when we want our children to act with compassion and courage and integrity. The times when good qualities really count are the times when it's not convenient to display them. If we discourage our son from befriending a teammate who can't seem to pass history without help, why do we think that same son will interrupt his busy life to care for his own children—or to care for us when we're old?

So I think you need to make clear to your children that their most important job is to be a good person. If your children can jump through all the hoops that schools set up, and still maintain their integrity, that's great. If they can't—if acting with courage and compassion and integrity means not getting an A on a paper or nailing down that last bit of detail for a science test—then you need to support them in their decision. Just keep asking yourself, What kind of world would I rather live in? One that is filled with people who got straight A's in school, or one that is filled with courageous, compassionate, honest people? Do your part to make sure that your own little world, at least, is filled with good people.

Some of my saddest interviews have been with kids who felt that, in order to get top grades, they had to give up something important about themselves.

## Second Goal: You want your child to have an independent intellectual life.

I think your primary *intellectual* goal for your child should be to love learning, and to pursue learning for the joy of learning itself.

Although I have made this the second overall goal, I don't think it conflicts much with the first goal. If anything, it complements the first goal, since a person who has the self-confidence and drive to pursue independent learning will also probably be an individual with the courage to stand up and do what's right.

If your child is an avid reader, he'll achieve this goal sooner or later—even if he's only reading Michael Crichton novels now. He's acquiring frameworks of knowledge, remember? Sooner or later all of these frameworks will blossom into a full-blown interest in DNA or early life-forms or sex-discrimination laws. I've seen it happen again and again.

I think that knowledge is exploding so fast now, that, in practical terms, we *have* to produce children who love learning for its own sake, if they are ever going to be top performers in a professional field. Future scientists and doctors and lawyers and bankers and investment counselors and engineers are going to have to have the motivation and ability to seek out, understand, and assimilate new information, probably on a daily basis.

Your child won't start out loving information about investment banking. He'll start out, maybe, loving baseball cards. He'll want to collect them, trade them, read about them in his *Beckett* magazines. That's fine. He has an independent intellectual interest that he's pursuing. He'll branch out later.

Does this goal conflict with school achievement? Sometimes. My experience with my own students indicates that it interferes most seriously in junior high school.

In elementary school, kids with independent interests are usually also good readers, and so find the work in elementary school very easy. They do it in school; they do it on the bus. And elementary teachers are more accustomed to having students work independently. Many of my excellent readers told me that their elementary school teachers allowed them much latitude in choosing books and doing assignments. I also think elementary teachers are more likely to be realists. A nine-year-old who is bored and turned off is also probably jumping around the room and making life hell for everyone. Let's find something that kid will do! By junior high or high school, that same kid has gone underground. He slumps down in his seat and just quietly fails, or does the minimum required to pass. So it's easier for everyone to ignore him.

I think that's why students with active independent intellectual lives often stop achieving in junior high, when teachers seem much less willing to allow them to do individual assignments. Of course, junior high and high school teachers normally teach as many as a hundred and fifty students a day—sometimes more. It's pretty hard to know that many kids as individuals—and to help them plan their schoolwork accordingly.

Often these independent learners are far ahead of the rest of the class. One girl who had loved biology since the age of six—who used to read anatomy books for fun in elementary school—told me her eighth-grade science teacher accused her of cheating because she finished her science workbook ahead of everyone else. So that was it for science class. She didn't want to do any of the other work.

Another boy, one of the best English students and one of the best poets to go through my high school, described his middle school* experiences this way:

> Middle school was horrible. I was learning just from books because I hated classes. By the time I was in middle school I could write pretty well because I did so much reading. I wrote this paper and the teacher said there was this national contest and he wouldn't submit mine because he said it was plagiarized, and I've never plagiarized a thing in my life. He wrote all over it "Are these your words?"

High school often becomes a bit easier. For one thing, there's a good chance that the high school teachers your child has are a little better prepared in their field, and so are quicker to spot and appreciate kids who have already mastered much of the subject matter themselves. For another, in high school there are often clubs or activities that incorporate and showcase independent learners. My high school has a science team and a math team that

---

* In Massachusetts, junior high schools are called middle schools.

win all kinds of prizes. We have a model United Nations, for kids fascinated by history. We have a literary magazine and a school newspaper for students who love writing. We have a French club and a Spanish club, and even a Russian club. In high school, independent learners can make friends with similar interests, and enjoy the accolades and recognition that their learning never garnered them in a junior high classroom.

But in high school, grades really start to matter, since college acceptance is, to a large extent, dependent on high school grades. Which brings me to my third goal:

### Third Goal: You want your child to have a respectable academic record.

Please note that this is your *third* goal. It's great if you have a child who, with enthusiasm and dedication, learns everything his teachers have to teach. But this isn't as important as having a child who develops an independent intellectual life, or a child who develops the qualities of integrity, courage, and compassion. Don't let this goal interfere with the first two.

You may wonder why I'm making this only the third goal. Isn't an outstanding academic record necessary to get into a prominent college, such as Harvard or Yale or Princeton? Surely your child's whole future depends on how well he does in school.

Let's see if we can sort this out. First of all, college, of course, is only one small part of your child's future. Let's say you have a daughter who does manage to get into Princeton as an undergraduate, and then into Harvard Law School. It certainly seems that her future is assured. But how is it assured? Yes, she'll probably be able to get a high-paying, high-pressure law job right out of law school, so she'll be able to make lots of money. Does this mean she'll be happy?

I would argue that the ability to make a lot of money is not a very important part of future happiness and well-being. An ability to form loving relationships is crucial. An ability to find satisfying, absorbing work is crucial. An ability to laugh at the inherent absurdity of life is crucial. Will going to Harvard Law School help with these goals?

Going to a prominent college is necessary for some students. I think students with a burning inner drive to be the best doctor or the best lawyer or a great scientist may need to attend a top-ranking college to achieve satisfaction in life. But a student like this carries his or her own motivation. If you have a child like this, enjoy her academic success, but don't expect your other children to be similarly motivated.

Your children don't need perfect academic records to be well prepared for life. There is such a multitude of excellent colleges and universities in this country that even students with very mediocre academic records can get into a good college. The critical element in college success is having a son or daughter who loves reading and has a well-developed, independent intellectual life. Having a child who is enthusiastic about learning is much more important than having a child who got all A's in high school.

I can't stress this enough because, every year, kids seem to be under more pressure from everyone to get high grades. I've had parents call me to complain about a B-plus their child has gotten. I've even had parents complain about an A-minus. These parents never seem concerned about what, if anything, their child is actually learning. Grades are everything.

This is such a poor message to give a child. Personal qualities are important. A love of learning is important. A habit of reading is important. But grades?

And the final irony is that high grades don't even ensure acceptance to a top-ranking college. I heard the director of admissions at Harvard speak a few years ago, and she noted that they had had over 14,000 applications to Harvard that year, for 1,800 places. She said that at least ten thousand of those applications were from top students who could do the work at Harvard. In fact, she said five thousand of them could do honors work. But most didn't get in.

From my vantage point—a high school teacher who writes an average of thirty college recommendations a year, and tracks acceptances—the whole process seems pretty random. Every year I'm surprised. How did this student get in? Why didn't they take that other student? Who knows?

And this is another reason why you should focus on qualities that really matter for your children, such as integrity and a love of reading and learning. These are qualities that will stand them in good stead their whole lives. Going to a prestigious college gets you that first job interview, but after that? Do you know where your most admired friends went to college? Do you care? Does it make any difference in their work? In their personal lives?

But, having said all this, I will admit that a solid academic record does open doors for students. It does give them options, such as going to medical school, or a top business school. Good grades can also boost a child's self-esteem. It's fun to be one of the "smart" kids. Sometimes high grades open to a student classes and subjects that would otherwise be closed. So grades certainly are important. I think the issue is one of perspective.

So, keeping in mind that grades aren't everything—that other things are much more important—how do you try to ensure that your child ends up with a respectable academic record?

## 1. Help your child to achieve a respectable academic record.

There is much conventional wisdom regarding how to help your child get good grades. A typical book that embodies this set of ideas is *Helping Your Child to Learn*, by Gordon W. Green Jr., Ph.D. (Citadel Press, 1994). In his principles ("Principle 1: Plan a course of study for children, and work hard to keep them on the right track"), he espouses the philosophy that parents need to organize and supervise their children's schoolwork. I'm sure you're familiar with the precepts: Make sure your child spends an hour or two a night—or longer—in a quiet place, either studying or doing assignments; check to make sure he understands the work and completes everything; keep in close contact with your child's teachers.

What could be wrong with this, you ask? Well, this philosophy has one major flaw: *It doesn't work.* It sounds sensible, it looks good written out in advice books, it's convincing when you hear it from education experts on talk shows . . . but it doesn't work.

Somehow, kids who are closely supervised are not the kids who, by high school, do the wonderful work. I'm not sure why this is, although the obvious reason—that maybe the wonderful workers *always* did wonderful work, and so never had to be supervised—I *know* isn't true. Too many of my top students tell me of periods when they did very little homework. Other top students always did homework, but still reported never being supervised.

I've been talking with kids informally about this for years, but finally decided to ask all of my classes to write, whether or not they did homework, and whether or not their parents supervised. I asked them to tell me about elementary school, middle school, and high school. I received no surprises—it's what I've been hearing from kids for years—but you might enjoy some of their responses.

The first group—consisting of my excellent students who report not always doing homework—aren't the students who always hand in every assignment on time, but they do the important work, and the quality is always wonderful.

### First student (one of the two best writers in the class):
Elementary: Nerd. I loved homework and took pride in it.
Middle: Downward spiral: did little if any homework by eighth grade.
High: Did some homework: I'll always do the minimum. My parents don't ask me about homework. I'll never do more than one hour of homework a night.

### Second student (one of the best readers in the class):
Elementary: My parents expected that I do my homework and I always did.
Middle: My parents expected that I do my homework, and I rarely did. They never knew.
High: My parents expected that I do my homework, but my slacking became exponentially worse and worse until I became the totally

irresponsible slacker that I am today. They still never knew.
Parents should only help their children when asked.

### Third student (the other best writer):
Elementary: There was no homework.
Middle: My parents never supervised. I did it on my own.
High: My parents nag me but I never listen. Sometimes I do it; sometimes not. There's a thin line between working and slacking
   where you still learn with minimum work. If you can walk that
   line, you're in good shape.

I do have some excellent students who report always having
done homework. But notice that they were never made to do
homework by parents:

### First student:
My parents never made me do my homework because I just did
it on my own. I don't know why, but I did. If my parents ever
made me do my homework I wouldn't have so I guess it's a
good thing they left it up to me.

### Second student:
My parents never checked my homework, not now, not then, not
ever. I always did my homework. My parents check my brother's
homework *every single* night. He never does his homework if
they don't nag him to.

### Third student:
I have always done my homework. For my entire life I have done
every damned assignment I've ever been given. Was I forced to
do it? No! I just *did* it. I don't know why I wasted my precious
youth at my desk doing homework.

As you see, even the best students who always did homework
don't really know *why* they did it. But they are very clear that they
didn't work because of parental pressure.
But what about the students who did have a lot of parental

supervision? Only one student who is an avid reader reported having parents who checked homework, and he is the only avid reader I have who is not a very good writer. This was his comment:

> In middle school and elementary school I always did all my homework. My parents made me do it, set up times. Once I got to high school I started to slack off, didn't do homework. In ninth grade I didn't do anything. Now [eleventh grade] I do it most of the time. I always do all the big stuff.

None of my other students who reported having parents who supervised homework were avid readers. Maybe this was just happenstance—over the years I do get an occasional avid reader who had his homework supervised—but now I seem to have only the student quoted above. The typical comment from my kids who were not avid readers but had parents supervising went like this:

Elementary: My parents always made me work for an hour. If I didn't I was supposed to read. (Never happened.)
Middle: I went to private school so my parents always made me do it but they never looked at it.
High: My parents try to make sure that I spend more time on my homework than on the phone. (It's a hard job.)

So what's a parent to do? With the help of my students, I have a few suggestions:

## 2. Don't make your children do homework.
My students are unanimous on this point. They are convinced—and I've been convinced for years—that it doesn't work. You might get a short-term gain—your children might do their homework a little better for a while—but the long-term cost is too high.

What are the long-term costs? The biggest one I see, by high school, is a loss of enthusiasm and creativity and competence in the student's work. The kids who do terrific work are not the students who were forced by parents to do homework.

I've thought about this a lot, trying to figure it out. Perhaps the fundamental flaw in making kids do homework is that they learn to do it quickly and in a cursory manner, just to get rid of an annoying parent. They don't feel like they own the homework themselves; they're tenant farmers, so to speak.

A second cost of forcing kids to do homework is that you risk starting an all-out homework war with them. I see this every so often. A few years ago I had a student who did no work at all, either in school or at home. Now, I'm pretty good at setting things up in my classes with assignments so that kids are motivated to work. It's very unusual that I get a student who does nothing. But this kid did nothing.

So we had a parent conference. The mother told me that she couldn't understand what was going on. Jake (not his real name) *always* did all of his homework with her before this year. "My friends say to me, 'What do you do?' " she cheerfully explained to me. " 'Do you work or play tennis or cards?' And I say to them, 'What I do is help Jake with homework. I never go out at night because he needs my help all evening.' " I'll never forget her explaining that to me, in her cheerful, sweet voice. She was an absolutely charming lady who was absolutely clueless.

Jake was a sophomore now, and was in all-out rebellion. He was going to do *nothing*.

I tried gently suggesting to the mother that they get some family counseling. No way. Could she at least back off a bit? No. Finally, in complete frustration, I asked her what she planned to do about Jake's homework when and if—a big *if* now—he went to college. "We'll get fax machines," she explained, "and fax the homework back and forth." I'm not making this up.

I don't know what eventually happened to Jake, since his parents pulled him out of our public school soon afterward, and sent him to a fundamentalist Christian school. I lost track of him, but his friends told me that he still continued to resist doing any work.

There were obviously problems in that family that were greater than simply trying to make Jake do homework—but the homework war at home, I believe, was the major reason I couldn't even get him to do any work in school.

Forcing children to do homework doesn't usually have such disastrous consequences, but I think it does significantly erode both the quality of the student's work, and the student/parent relationship.

"Kids won't do anything if you force them to—let them make mistakes—they'll learn that way," one student wrote. Another student was even blunter: "I get less done when my parents tell me to do my homework. When they don't enforce anything, I take it upon myself to get it done. I hate being told to do anything!" One young man who had been closely supervised by his parents wrote that he wouldn't advise parents to give so much help: "It makes kids lazy and then they will depend too much on their parents or other people." And, finally, a couple of students mentioned that they started lying about homework to avoid parental consequences: "In middle school my parents nagged me about it, and they would always ask if I had any. If I hadn't done it, I couldn't go out. So I started lying."

The cost of forcing homework can be huge. Frankly, I don't think it's worth it.

## 3. Don't call teachers to check up on your children's work.

I know that this suggestion again goes against accepted wisdom. Aren't you supposed to show interest in your children's schooling?

The problem with constant calls to the teacher is that your children will think you don't trust them. And you don't, right? Why else would you be calling teachers? Why not just ask your children? One of my students described her feelings about parental calls to teachers this way:

> I wish that my parents had given me my own responsibility when I was little. It's degrading to high schoolers to have a parent breathing down their back or calling teachers all the time to see if their kid is up to date. A kid usually knows if they're missing work and it makes them less likely to do it if

their parents keep annoying them. It's the kid's responsibility, not the parents. If the kids aren't going to do it, they're not going to do it.

As you can see, my student is quite passionate on this point. I know I've learned, over the years, that if I form the kind of alliance with a parent in which I'm calling every time a student misses an assignment, I ultimately lose the kid completely. This hasn't happened to me for a number of years, because I simply refuse to do it. Every so often I get a request from Guidance or Special Ed to call a parent if an assignment is late or missing. I just smile sweetly and say, "I don't do that." I *can't* do that, because if I do, I risk having a student who pretty soon will do nothing. Or a student who does assignments in only the most cursory, perfunctory manner.

What I usually do now, when I get a request for a phone call to parents to update them on their child's progress, is to find that student, have a conference with him on grades, and then ask him to talk to his parents. And when, because of time constraints or real concerns, I end up talking to a parent on the phone about a student's progress, I always try to find that student immediately afterward and report the substance of the conversation to him. No surprises or talking behind a kid's back—that's my goal. And the closer I can adhere to it, the better results I get in terms of student work.

But so far all I've given you are negative suggestions. Is there nothing positive you can do?

## 4. Show interest in your children's studies, and be available for help.

This was the most common suggestion from my students. They like having parents admire their work, and they like parents who are willing to help—but only if they're asked. My students were adamant about this. One of my avid readers describes his homework experience:

Elementary: Teachers organized it, parents helped me, didn't make me, I did most of it.
Middle: Parents helped me more, didn't make me, I still did most of it.
High: Parents don't help me as much, don't make me, I try to do most of it.
I say to my parents, "Keep it up, you're doing fine."

There are many things parents can do to support children. "Give them a place to study, if they want it, and make sure they have time to do it if they choose. But don't tell them to do their homework," suggested one student. If kids stop doing homework, "Talk to them, make them take enough pride in themselves to learn for themselves and do work," suggested another kid. One of my current students, who was an avid comic-book reader as a kid, and is now reading Dante's *Inferno* for fun, offers this advice on homework:

> I do as little homework as possible. I do fine on tests; I just don't feel like doing any homework. Most of it is busy work. If you already understand it what's the point. If I haven't read the required book I'll read it. I'd already read the Tale of Two Cities. I get fine grades. They're high. I just don't do any homework. Got in a little trouble for not doing homework. In middle school I bombed out in social studies, math was a mess, and science was terrible.
>
> Never say to your kids you have to get this done now. Parents have to make it clear that education is a value but they should make you self-sufficient. Always support your kid. My parents always supported me but they left me alone enough that I could take care of my own schedule.

## 5. The time element is really important by high school age.

I don't think some parents realize what packed schedules their children have, or how hard it is for kids to do high-quality work—

or any work—when they are exhausted from a job or a sports activity. One mother constantly called me on the phone to tell me how her son needed to get all A's. Of course, she told me, he was also practicing a sport six hours every day—but somehow she didn't see that that might negatively affect his schoolwork. He was a ranked player in that sport, and she was convinced that he could be—*should* be—the perfect kid, who was a top athlete, a top student—tops in everything. I felt sorry for the young man, who coped with this kind of pressure by starting to be a real goof-off in school. Making sure your child has time to study is very important.

My own guess, after years of teaching in a very affluent, high-pressure high school, is that it's impossible for a student to do everything well. It's impossible for a student to have an interesting, supportive social life, top grades in top classes, a rich extracurricular life, and an avid reading habit. Something has to give.

I find that, with boys, what often gives is homework. While homework is sometimes likely to suffer with girls also, it's more likely that avid reading will suffer—which is another reason that girls' standardized test scores fall behind those of the boys by senior year of high school. Doing all of the homework required for top grades doesn't necessarily bring up standardized scores—especially verbal scores. Reading brings up verbal scores. And not only do girls have more trouble finding interesting books in high school, they are less willing to let homework slide to make time for reading. So, as Myra and David Sadker point out in *Failing at Fairness*, girls have higher grades and lower scores.

### 6. A tutor might help.

Another way you might support your child is by offering to hire a tutor if there is one subject that is causing particular difficulty. A really good tutor—and you should check around ahead of time to make sure you are getting the best—can be very effective and an incredible bargain. With a tutor you don't have the emotional complications that sometimes arise when you try to teach your child yourself. If you supplement your child's public school experience with carefully chosen tutors for difficult subjects (only if your child is agreeable, of course), that child is getting at least as much individual attention as he'd get in a private school, at a fraction of the cost—and without all of the perils inherent in your trying to teach him. I love the description one of my students gave of his parents trying to help him with homework:

> I tell my parents to leave me alone because when they get involved they ask questions and make it harder by making me teach them. . . . And they try to figure things out and end up doing the homework themselves and you're more confused than [when] you just started. So don't let parents touch your homework.

But there are some specific things you can do to help.

### 7. Help with the little things.
One way you can show your support for academic performance is by willingly helping your children in the day-to-day demands of school. Buy them all of the notebooks and pens they want. Drive them to the drugstore after dinner to get the poster board they need for the science project they just remembered they have to do. Try to do these things without complaining too much. Be enthusiastic about any work they bring home to show you. Be willing to buy them any books or magazines they need for class projects. Rearrange your schedule so you can attend events at school, such as authors' breakfasts, or back-to-school nights. Be there for your children in a friendly, supportive way.

And the most important suggestion:

### 8. Believe in your children.
Probably the most crucial thing you can do for your children is to believe in them. Of course they're smart—maybe not in every subject, but in subjects they care about and are interested in. The worst effect of low grades isn't that they put college acceptance in jeopardy—they really don't need to—but that children might start feeling that they're dumb. Keep telling your children how smart

they are. Tell them that you know they can do well in whatever they work at. Cheer them on.

Especially cheer them on if they've decided to put their time and energy in an activity outside of the classroom. It's very tempting, when this happens, to say something like "Oh, yeah, great soccer game. Too bad you can't put that much energy into your biology homework."

Don't do that because, to start with, your snide comment is not going to make him more anxious to study biology. What it *will* do is take the shine off his winning soccer performance, make him feel less good about himself . . . and make him feel like a failure in *everything*. Success is contagious. If he's doing very well in an outside activity, chances are that his self-esteem and energy level will rise, and he may even start to do better in his academic subjects.

So believe in your children. Encourage them in whatever activity they choose to pursue. Be proud of them.

And I have one final thought:

## Realize that school is only a very small part of your child's life.

One of the perils of being a teacher is that people come up to me at social gatherings and start telling me about their school experiences. I can't begin to tell you how many adults have told me that they disliked school and didn't do very well in school, but are now (finally freed from teachers like me, I guess) living rich, full lives. They read now, when they never read in school. They have great jobs. A great family. Life is wonderful. School is just a dim, distant memory.

So relax. Your love and belief in your children will shape them much more powerfully than any school experience.

# Questions and Answers

Talking to people about reading has been one of the most enjoyable, unexpected highlights of publishing a book. I am asked questions everywhere, often from the most unlikely people. Many of the questions have come from the invitations I've received over the last year and a half to talk to parent and education groups. But I also receive questions during interviews, book signings, and ordinary, friendly gatherings. People always ask great questions; unfortunately I'm not so adept, sometimes, when it comes to thinking up a good answer on the spot. At two in the morning I wake up and say, "*Why* didn't I think to say that?"

So here's my chance. I hope the lovely cabdriver who asked about his daughter's school problems while he drove me around New York finds this book. And the reporter who asked me what to do about her special-ed son who was assigned to read the same, hated book two years in a row—by his special-ed teacher! And all of the funny, charming parents with their homework horror stories. I hope my answers make more sense to you here, and I hope you take the time to write and tell me what else I should be saying.

So here goes. The first set of questions concerns school problems. These questions were, by far, the most common.

## SCHOOL PROBLEMS

**Should parents have input to the school? Should they be talking to the teachers?**

In my first book I discouraged parental input to schools on the theory that, by high school, too much parental input will turn off children and either make them rebellious or passive. But at that point I hadn't heard the horror stories I've heard since then. I still think there's a real risk in frequent calls of complaint to your children's teachers—but I've decided you have to balance that risk with the risk of children becoming totally turned off to school, and to learning in general.

And there's another aspect I hadn't realized until I did some traveling, and talked to teachers in a number of different areas of the country. I recommended in my first book that teachers let students choose much or all of their own reading material. But teachers are very afraid of doing this. They think parents and administrators and community leaders—and God Himself, apparently—are going to descend on them in fury if they stop making all of their classes read *Great Expectations*. Doing what I recommend, which is using whatever reading material it takes to get kids reading, seems like an impossible dream to them.

So I think, now, that parents need to encourage and support teachers in doing this. I have great faith that the vast majority of parents in this country want school to be a happy, effective learning place for their children—and if that means their child is free to read twenty-seven horse books rather than a basal reader, I think few parents would see that as a problem. Actually, I think most parents would be delighted. Parents aren't stupid. They know practice and motivation are *everything* when a child is learning a skill. You can't be a parent and not realize, sooner or later, that when a child loves a task, the odds of his actually doing it increase immeasurably.

And the other advantage of allowing children to choose their own reading is that parents will have much more input. I frequently have students who choose to read Christian authors—the books of Frank Peretti are very popular—and that's fine. Their descriptions of these books enrich our classroom. And I have other kids who only want to read "politically correct" authors— i.e., those who make a point of validating the experiences of various minority groups—and that's fine too. The descriptions of these books also enrich our classroom discussions. Some kids read classics. Great. Some read horror. That's interesting too. Having a classroom where children choose books means that parents are finally empowered to be a major influence in the choosing of their child's school reading.

So my general recommendation to parents is to support any choice-friendly reading initiative you see happening in your school district, to support these initiatives loudly and publicly— and, while still respecting your children's control of their own education, to speak out about really outrageous educational situations that are hurting them.

Here, now, are some specific questions:

**My son was required to read *The Bridge to Terabithia* [Katherine Paterson] last year in his special-ed reading class. He hated it. Guess what he has to read this year? *The Bridge to Terabithia* again. Is there anything I can do?**

A reporter who was interviewing me for a column mentioned this situation—her own reason for interest in my first book. I was horrified by her story—special-ed teachers, of *all* people, should be trying to match up students with individual books they'll like. But I wasn't especially surprised.

What can a parent do? Since special-ed teachers are committed to ensuring that their charges reach their fullest potential, I'd argue here that a child can't begin to reach his fullest potential if he's assigned reading he hates. With kids, motivation is everything.

One thing about dealing with special-ed teachers is that they usually listen to parents—for a lot of good reasons, but also because an unhappy parent has extensive legal options that, if utilized, can be very expensive for school systems. So I don't think I'd sit still for this one, unless my son specifically requested I do nothing. Gently point out to the teacher the harm this assignment is doing.

**I have a bright first-grade daughter who isn't reading very well yet. She's starting to hate school, and the teacher wants me to hold her back. Should I?**

A mother phoned me to talk about this problem. Her daughter came home nightly with so much hard homework that she and the mother spent all evening on it. Consequently, the mother felt that my first suggestion—that she get the daughter doing as much fun reading as possible on her own so she could quickly catch up—wasn't practical. The little girl literally had no time to read. She was doing homework all the time.

I was so appalled by the problem that I can hardly remember what I told the mother to do. A first grader who had to spend her whole evening on "hard reading homework?" That's ridiculous! The mother really felt she was in a catch-22 situation. If she held the daughter back, as the school wanted, she'd have this teacher for another year! But if she insisted on her being promoted, she was afraid her daughter would experience another year of falling hopelessly behind.

This phone call highlighted a problem I've since heard about often. The problem is that some schools seem to be putting enormous pressure on kids to learn to read right away. If a child isn't reading pretty well by the end of first grade, somehow he's a failure. Reading skills are everything in these schools; forget about a child developing a love of reading and a habit of reading. Personally, I'd rather see a child at the end of first grade who loved looking through books, and was just starting to figure out some of the words, than a kid who had a much larger reading vocabulary, but had decided reading was a hated chore. What can these schools be thinking of?

If your child is in a first grade like this, I really think you have to take action. Discuss the situation with some of the other parents. Almost certainly if your child is overwhelmed and unhappy, other children are too. Go in a group to see the teacher. If she isn't willing to make changes, talk to the principal. Talk to the superintendent, if you have to. Do anything you can to turn your child's first grade into a more nurturing, friendly place.

If there is also a question of grade placement for the next year, arrange for some independent testing to see what grade your child truly belongs in. Armed with the test results and, I hope, the school's assurances that both first and second grade will be amenable to children experiencing difficulties, you should be able to make a decision on placement.

If you can't get any assurances that the school will change, I think you have to consider moving into another school district, or paying for private schooling. Your child has many years of schooling ahead of her; you certainly don't want her unhappy in school year after year.

Here's another first-grade horror question:

**My first grader is given long phonics worksheets to do every night, and he hates them. The school district stopped the whole-language approach because they were afraid of censorship. What should I do?**

This question was asked by a lovely, sensible woman whom I met in Minnesota at a library talk. In most respects she loved the school her son attended; an older sibling had been gravely ill, and the school had really rallied around him. The whole-language approach, in which a school essentially uses regular children's books to teach reading, rather than just programmed readers or skill sheets, had worked well with this older child. But now these worksheets that her younger child had to do every night were killing all interest he'd ever had in learning how to read. Another woman at the talk mentioned that, because of this approach to reading, she'd started home-schooling her children. The situation was that serious.

This mother needs to do two things. Since community pressure resulted in the removal of regular children's books from the curriculum, she needs to organize other parents to bring pressure to bring the books back. We must not give in to zealots who always want everything their own way.

And, meanwhile, she has to work hard to teach her own child to read and to love books. Since her family has deep roots in this school and community, moving would really be a last resort for them. I think that with some savvy and courage, they could at least ride things out, and maybe even change the reading situation for the better.

## My son can't read the books he likes for book reports because his teacher says they're too easy for him. What should I do?

I've heard this question again and again—and it's a tough one because, of course, what you want to do is storm into that classroom and yell, "You idiot! Don't you know my son is just starting to like books? That he's just starting to feel good about reading? And now you're telling him that the only books he likes are dumb, baby books? Where did you get your teaching degree? Off a Wheaties box?!"

But of course you can't do this. So here are some other options:

1. *The "I'll Try to Deal with the School in a Reasonable Way" Option*: This option is certainly worth a try. Phone the teacher and explain the problem. Maybe he'll be reasonable. Offer to try to find an easy book that looks like a chapter book, so it won't appear that he's letting your child slide. Of course, you can't call and advocate for your child very often because after a while it will turn both teacher and child off to you, and no one will listen. But once in a great while I think you can get away with it.

2. *The Help Your Child Option:* This is the most commonly chosen option. Take that teacher-approved book and help your son read it. Read him parts of it, if he'll let you. Read him the

whole damned book, if he'll let you. Just make sure that he continues reading books himself that he enjoys.

The risk here is that you, and your child, get in the habit of your doing a considerable part of his homework for him. There's no future in that. Sooner or later he'll either rebel or gradually become more and more incompetent about finishing any assignments himself. So probably you should take this option only in an emergency.

3. *The Laissez-faire Option:* Ultimately, as I've said, this is the only way to go with homework. When your child comes home and, in disgust, shows you this book that he's already decided he's going to hate because it's too hard, you just smile vaguely and say, "Oh, I'm sure you'll do fine with it." When the teacher calls up to complain that he's not reading his book, say, "I think he's having trouble with it. Maybe it's too hard." If the teacher suggests you help him, say in bewilderment, "You want *me* to read the book? I thought it was for *him.*"

A few possible things can happen.

The unexpected thing might be that your son ends up actually reading and liking the book—and feeling proud that he read such a hard book. I wouldn't count on this happening but, if the teacher is pretty good, there's a chance. He should know what kids like and what they don't.

Your son might try the book, fail, and have the teacher berate him for being lazy and not reading it. This is a really bad thing to have happen, of course. And if it happens very much, you're going to have to give up the laissez-faire approach and go back to one of the first two options.

Your child might try the book and fail, and the teacher might say, "Oh, I guess that wasn't a good book for you. Let's find one next time that's not so long." This is a great thing to have happen. The teacher has shown he pays attention, cares, and will individualize his curriculum for your son. Make sure all of your children get this teacher.

Your son might not read the book, and manage to get away with it in school. From what my students tell me, this happens much of the time. I have kids swear up and down to me that they *never* read a book until they walked into my high school class-room. This isn't such a bad thing to have happen to your child if you're making a full-press effort at home to get him reading, doing all of the things I suggested earlier.

But what if all of these reasonable options don't work? Well, there's always this final option:

4. *The Take No Prisoners Option:* Phone the teacher and politely request a conference. Show up dressed to the nines and carrying a tape recorder. Politely inquire, as you prominently display the tape recorder on the table and click it on, "You don't mind if I tape this conference, do you?"

Now smile encouragingly at the teacher and say, "I'm so glad you're encouraging Joshua to read really difficult books. I'm especially glad because we were debating whether or not to request a full core evaluation and special-ed services. We've hired an advocate, and with these kinds of assignments you're giving, the advocate assures us that Joshua should be eligible for up to ten hours of individual tutoring a week. Right after we finish our conference, I'm having a chat with the principal about scheduling it."

After the teacher's heart slows down so he can speak again (it is an almost laughable understatement that special-ed referrals are discouraged in public schools because of their expense), you may find that he is much more willing to consider a wider selection of books for your son.

It's interesting that I've heard this concern—about pressure for children to read too-hard books—from teachers as well:

**Some of my students are still happily reading picture books, but their parents worry that their child is "behind" and should be reading chapter books. What can I tell them?**

I wish there were some way to get these flexible, open-minded teachers and parents together. Actually, what I really wish is that all elementary teachers were like the teachers who have expressed this concern to me. I have really met some wonderful, caring teachers over the last couple of years.

I suggest they tell parents that children learn at different rates, and if everyone is warmly supportive of *any* reading the child is doing, two years from now no one will be able to tell which children first progressed to chapter books. I also emphasize the point I made in my first book: that some children are very visual and simply love pictures. And that's fine. Go with it!

**My daughter just chose a two-hundred-page biography for a book report. I know it will be murder to get her through it. I'm already thinking that she's going to have to read two chapters a day—maybe before breakfast—to finish in time. What should I do?**

All stop! Forget the reading before breakfast, and especially forget trying to figure out how she's going to get through it.

First of all, take a good look at the book. If it's a book written about a subject she finds very interesting—horses, say, or a singer—there's a good chance she'll not only get through it, but enjoy it. Remember, interest is everything. I've had kids who I thought could barely read enjoy four- or five-hundred-page books about singers or athletes they loved. She may not finish it in time, but she'll probably be able to fudge her book report so it looks like she finished. Or she'll turn in her report late. Whatever the case, if it's a book she has a good chance of liking, stay out of it.

But suppose it's really a boring book. Kids who don't read much tend to choose boring books because, as I finally realized, they don't know there's such a thing as an interesting book. To these kids, all books are boring—so one boring book is the same as another.

Here's what I do. I let the student try to read the boring book for a while—a day or two—and then I casually present him with another book, saying, "You know, a lot of kids pick up that book you have because it really looks interesting, but they end up not liking it. Here's one most kids like much better." The idea is that you don't want to insult her choice. That's why you mention that the book *looks* good. With any luck, she'll be willing to try your choice.

Of course, she may be hell-bent on sticking with that book she chose. Fine. Leave it alone. But don't organize her reading for her. If she reads it, she reads it. If she doesn't, it won't be the end of the world. Life goes on when kids don't finish school assignments.

A related question:

**My third grader can't do alone the reports he's assigned to write on his reading. How much help should I give him?**

I've had this question in a variety of forms. Apparently large numbers of elementary school children are being assigned boring, difficult questions to answer about their reading. Large numbers of parents seem to be spending an inordinate amount of time helping their children deal with these difficult assignments.

I vote that you stop giving help unless your child specifically asks for it. And even then, I'd help as little as possible. Here's why:

Walking children through assignments is ultimately very destructive to their self-confidence and sense of competence, not to mention their sense of responsibility. There's no future in providing this kind of all-encompassing help. Your child gets much more out of completing a job on her own, even if the result isn't terrific, than she gets out of completing a job with extensive help from you. *Don't give that kind of help.*

Dig your heels in. When her teacher calls to complain that her assignment wasn't done properly, tell the teacher that she worked hard on it and that if the teacher is not happy with the result, she should give her a more appropriate assignment.

And, for heaven's sake, don't worry about the grade she gets. It doesn't matter what grades she gets in third grade. Learning to work independently will help her much more in the future than getting high grades with extensive help from you will.

**How do you get around kids being so busy they have no time for reading, other than school assignments?**

This is another question that comes up frequently, especially from parents of older students. I talk about this issue in some depth in *Parents Who Love Reading, Kids Who Don't,* and suggest ways that parents can support pleasure reading for teens (de-emphasize grades and sports; provide spending money so teens don't have to work at minimum-wage jobs for pizza money, etc.), but there is really just so much parents can do about this problem. The real solution to the problem lies in the curriculum of junior high and high schools.

Schools simply need to make student-selected pleasure reading an important part of the curriculum—as the best elementary schools do—and then kids will keep reading. When I give a grade every week based on how much reading my students do—they have to read at least two hundred pages of a book of their choice to get an A—my students all read. They all do lots of reading, and many of them tell me they read more during the semester or year that I have them than they've read before in their whole lives. They find out how much fun reading is, and many keep on reading even when I no longer have them. In later years we compare book titles while passing each other in the halls. If you set up the curriculum properly, it's easy to get even the busiest kids reading.

**In a big family with lots of kids, some get lost in the shuffle, and kids who might like to read get caught up in other things, such as school activities and sports. How do you prevent this?**

First of all, you have to stop feeling guilty. Children from large families get so much warmth and support from all of their brothers and sisters that they don't need as much individual attention from parents, even as regards to reading.* I'd do the obvious things, such as having comics and magazines in the car, so they can read on the way to all of their activities. I'd have lots of reading material in the kitchen, and insist that all snacks be eaten there. I'd encourage older siblings, when cleaning out their rooms, to pass books and comics along to younger siblings. A real advantage of big families is that there is usually a good deal of reading material—of all kinds—lying around.

My own experience is that kids from large families are *more* likely to be avid readers. I think it's because of the presence of many books, as well as the knowledge these kids acquire that the world doesn't owe them a living—so if they want to be entertained, they'd better find something themselves that is entertain-

---

* I came from a large family, and the benefits far outweighed the drawbacks.

ing. What could be more entertaining than books? And it probably doesn't hurt that they rarely have a television or VCR to themselves.

## READING COMPREHENSION QUESTIONS

**How do I know if my child is comprehending what he reads? Should I continue to make him give me a book report after every book he reads?**

A lot of parents have asked me about reading comprehension, but only one actually mentioned that she was making her son do book reports for her after every book. To that mother I say, "Stop!"

But let's talk about comprehension for a minute, because I found that it was a universal concern. This is how I see it:

It takes young children a long time to comprehend oral language completely, but that doesn't stop us from talking to them. We talk to babies all the time. We know that they don't get everything out of what we're saying, but we figure they're getting *something*. Gradually they understand more and more. Of course, then they become teenagers, and understand less and less. "Wash the dishes?" they say in disbelief, until you're reduced to saying, "What part of the sentence didn't you understand?"

But anyway, I think reading works the same way. Kids initially understand only literal meanings—and sometimes not *all* of the literal meanings. But if they're absorbed in the book, and happily reading, don't worry about it. After a while—after many hours spent hunched over fascinating books—they'll be getting more out of their reading. It's why good readers get bored quickly with formula fiction. They're getting *too* much out of those books—they see through the magic curtain an author hangs to keep our interest.

If your child is spending many, many hours happily curled up with reading material, don't worry about comprehension. It will come.

**How can I make sure my daughter is really reading the magazines I buy her? If she's staring at the pages, does that mean she's reading?**

No, she might just be looking at the pictures. But *that's okay*. If she's a kid who hates reading, looking through magazines is a good way for her to ease into reading. After a while she'll start reading short articles.

If kids are enjoyably looking through reading material, I don't think it matters very much whether they're actually reading or not. Sooner or later they'll read. They just need a get-acquainted time first. Bide your time. Keep buying those magazines.

**How do you judge the level of difficulty of reading, so you know what books or magazines to get for your child?**

Don't worry too much about the level of difficulty, except in a broad sense. Obviously you're not going to buy *War and Peace* for your daughter if she's just starting chapter books. Interest should be your key criterion. If the subject (horses, sports, twins, etc.) is interesting for your child, you're probably okay. Try to select books on her reading path. There are some other general guidelines as well.

I pointed out, in *Parents Who Love Reading, Kids Who Don't*, that a first-person narrator is usually easier to follow. I find now that this is especially true for children who like relationship books, since they often identify with the narrator.

Series books—especially after you've read one—are usually easier to follow than other books. They're written in a set pattern that readers quickly get familiar with. While some series are very complex—those of John le Carré, for example, or Anne Rice—on the whole, series books are easier.

Category fiction (e.g., mysteries, science fiction, romances, suspense) is usually easier to read than mainstream fiction. I think the reason these books tend to move more quickly is because the writers of these books usually aren't trying to change the world; they're just trying to tell a good story.

Contemporary books tend to be easier to read than books written a long time ago. Our language and expressions have changed.

My own guess is that people used to read more often for entertainment, and so could handle more complex language. Whatever the reason—please believe me—*Little Women* is not a good choice for a poor reader. Try a Baby-sitters Club book instead.

## CHOOSING BOOKS

### Will comic books make my son violent?

No. In chapter 1 I discussed how reading—any reading—really gentles kids. But, more important, I can assure you that the violent kids are never the readers. Kids who love comics go on to love books. Boys who love books, by high school, are not the ones packing hidden knives to protect their drug deals, just as the girls who read bodice-ripper romances are not the young ladies offering a variety of services to adolescent males. My general observation is this: Kids who *read* about dangerous practices are actually less likely to *do* them.

### Should we move kids from comics to other books?

I don't think you have to worry about doing this. It will just happen, though you might speed up the process by making sure there is a nice selection of other books in easy reach of your comic-book readers. Check my suggestions in chapter 7 for Path 3 readers.

The other thing to keep in mind is that it's usually not an all-or-nothing situation with comics. Kids tell me that, long after they've started enjoying other reading, they still read comics. I know one young man who loves a wide selection of classic writers—and still keeps his subscription to his favorite comics.

### But aren't there things to be learned from the classics?

Yes. Most classics present a rich, complex view of life. They help children understand that there are few easy answers to life's problems. Many are written in the kind of breathtaking style that makes past centuries come alive. Dickens's lavish, tragicomic view of nineteenth-century London has never been equaled. Richmond Lattimore's translation of the *Odyssey* is dazzling in its imagery. Jane Austen's ironic vision of the foibles of society is as realistic today as it was almost two hundred years ago. We learn about our past from the classics, and, even more importantly, we often see truths that transcend centuries.

But it's usually only sophisticated readers who can appreciate classic literature on this level. A beginning reader will miss Dickens's comedy and color and life, and focus in on his unrealistic heroines who achieve success in life by marrying rich men. They'll read *The Great Gatsby* and be dazzled by the glamorous lifestyle of the flapper era, without understanding the savage social commentary that underlies F. Scott Fitzgerald's masterpiece. *Romeo and Juliet* will just be a love story of two dumb kids who did all the wrong things. They'll miss the tragic sense that Shakespeare captures of what happens when family pride and arrogance become more important than love.

That's why you want to save the classics until kids are ready for them. I've seen too many classics ruined for students when they're forced to read them too early.

### Do kids really turn to classics when they run out of Nancy Drews?

No, not all kids. And we have to say that many, many people lead rich, rewarding lives with no knowledge of the classics at all. But I do think that all people who have fallen in love with reading, and formed a habit of reading (and Nancy Drew books are a great beginning for this) will eventually move on to richer, more complex writers, be they classics or not. Don't forget that we have many wonderful contemporary writers whose style, imagery, and complex vision of reality rival that of the best classic writers. I'm thinking of John le Carré, Anne Tyler, Cormac McCarthy, Anne Rice, Barbara Kingsolver, Jane Smiley, and many more.

The other thing I notice is that many adult avid readers move over to nonfiction, and read from an incredibly rich selection of biographies, histories, books on science, culture, psychology—you name it. By junior or senior year in high school, I see a large number of my avid readers, especially the boys, start to do just this.

So no, you can't count on a former Nancy Drew reader going on to classics, but you can count on her going on to better written, more complex reading.

### Do you ever come across a book about which you thought, "No way, this one isn't going?"

A parent who volunteered as a school librarian asked me this question, but I get the same question again and again from teachers also. "Aren't there any books you censor?" they ask. It's interesting to me that I've never gotten this question from a parent who wasn't working in the schools. It's made me think that schools are much readier to censor than parents.

But apart from one hard-core S-and-M porn novel, which I took from a kid who was passing it around in one of my classes about fifteen years ago, I haven't censored books.

I think, again, that teachers run into problems with books when they have required reading—i.e., when everyone in a class reads the same book. I can understand that there are some books that some parents—for a variety of reasons—don't think their children should read. Sometimes these reasons are religious, but not always. Sometimes there are very good emotional reasons for steering a child away from a certain book. For example, one of my African-American girls stopped in the middle of a book titled *Your Blues Ain't Like Mine*. I was surprised that she stopped reading it, because she'd been enjoying it. But then she told me it was too sad because a main character in it had just been shot dead. I was stricken, because I knew she'd lost a young uncle, and a friend, to gunfire within the preceding two years. If I'd known the plot of that book, I'd have tried to move her to another book earlier. It was not, for her, a good book to read at that time in her life.

So, as a parent, you might have very personal reasons for thinking your child shouldn't read a certain book. If that book becomes part of a required class reading list, you're in a very awkward position, and you have to weigh the relative harm of making your child different—by having her be the one child who can't read a certain book—or hoping she can get through the book unscathed. This is another reason why I think class-mandated reading is so hard to defend. If all children can choose their reading, the danger of a child's being assigned to read a book that is not good for that particular child disappears. She may inadvertently pick one up, but an alert parent or teacher can intervene.

But should some books be censored so that *no* children can read them? I don't think so. Actually, even reading magazines like *Playboy* and *Penthouse* seems to be a stage that many perfectly normal boys go through.

The other side of censorship is that censoring a book is the fastest and surest way to get it into the hands of kids. One of my colleagues tells the story of the time he was planning to assign a book for his class to read, and a parent called to tell him that there was inappropriate material on pages 15 to 27 of that book. "Okay," he told her, "I'll take care of it." He walked into class, passed out the books, and told his students to skip pages 15 to 27 because of "inappropriate material." You can probably guess what happened. Every kid went home and immediately skipped to the forbidden pages. The parent called up furious the next day. But the teacher said, with a straight face, "I was just doing what you told me to do."

So, outside of extreme, hard-core porn novels—the kind you buy in those special "adult" stores—I can't think of any books I wouldn't let my students choose. And the funny thing is that, when allowed to choose, few of my students opt for books that have much profanity or sex. Somehow, when they know I won't forbid "dirty" books, they lose their allure. A couple of kids tried *Private Parts* by the radio personality Howard Stern, but neither one finished. They told me the book got boring in the middle.

## How would you get ideas about what books to buy for your children?

First, review chapter 7 on reading paths. By studying your child's interests, you can get a pretty good idea of the kinds of books to buy.

Also, talk to librarians and booksellers. They see what kids are reading, and are usually more than happy to help with book selection. And, as you'll see in the next question, my experience is that most booksellers aren't just trying to make money; they truly are interested in finding books that kids will love—if for no other reason than a hope for repeat business!

You might talk to your children's friends, also, especially if you're looking for some titles to get your children as presents. If you've been cultivating "reading friends" for your children all along, they should be a big help.

Or you might look at the reading lists in *Parents Who Love Reading, Kids Who Don't.* I updated them for the paperback version.

Now here's a question from a bookseller:

**I have such a hard time when parents come into my store and won't let a kid buy a book he really wants. They want him to get something else. What do I say?**

The person asking me this question was co-owner, with her husband, of a Little Professor Bookstore. She was the nicest lady, more concerned with making sure children got books they'd love than with making a quick profit from selling anything. She told me that it happens often that parents, with the best intentions in the world, try to force books on kids that the children just aren't ready for yet, or don't want.

I suggested she remark to parents that this particular book the child wants—let's say it's a Baby-sitters Club book—is often a book kids read *before* they go on to read classics, or harder books. It's not a book they read instead of classics, just *before* classics. She might talk about how many of the best readers coming in have read Baby-sitters Club books.

Of course, if a parent is adamant, graciously sell him or her the wrong book. At least the parent is buying the child a book. Who knows? Maybe the kid will pick it up years later and love it. Maybe the parent will realize the truth of what the bookseller is saying, and return for the first book. Surely it's always better for a parent to be buying books for children, even not-terrific books, than *not* buying books.

## LIBRARY QUESTIONS!

**In my school district, with the cutbacks, it's hard to get funding for the school libraries. How do you get kids to use the public libraries more? I know lots of kids who have library cards and never use them.**

A school librarian—frustrated because he lacked the money to buy the books he wanted—asked me this question. First I needed to say that I thought it was appalling that schools were cutting back on book buying. On book buying! That's the last thing that should be cut from school budgets. Schools should disconnect the phones and sell all of the computer equipment and central office carpeting before they stop buying books. How can you educate children without books?

What's happening is that libraries have become "media centers," and budgets that used to go primarily for books are now being used for computers and CD-ROMs and Newsbank and other sexy new technology.

I've talked with librarians a good deal about the problems they have getting kids into town libraries to check out books for pleasure reading. Kids tell me they wish libraries would organize books the way bookstores do, with a mystery section, a romance section, and so on. Librarians tell me it's too hard to keep track of books that way. Kids also tell me that if most of the books were paperbacks, and if they were facing out, as they do on bookstore shelves, they'd be more appealing. Librarians tell me they lack the room to face books out, and paperbacks don't hold up when heavily circulated. But some librarians are finding ways to make changes—and if we could just help kids fall in love with reading, they wouldn't care so much how books were shelved. I did find, in my talks with librarians, that librarians care very much about getting kids reading. I think they are a wonderful, underused resource in the war against illiteracy.

**I'm a librarian for grades four to eight, and I find even some of the very good students don't love reading. What can I do about it?**

Fourth graders are at the perfect age for series books. Librarians should flood the library with as many Baby-sitters Club, Star Trek, and Nancy Drew books as they can beg, borrow, or steal. They should haunt flea markets, put out a call for community donations, and check used-book stores, and start bringing in adult authors for the seventh and eight graders, and magazines and comics for everyone—piles of fascinating reading material. That's the ticket.

## MISCELLANEOUS QUESTIONS

**What do you think of the E. D. Hirsch books, such as** *Everything Your First Grader Should Know,* **and** *Everything Your Second Grader Should Know?*

A reporter who had called to interview me for an article asked me this. She said she was curious because they were selling so well.

As I mentioned in chapter 1, Hirsch has the right idea in that he understands kids can learn information more easily when they have knowledge frameworks. I'm just convinced that most kids don't learn anything very well simply by being read a short paragraph or article about it. With children, interest comes first, then learning. Any parent who has patiently explained to a ten-year-old how to operate a washing machine, and then realized the ten-year-old has *no clue* which knob to turn—or push? Or pull? Who knows? Who cares? Ten-year-olds aren't interested in clean clothes. But a fifteen-year-old who will wear only two of her extensive wardrobe of jeans—and they're both dirty and you're not home—learns how to operate that washer in the flick of an eye.

Wide reading raises interest in diverse subjects. Interest leads to learning. So I'd say you're better off spending your money on a variety of fascinating magazines and books rather than on Hirsch's mini-lessons. Not only do I doubt they work, but they might turn your children off to reading.

## Should I buy Hooked on Phonics for my daughter?

A New York cabdriver, who was just learning English, asked me this. At the time I hadn't yet seen the program, but had heard it was expensive. "Buy children's books with that money," I told him. "Read to her. That's the best way to make sure she's a good reader."

By now I've checked out the program, and found that my advice to him was sterling. The total cost, if you live in the United States, is $245.95. For this you get thirteen tapes (which are mostly filled with a lady's annoyingly cloying voice chanting vowel sounds and words) and nine sets of small, flimsy flash cards with a sound (like "ar") written twice, a word containing the sound ("car") and a picture of a car. You also get seven workbooks. The workbooks look like something that was typed up at home before PageMaker was invented. The only pictures in the workbooks are of ears and cassette tapes (I'm really not making this up).

But appearances can be deceiving, so I gamely tried it out with my sixteen-year-old daughter (since it's supposed to cover skills from kindergarten to twelfth grade). We put on one of the hardest tapes, and she followed instructions—which are merely to repeat the words and sounds with the lady on the tape, while looking at the flash cards or workbooks.

"Do you think it will work?" I asked her after she was finished.

"Are you kidding?" she asked.

"What's wrong with it?" I persisted.

She gave me that disgusted look that teenage girls are genetically programmed to throw at mothers every so often. "What's wrong with it? It's *boring!*"

And even if it worked—which I doubt—there are many, many better, much less expensive ways to teach your children all the phonics they'll ever need to know. I describe one way in my first book, but there are also all kinds of wonderful, charming alphabet books and early-reader books, and even workbooks, available in any good bookstore.

By high school I almost never get a student who doesn't know all the phonics he needs. Everyone picks it up somewhere. But my classrooms are awash with kids who hate reading, and hate books. *That's* the problem to worry about. Use that $245.95 to buy X-Men comics, or *Beckett* magazines, or Berenstain Bears books. Please don't waste your money on Hooked on Phonics.

# *Appendix*

## *Conversations with Teenage Readers*

● ● ● ● ● ● ● ● ● ● ● ● ● ● ● ● ● ● ● ● ● ● ● ● ● ● ● ● ● ● ● ● ●

Throughout this book what you've mostly heard is my voice, telling you what I've gleaned about reading from years of teaching high school and raising my own children. Now I'd like you to hear the voices of some of the students at my school. The longer I teach, the more convinced I become that the heart and soul of the educational crisis is that we don't *listen* to our children. We don't believe them when they tell us that reading *Great Expectations* is not, for them, a good thing at this time in their lives. We know what's best, we say. Read this classic, or that multicultural book.

It's only when I stopped filtering the voices of my students through my own preconceived notions of what they should or should not like, that I became successful in building a love and habit of reading in my students. It was only when I listened, really listened, that I started to understand about different reading paths, and about the natural progression to more complicated literature that good readers follow. So I invite you to read through this appendix, and really listen to the voices of teenage readers.

I've divided the appendix into four sections, to correspond to the four basic reading paths I've been able to identify. In each section I've included an interview with a really avid, sophisticated reader, and fragments of interviews with more typical—though still avid—readers. The only exception is section 4. Since I found so few Path 4 avid readers, I thought it might be helpful to let you see some portions of reading histories of students just starting to like reading, in addition to the interviews with Path 4 avid readers.

I'm hoping you'll see how any path can lead to very sophisticated reading skills and tastes, and that you'll get more ideas of books to suggest for your own children. In addition, I think you'll be interested in these teenagers' comments about school experiences, about watching television, and about parental involvement in their reading.

## SECTION 1

### Relationship Reading with Unrealistic Elements

This first interview is with one of the most exciting students I've ever had in class, mostly because of her imaginative, metaphor-filled way of viewing life, her gentle, impish sense of humor, and her wonderful insight into books. When she described, for the appendix of *Parents Who Love Reading, Kids Who Don't*, Cormac McCarthy's *All the Pretty Horses* as "a pretty book, like black and white photographs. Kind of old-fashioned and symbolic, weighty but beautiful," I thought, "Yes! That's it. That's the book!" She tagged Barbara Kingsolver's books as "like salsa and chips. You go through the whole bag. They're really salty and spicy and fun to eat, and you can use your hands." I laughed at her description, but now I can't read Barbara Kingsolver without getting hungry for salsa and chips.

This is my interview with her. Notice her love of magic books, as well as of happy-family books (which function, I think, as wish books). She's branching out now, enjoying more realistic authors such as Jane Smiley, but she keeps her love of rich, imaginative language (Annie Dillard, Charles Dickens). Notice, also, her tough transition from a child-centered elementary school to a more curriculum-driven junior high school. I've found this to be typical of my students, but especially for these sensitive, imaginative, avid readers. By high school she's coping better, and instead of just hating a book like *Slake's Limbo*, she has fun "trashing" *Ethan Frome*.

*Do you remember what you read in elementary school?*

A lot of fantasy and family books. I really liked *Four Story Mistake, And Then There Were Five.* They took place during World War II, and are about a family of five kids and all the interests they have. I liked them a lot. I liked C. S. Lewis. He doesn't have a lot of humor, but I liked him. The Narnia series. Roal Dahl I loved. I was so upset when he died. I love his adult short stories too. I think they're wonderful. Terrific. I loved *Anne of Green Gables.* At first I didn't really see the humor in it until later. I wouldn't really see the humor in it and I'd take it seriously. I read it now and it's hilarious. Her speeches and everything. Wonderful. Mrs. Piggle-Wiggle. I loved those. Edward Eager, who wrote *Half Magic.* They're kind of like E. Nesbit books, but they're more modern. E. Nesbit, *The Carpet, the Phoenix.* They're fantasy books, really classic. Not [about] dragons. More about normal children who find something magic or get in magical situations. I loved that. I never really got into the more hard-core fantasy. I couldn't believe it. Fourth grade the teacher read aloud the first one of the Indian in the Cupboard books. I read through the rest of them. Actually she's still writing them and my little brother is reading them, and I still read them. They're really great.

*You like books about older times?*

A lot of them were like the E. Nesbit books and things that my mother had read and she gave them to me. A lot of them are family books. Animal books I liked a lot. *Charlotte's Web. Trumpet of the Swan.* Laura Ingalls Wilder. I must have gone through every single one of those at least three or four times. I went through a Baby-sitters Club period for about a year, and my friends and I read every one of them. I never liked Sweet Valley High. It didn't interest me. In middle school I really liked *All Creatures Great and Small* [by] James Herriot. I read through every single one of his books. His sense of humor is so wonderful. And they're so warm. I'd really enjoy them in winter. I'd snuggle up. *Gone With the Wind.* I loved *Gone With the Wind.* One of my favorite books. I think it was in middle school that I started going through my mother's books, although I still read children's books now, and even picture books. I started getting into mystery in middle school. I read Agatha Christie. She's the best. My father read Tony Hillerman, so I read all those. I usually read what's lying around.

*Do you binge on authors?*

Yeah, I read one and then I go through everything. I was like that with Anne Rice.

*Were you still reading any kind of fantasy in middle school?*

Not as much. I did read some Isaac Asimov. Daphne du Maurier. *The Strand* was my favorite. It had that element of going back in time. I like historical novels too.

*Did you go to the library a lot?*

Bookstores. My grandmother would always take me and let me go crazy. My mother would say, "Oh, it's so much money," and my grandmother would say, "It's books." And I would also reread them. And I also still have them. I never get rid of them. My brother, once he's read something that's it. I go back four and five times.

*Poetry? Nonfiction?*

No, not really. I think the only nonfiction person that I really like is Annie Dillard. She's wonderful. My favorite is "Seeing," in *Pilgrim at Tinker Creek.* And I just read *Charms for the Easy Life,* by Kaye Gibbons. It was so good. I read it over the summer. My mom's now reading it. She's in a book group. I tell my mom what to read and then she has her book group read it. I've read all of Kaye Gibbons.

*And you said your favorite Anne Tyler was* Searching for Caleb, *which was my favorite. And no one else even mentions it.*

I love the way she ties everything together. At the end the wife tells her husband's fortune and says, You will marry a fortune-teller and join the circus. And her daughter. She has a wonderful sense of humor. Like Kaye Gibbons.

*What about Jane Smiley?*

*A Thousand Acres.* I thought that was really good.

*So you like women writers now?*

Yeah, although just a few weeks ago I finished *The Rainbow* by D. H. Lawrence. I read *Sons and Lovers* and I liked it, but *The Rainbow* was so rich. It was like Anne Rice.

*Anne Rice is the magic again.*

Yes, but it also has to be realistic at the same time. I can't go completely fantasy.

*You don't like political fantasy, then? You like more the personal?*

Yes, family relationships. I'm about to start reading *Like Water for Chocolate.*

*You said you wrote a hundred-page story when you were in first grade. What else did you do?*

I always made books. I still have them. I had fancy covers. I was really big on haiku. I remember that I had this one big box, and I'd write the haiku, wrap it up, and then put a rubber band around it and put it in there. I wish I still had it. I was big on diaries. And especially had fun hiding them too, in all sorts of interesting places. I think I hid one once outside but then it rained. They're the funniest things. I love reading them now. For a while, I think it was in middle school, I would write down my dreams. Every time after I woke up, I'd write down my dreams. I was never very big on poetry. I really got into short stories in middle school. The people that I try to model myself after the most are Roald Dahl short stories. They're wonderful. And now Annie Dillard. She reminds me of Thoreau except she's more human. She goes on for pages about drying a baseball glove, and she just makes it so rich.

*You don't do much essay writing.*

What I do over the summer is write letters. I'm a big letter person. And actually a lot of the people I send letters to would read them aloud to their camp. I have fun with them. I just talk about what I'm doing. Single-spaced ten pages.

*How was school for you all along?*

Fifth grade was a hard year for me. Middle school was harder. Also I was doing a lot of moving around in middle school. Also the school wasn't good. I was in Colorado, and I think the reading level was way below what it should be, and I was very bored. School for me before fifth grade was really good. I had teachers who were big on reading aloud to classes, and there'd be a section of the classroom with books you could take out. I liked that.

*Maybe in fifth grade it gets more curriculum-driven, where everybody reads a certain book.*

Yeah, I think that may be it. Now, during high school, freshman year—no, eighth grade was the hardest. Being forced to read *Slake's Limbo*. I hate that book. Oh, it was awful. I got C's all the time. I just couldn't get interested.

*Was that here?*

Yeah. And also grammar. I can't stand grammar. I would flunk grammar. High school English has been good for me. I think a lot of it is coincidence. I just happen to like the books.

*Any books you haven't liked?*

*Ethan Frome.* I had a lot of fun trashing *Ethan Frome*. It's a horrible, frigid book. I loved all the Brontë books that we read here. I like Dickens too. All the books I read now have very strong female characters.

*It matters to you now?*

Yeah. It drives me nuts when women are either just the happy mother or the sex object. It annoys me.

*Are you going to go on in English?*

Oh, yes.

Here are a few snippets of interviews from other Path 1 readers. The first one is from a wonderful reader who was so disenchanted with school that she often refused to do homework. Once, this resulted in her being put in a lower reading group:

I read a lot of Dr. Seuss–type things. I liked having them read to me, especially when my sister did it and left off the first letter of each word. I thought that was really funny. Then I guess I read Choose Your Own Adventure and Richie Rich comic books. Then Dorrie the Little Witch books. Then Betsy-Tacy books, the Sweet Valley Twins. The Lois

Duncan books, Gift of Magic. I really liked that book. I read all the Little House books except the boy-on-the-farm one. I didn't want to read that for some reason. I read all the Narnia books. I didn't like them at first. Then we read one for school and I loved them. I read them all and used to play Narnia games with Jillian. I read random fantasies, like the Bunnicula [series] and one or two of the Piers Anthony books. I liked the Brian Jacques books, and the light fantastic ones. They didn't have chapters and were about weird magical things on different planets. Really cool. I loved Mrs. Piggle-Wiggle and Roald Dahl. They also had witches and stuff. All magic. I love magic. . . .

Let kids pick their own books. Don't put kids in different groups. One time in grade school I got put in a lower group and I felt so stupid. . . . Don't give everybody *Jane Eyre* to read. If kids don't like it, it's going to be hell. Like *Great Expectations*. I couldn't read it. It was so slow it was awful.

The next student was number two in her senior class—showing that Path 1 can produce outstanding students. She also scored a perfect 800 on the verbal section of the SAT exams. She's a talented writer, a musician, and so good in science that she's thinking of a science career. At first glance it seems she might be a Path 3 reader, since she likes so much fantasy, and even a little science fiction. But her insistence on happy endings, and her need to like the main characters, puts her pretty firmly, I think, into Path 1.

I used to love reading a lot as a kid. I was never the kind of kid that Mom would have to make me read. She had to make me stop reading and make me go out and play because she was worried that I was reading too much and not staying in reality enough. I read Nancy Drew—I liked the early ones. I really liked the Anne of Green Gables books. I liked the Little House Books. I read *Cricket* [magazine] and liked that. Later in elementary school I liked mysteries and science fiction. I'd get into one author and read everything they ever wrote. I liked the books with no sex or violence. I liked mystery and nifty robot stuff.

In fifth grade I really liked the Lloyd Alexander books, the Chronicles of Prydain—Madeleine L'Engle I read in middle school—I read one of the EarthSea trilogy, but I didn't like those as much. I like the ones with human interaction.

*Is it important that you like a main character?*

If I like a main character, I'll like the book. Even now, that's how I decided what books I like, basically. Like in some books that are better written, I still won't like them so much because there're no characters I really like.

*You read fantasy?*

I read the Narnia books twice. The books that I really liked I read a lot and I remember the summer of fourth grade I read *The Lord of the Rings*, and I just read it straight through.

*Mysteries?*

I liked Agatha Christie. I like plots too, and her plots are good.

*I liked her world. I wanted to live in her world where people brought me tea in the morning.*

I think that's why I liked science fiction. You could make up the world. I like escape books. The Xanth books I really loved—all fifteen or something. I like books with happy endings. I loved *Pride and Prejudice*. That has a good ending.

I started reading poetry in ninth grade. We did a poetry unit and I liked it, and I started reading. We got a chance to do an independent project, and I did Edwin Arlington

Robinson. I really liked that. And then I read a fair amount of Robert Frost, and Emily Dickenson. Now I'm reading *One Hundred Years of Solitude*, and I'm still working through *Gödel, Escher, Bach*, by Douglas Hofstadter. I'm ten pages into *Memoirs of a Dutiful Daughter*, by Simone de Beauvoir, and I'm planning to start *Chaos* by James Gleick.

## SECTION 2

### Relationship Reading with Realistic Elements

These readers are very different from Path 1 readers in that they tend to be better organized, and they tend to do well in school all the way through. They're realistic! The young woman in this first interview was the kind of student every teacher dreams of having. She was very independent about doing her work, and everything was always beautifully done, and handed in on time. She was active in student council, and in her church. She played in the band. When I asked if I could interview her about her reading, she responded in her typical, helpful, responsible way: I walked into my office the next morning to find a list of her reading already on my desk. What follows is that list. Notice that, although the majority of her reading is about everyday relationships, she does read some "magic" books, such as the Mrs. Piggle-Wiggle books, the Oz books, and books by Madeleine L'Engle. But, on the whole, her favorite authors are much more likely to be writers who deal with problems in a fairly realistic way—at least realistic from a child's or teenager's viewpoint. Not many witches or vampires are on her list, and she doesn't seem to mind books with realistic, less-than-happy endings.

## Series books

Baby-sitters Club
Anne of Green Gables
Sweet Valley High
Ramona Quimby
The Berenstain Bears
Mrs. Piggle-Wiggle
Little Miss

Curious George
Oz books
Nancy Drew (the new series)
Amelia Bedelia
Class of '89
Sweet Dreams Romances

## Favorite authors

Judy Blume
V. C. Andrews
Lois Duncan
Stephen King
Agatha Christie
John Bellairs
Danielle Steel
Farley Mowat
Christopher Pike
Joan Aiken

Mark Twain
Shel Silverstein
Beatrix Potter
Cynthia Voight
Jane Langton
Madeleine L'Engle
Mary Higgins Clark
Robin Cook
Daphne du Maurier
Lois Lowry

## Recent authors

John Grisham
Amy Tan
Margaret Atwood
Jean Auel
John Irving
Jane Smiley

Anne Rivers Siddons
Milan Kundera
Barbara Kingsolver
Michael Crichton
Toni Morrison
Sue Grafton

I had a very pleasant interview with this student, because we didn't have to worry about her remembering book titles. Probably the thing that most stands out about this interview is how important her family has been in shaping her as a reader.

I do remember sitting in the bed with my mother. When I grew older and learned to read, I always read to her, like when I was five. I went to story hour when I was younger because we lived across the street from the library. So I'd walk over myself and go to story hour and in the summer we'd go to Nantucket, and I'd go to story hour there. It was a big thing for me. At the time my mom was working at a college library in New Hampshire, so I'd spend a lot of time at her library as well.

Baby-sitters Club was fifth grade when they first came out, and I would read every one religiously, and I would bother the Concord bookstore. I'd go in every day and ask, "When's the new one coming out?" I was really annoying.

*Did your mother buy them for you?*

I used to do a lot of baby-sitting and had an allowance so I used my own money because the library never had them until really late on in the season. I use the Concord library mostly for research, but I use the Carlisle library a lot. I never use the school library much.

*Do you still go to the library to get fiction books?*

Yeah, but I don't sit there for hours on end. My dad does that.

*Where did you get those great new authors in Brit. Lit.?*

I got a lot of those from my sister because she's spending a year in Oxford. She got a lot of new British authors and stuff, and she's like, "Oh, try this book." We have a lot of the same taste in reading.

*Do you have a lot of books in your house that you read?*

So many. My mother says that we don't buy books in our family, but we do. My dad likes to buy books from bargain places. He'll go to the book fair and just buy thousands of books and they'll just sit around the house.

*Why does your mother say you don't buy books?*

Because she used to be a librarian, she's big on getting books from the library.

*Did she used to get you books?*

Not a lot from her library because it was college level and it was beyond my reading level at the time. But she goes to the Carlisle library a lot now and will oftentimes bring me back books because she swears by the Carlisle library. She says they have the best new book collection. She brings me books a lot. She makes me try different books. She likes to bring me books and see if I like them.

*Do you usually?*

Sometimes. Right now I'm reading *Nicholas and Alexandra* for a class. I don't have a lot of time during classes. During vacation I like Anne Rivers Siddons. I read *Colony* and it was really good. I'm hoping to get a lot of reading done.

*Can you think of any common element in the books you really like?*

Not really. I've never been a huge mystery fan, but I like John Grisham a lot. V. C. Andrews for the same suspense thing, and also the plots. I'm a real fan of Danielle Steel because she's real escape reading.

*Plus she has strong women characters. In fact, looking at your list, you have a lot of women writers.*

I do like women writers, probably my mother and sister's influence. My sister's a borderline feminist. Aren't we all?

*Yeah, you had Jane Smiley and Barbara Kingsolver. Fantasy?*

I can't remember. I remember Douglas Adams. I'm not really a science-fiction fan. My mother was when she was little, and she always tried to get me into it. I liked Madeleine L'Engle.

*You seem to like books about personal relationships.*

Yeah, more than anything. I like psychology.

*When you try to find a book now . . . ?*

I go to the library and look through the paperback section. If there's an author I like, I'll go to the hardback, but I think it's easier to look through the paperbacks.

*Does your whole family read?*

My dad's the slowest reader in the family, but he reads religiously every single night. And my mom always has two or three books going. And my sister reads. She's always coming up with new books she likes. She lives in Chicago now, and if there's a really good one she'll send it or tell me about it.

*So there's a lot of interaction in your family?*

Yeah, books are a big thing.

*Did you ever get pressure from your mother to read? Like "Read now, turn off the TV"?*

Not really, because I always liked reading and I just did it normally. In seventh and eighth grade, before we had to read books for English, when we could just pick any ones we wanted, I read the whole selection before any of my friends finished the first book. Because I'm a fast reader and I've been reading since I've been five, and I learned how from watching "Sesame Street." My mother said she didn't care what I read as long as I was reading something. She didn't care that I read Sweet Valley High. If she had been sitting me down, saying, "You must read Charles Dickens," I would have been annoyed and I wouldn't have liked to read so much. But she said, "Read whatever you want."

*How has school been for you?*

Assigned reading is no big deal because I've done so much reading on my own. The only thing I don't like is when teachers ask me to take notes on books. You sit there with a notebook open and take them in a specific pattern, but then I can't focus on the book. Usually what I do is read through the chapter once and then go back.

*And you've always done really well.*

I like school. I'm glad to get out, but I've always liked school.

The following partial interview is from another very good student, one of the top students in the school. And again, she was very organized, so organized that not only did she conscientiously write reading journals, but she also used to arrange to meet with me to chat about books.

Realistic fiction. I liked that a lot. I read biographies. Also Little House books. One book that I really loved and am still reading [is] *Life Without Friends* by Ellen Emerson White. I also read Sweet Valley High and Baby-sitters Club. My mom said they were like popcorn. I read them when I was younger. They were about older kids. You want to look into that life and see what it will be like. Jealousy and that kind of stuff. I never really liked to read fantasy or science fiction. But I read the Narnia books. I liked that. *The Lion, the Witch, and the Wardrobe* I read a couple of times. It's not really about people, but about war, actually.

I learned how to read when I was about four, and when I was in third grade I was reading on an eighth-grade level. I liked mysteries. I read those a lot. I read Nancy Drew, the Bobbsey Twins, the Betsy-Tacy books. They took place in 1900 or something like that. But Anne of Green Gables I didn't like. I think I was too young and I never went back to them.

I read Holocaust books, like *I'm Fifteen and I Don't Want to Die.*

The following student, who is also very conscientious, was the most adamant about liking books set in the present.

I've always liked mysteries, and my parents and sister do, so we have a lot floating around the house. I never actually got interested in all that Anne of Green Gables—anything that didn't take place in my time didn't interest me. My mom would always buy them, but they didn't interest me. Life was so slow back then that I'd read the books and ZZZZZZ. Danielle Steel was reading that you do on the beach. I've read all of those. Sidney Sheldon—he's really good. I've read every single one of his. I really like Sue Grafton. I've read all of those she's written. The Cat ones, oh, those are awesome. I can't remember what they're called. *The Cat Who . . .* We have a lot of those.

I love books that have multiple people involved. I like

basically two types of books: books about one person and they tell about their whole life, or they tell about their granddaughter and stuff like that, the legacy of the whole family. I think that's really interesting. Or I like books that go back and forth between different characters, like Sidney Sheldon. I always read V. C. Andrews. Those were really good. I read those a lot in my trashy-book stage.

I like stories about women. Maya Angelou, [*I Know Why*] *the Caged Bird Sings* and a collection of her poems. I like poetry a lot. I really like it because I write it. I like Sylvia Plath, *The Bell Jar*. Interesting book, kind of weird. I liked it. I loved Shel Silverstein as a kid. I read Agatha Christie but don't like her. All that olden stuff. I like things I can more relate to.

I loved *The Great Gilly Hopkins*. The stuff in elementary school was kind of fun to read. I loved Judy Blume. I read all the Ramona, and then I watched the show. That was great. I read some good stuff this summer. I read *The Cider House Rules, The World According to Garp*. I liked that author [John Irving] a lot. Virginia Woolf, *To the Lighthouse*. I liked that. I can't get interested in books that talk about history unless you tell it through the eyes of one person.

Advice to teachers: Make reading part of a class assignment. Maybe say, "Once a week bring in a book and read it." Bring in whatever you want. I like it when teachers say, "Read a book and then do something creative with it. Do a cartoon or whatever." I like it when teachers leave things wide open.

The following reader of relationship books with realistic elements is a brave young woman who had a bit of a tumultuous time in high school. I think at least part of the appeal of the problem-laden books she read was that they gave her models of young people who overcame problems. And she did manage to overcome her own problems, excelling in school by her senior year, and being accepted by a host of competitive colleges. My favorite thing about this interview, however, is the advice she gives at the end. I wish all of the educational specialists I've met had her insight and compassion.

I first started out with the Baby-sitters Club. I liked the relationships, the stories about them because I was the same age as they were. I moved on to other juvenile novels, such as Judy Blume and Sweet Valley High. I bought them; my parents gave me the money. I collected a lot of them, Sweet Valley Twins, Sweet Valley High, and Baby-sitters Club.

*Any books you loved and read over and over?*

A Day No Pigs Would Die. I loved that book, and read it over and over. It was so sad. I cried.

*Anne of Green Gables?*

No.

*Betsy-Tacy?*

No. I tried reading those at a young age, but couldn't really get into them.

*So you like books set in modern times more than [those set in] older times?*

Yes.

*Middle school? Anything else you read? Magazines?*

I read *Cat Fancy,* and I started reading fashion magazines: *Seventeen, Teen Beat, Teen.* I read a lot of Judy Blume, just about all of her books.

*Did you read any mysteries? Nancy Drew?*

No, just pretty much about high school relationship-type things . . . Then I started reading a lot of Michael Crichton books, and science fiction/horror books. I read all Michael Crichton and most Stephen King books. And I've gotten the college edition of Sweet Valley, and I've read some because of the writing style. And they're fun to read. I also read *Ellen Foster* and really liked it. I've read some Alice Walker, *The Color Purple* and *Possessing the Secret of Joy*. I've liked them both, very powerful and kind of disturbing, but it's reality. Kind of shocking, but it really does happen. They're great books. I liked *Wuthering Heights*. I liked it a lot. *Pride and Prejudice* I liked. One I really liked a lot was *Sons and Lovers*. That was a great book. I could read that again. I like not out of the ordinary relationships but typical family and friend relationships.

*If you go into a bookstore . . .*

I drift to Stephen King and the nonfiction section. And I look at the Anne Rice books. There are so many things that I want to read and hope to read.

*When did you start writing?*

About seventh grade I started doing it on my own, but I had done it for school earlier and got recognized for it.

*Did you start writing fiction?*

Yeah. There were some times in high school that were too rocky, but I did still write.

*Advice?*

Let kids read what they like to read. Because if you're reading, that's what's important. Don't force kids to read books if they don't like them, or don't make them read too fast. Because some kids are slow readers, a lot of the kids I know, and really don't read on their own and aren't familiar with reading. A lot of the kids I know don't read outside of school. Just be patient.

## SECTION 3

### Action/Adventure Reading with Unrealistic Elements

I had a very hard time settling on a main interview for this section, because so many of my top readers have come up through Path 3 reading. The interview I finally selected, however, is with a student I never had in class. Another teacher, just about to retire, recommended him, saying he was the best English student she'd taught in years. Since she was an incredible teacher who had taught, at one time or another, most of the top students in the school, this was quite a recommendation. As I got to know this student, I could easily believe her assessment. And I found out that he was not only a terrific English student, but a very accomplished poet in his own right.

Notice that, although this young man started out with the most sensationalized Path 3 reading of all—superhero comics—he quickly expanded his reading, and his real love today is poetry. This isn't surprising; the imaginative worlds of Path 1 and Path 3 help children love metaphor and images. Notice also the central role his father played in his love of reading, and the peripheral, almost negative, role that school played.

I loved comic books. Before I could read, my dad used to read comic books to me and show me the pictures. Spider-Man, The Incredible Hulk, X-Men, The Adventurers, Daredevil, everything. I probably really started reading them myself in the first grade. I still read comic books regularly. I just don't read as many. My third-grade teacher had a relation who worked at Marvel Comics and he'd bring free comics and hand them out. I loved it. The stories. Comics got me reading.

I liked *Treasure Island* when I got old enough for that, Tom Swift, some of those. I used to read some science fiction. I read *Princess of Mars*, which almost no one has anymore—Edgar Rice Burroughs—no libraries carry that series anymore—but I loved that series. *The Red Planet.*

*They were just books you had at home?*

Yeah, my dad has a huge number of books and I would just walk up to the bookshelf and pick something that looked interesting and start reading. Then when I moved to Concord I would ride my bike down to the library every day and so for a lot of that summer when my mother was working I'd end up reading a book or two a day.

*Do you remember what kinds of books?*

I read *Over Sea Under Stone* [by Susan Cooper]. I loved those. And I read all the Madeleine L'Engle books.

*Do you remember by fifth, sixth, seventh grade what you were reading?*

I was reading a lot of poetry. From the very beginning I liked poetry. I loved Robert Frost. I read everything of Robert Frost I could find. Wordsworth. One of the first poems my dad ever taught me was "I wandered lonely as a cloud." And I liked Ben Jonson.

I loved the *Odyssey*. About sixth grade I read the *Odyssey* through once and then I started it again. I liked *Midsummer Night's Dream*. I've read through that many times. I didn't like to start at the beginning of books—that's one of the reasons I like poems. I'd open up the book and read through places, and then, when I'd felt I'd gotten to know the book, I'd start at the beginning and read through, I don't know why. It's just a little quirk, I guess. Oh, *The Neverending Story*, by Michael Ende. I was so disappointed by the movie, but I must have read through that fifty times.

*Did you watch television?*

I watched it not a whole lot, but at one point I was getting very into television and my parents did something that I'll always be grateful for. By fifth grade or sixth grade they told me they would give me a hundred dollars if I didn't watch TV the whole year. And a hundred dollars was to me at that time . . . wow . . . I thought I could retire after I got a hundred dollars! So I didn't watch television that whole year, which meant I had a lot more time for reading, and I found after a year of not watching television when I turned it on again I was absolutely disgusted by it. You know, it was mindless, not even funny. So I kind of shy away from television.

*How was school for you?*

I hated middle school so much. Middle school was horrible. It was pure hell. I really had no friends. I would just sit up in my room and write most of the time. And the classes I hated. For me it was everything. Even English . . . usually I could get through English with my eyes closed, but I was paying so little attention in middle school English that I would not even finish the test. Most of my F's came in math. I just wouldn't do any of my homework. I learned biology by reading through the biology book. And that's how I learned grammar. I read through the grammar book. In most classes I would just read the book. When I got to high school it was almost completely the opposite for science. I didn't open the book until I got to advanced physics.

High school was a lot better. Socially it was better because I met the Carlisle kids and they ended up being my closest friends. And I'm friends with the musicians there. I've always been very interested in music. Things were better when I came here. Classes allowed you a little more scope.

*What kind of grades do you get?*

In middle school I got a couple of F's, C's, and B's. All this year [his senior year] by putting in about fifteen minutes at home a day, I've been on the high honor roll for college. I still work on Latin at home because I love the language, and English, you know, I read the books.

*Papers?*

Papers I would usually write the night before. I'd start the research when I got home from school and I'd write them until one that night, and turn it in the next day. The thing is, I wouldn't do that with subjects that I liked, when I got to choose my own topic. Then I read lots and lots of books and spent a long time. But if we were assigned a character study or something, I would usually write it the night before.

*What kinds of things do you read now?*

I read even more poetry, and I'll read some poems over and over again and find anything there that I can. Just going through the bookshelves, too, in my house. Just now I'm reading *Victory*. I love it, so now I'm getting *Heart of Darkness*.

*So you binge on authors?*

Oh, yeah, I did that with Saul Bellow. I went through just about everything. I've been reading Dylan Thomas, a couple of biographies of him. For a long time Keats was the only thing I would read. Obviously he didn't have a great outlook, but I read everything Keats ever wrote.

I like biographies. I'm not really fascinated by the political goings-on. Some history I like. I like to read Confucius. Plato, of course, is my favorite. I haven't read much Aristotle. I should.

*To get books now, do you go to the library?*

A lot of times I go to the library, in which case it will cost me money because I always forget to bring books back. I also like to buy books because then I have them and they're mine. I like to buy books more than anything.

I want to major in everything. I'm going to take quite a few English courses. I don't want to give up physics. I'd like to take music. I'd like to learn some art history because I don't know much. I'd like to continue taking math if I can. I want to take philosophy. First thing I'm going to do is take as many courses as I can. You don't have to declare a major until your junior year. Whatever I do, I'm going to go on to write afterward, so I'm not going to worry if what I take leads me toward a philosophy major or something.

*You don't do leisure reading? Michael Crichton?*

I usually read those things if I'm not exerting myself, if I'm in the mood to relax. I've read *Jurassic Park* and *The Andromeda Strain*. I like those, but as I get older I like the classics the best. I like poetry. I like reading those things, and it's not that I think people shouldn't read those novels, but that I think I shouldn't myself. It's just not what I think I can learn the most from. I got very excited in *Jurassic Park*, but there are poems I've read that I'm still hurting from. You don't get away from those.

Path 3 is really the only coed path I found. Although the majority of readers are boys, a significant number of girls also love these unrealistic action/adventure books. I've found that the girls who read in this path are often more reliably good students than the boys. The following girl was an excellent student.

I read a couple of Baby-sitters Club [books], but I couldn't really get into them. Once in a while they'd be interesting, and other times, *eeee*. I didn't want to read about that. Actually, I read science fiction and fantasy. I loved them; I still do. I also read a lot of mystery. I started off with Lloyd Alexander, then Narnia, then I went on and got into the Xanth books and Piers Anthony's other ones. I branched out and read other types of fiction things. I really liked Catherine Kurtz. I really loved the Deryni. I loved her. *Darkover, The Landover.* Then I'd read science fiction and then I'd read books that combined the two. I loved the Redwall books. I still read those because they keep coming out. They're so unbelievable. I just love reading them. I think a lot of the time what I liked was fantasy because often fantasy is historical and I liked going into the past, like I've always liked historical fiction and books that dramatized historical events. And also, as an only child I had to play by myself and I role-played a lot. So even now, when I read a really interesting part, I'll project myself into that role.

I read DragonLance. They're great. You read them over and over again, and I played Dungeons and Dragons. I read some of Asimov. I read history, but it has to be interesting history, not just dry, dull facts. I like biography.

Other books, the ones about people with problems, Judy Blume, I never liked those. I hated *To the Lighthouse*. It got to the point I walked into my class after we started reading *To the Lighthouse* and all the girls were saying, "Oh, I love it." And I was the only girl saying, "I hated it. I absolutely hated it." And all the guys were like, "Yeah!"

I usually like school. I can't imagine not being in school. I like working and sitting there learning. One author I really like now is Shakespeare. I read my favorite plays over and

over. I love history, especially English history. I love historical fiction.

The following interview excerpt is with a very charming, funny
young man who is one of the top students in his senior class. His
very casual attitude to homework, however, I found typical of
Path 3 readers.

I remember reading the Hardy Boys and the Chronicles
of Narnia. Then I read Judy Blume—I don't know where
they fit in—I used to read anything I could get my hands on,
regardless of how good or bad it was.

In sixth grade I started reading all the DragonLance
books. I would go through one a day. I would get home from
school and lay on my bed and read. After that I stayed in sci-
fi fantasy and then went on to Asimov, which was really
good—all the Foundation books. I played Dungeons and
Dragons a lot on the computer. The King's Quest. I read
L. Ron Hubbard books. I did a lot of the Arthurian legend
books.

No, I never did homework at all. I was completely the
opposite of my brother. I don't know how I got by. But I did
a lot more reading. I kind of feel bad for people who don't
read a lot. I would never do homework. It's not so much I
wouldn't want to do it—I would get home and forget about
it. I would feel awful, but I wouldn't do it. I'd just have so
much other stuff to do. I'd be reading other things. I'd play
computer games endlessly. I'd forget about it and wake up in
the morning. Sometimes I could get it done on the bus. I
didn't start homework until freshman year. I wanted to go to
a good college. And because my brother did so well. I used
to see him doing his work and I'd think, "Oh, yeah, I could
do mine too." I do all my homework now; I'd get marked
down.

Robert Jordan—I love him. That was eighth and ninth
grade. Some of the best books I ever read. I read all the Anne
Rice books. I like historical fiction a lot. I go to the book-

store and look around. I always buy books because I like to own them. They're strewn around. *Pillars of the Earth* is great. *Lonesome Dove* is great. I read *Dune*. Definitely. I liked those.

I never really pick up a book and read it alone because I always go through authors and series. I just read the most recent Follett one, *The Most Dangerous Game*. I read *The Prince of Tides* [by Pat Conroy] and the Citadel one, which I liked [*Lords of Discipline*].

I basically like everything we read in school; I just don't always do it all. *The Great Gatsby* is a great book, but there are a couple of chapters in the middle I never got to because I was doing other things. Freshman year I read Vonnegut. I'm a big fan. I read five Vonnegut books and I really liked him.

My parents only let us watch television on Fridays. I used to hate them for doing it, but I'm also positive I'll do the same thing with my kids.

## SECTION 4

### Action/Adventure Reading with Realistic Elements

When I started this section, I realized that I didn't have any avid readers who started out in this path, probably because there are so few children's books that fit this category. Most of the avid readers on this path are either boys who started out doing Path 3 reading, or boys who didn't read much at all until they could read adult authors.

The main interview of this section is with a boy who fell in love with science and, after some early combination of Path 3 and Path 4 reading, diverged into nonfiction. He certainly isn't a typical reader in any sense. His avid science reading earned him a place as one of five high school seniors on the U.S. physics team. They competed in Australia, and earned a silver medal. As I write this, he's beginning his freshman year at Harvard.

I read lots of Hardy Boys–type novels. I used to devour those. I read a lot of random science-fiction/fantasy things, *The Hobbit* and the Fellowship of the Ring series, a whole bunch of Asimov (Foundation, Robot series), lots of Heinlein novels, all sorts of Star Trek novels, and lots of Piers Anthony. I also read a lot of mystery stuff, like John Bellairs. I loved that.

My parents were pretty strict about television. I only watched PBS and "The Smurfs." I loved "Nova" and watched it every week and got this wonderful science background about it. I didn't watch much else until middle school. I never felt deprived.

I used to write a fair amount on my own. I wrote some pretty good science fiction. I was careful to make it realistic. I used zero gravity, stuff like that. But my handwriting was horrendous. My teachers kept harping on that, and it made me detest writing. No matter how hard I tried, they would make me write it again. I don't mind about writing now, but the creative writing I do seems contrived. It's depressing. Critical writing I enjoy moderately. I seldom really, really enjoy writing, unless it's going really well. At least I'm satisfied with my style now.

Middle school was pretty bad as an experience. I did okay on schoolwork. I got through even things I detested. Socially it was horrendous, but that improved a lot by eighth grade. Middle school was the first experience I had with people who were anti-intellectual. I got really isolated. I loved math and did it on my own, but most often my teachers ignored me. A great deal of my encouragement was from outside of school. The most I got was in high school. It's revived my interest in other things, like English, that I wasn't that keen on.

*Tell me about your science reading.*

I'll start when I was really young, in elementary school. Then I didn't read much science and math. I read lots of practical books. Interesting things about electronic stuff and books on physical experiments you yourself can do. I had lots of fun with stuff like that for a while.

I guess I really didn't start reading much science and math, much dense stuff, until I tackled around sixth grade *A Brief History of Time*, which I had gotten as a present and which I had heard wonderful things about. So I started reading it, and it was really exciting and really interesting and then suddenly I found that I understood nothing, and I just had reached my limit of being able to interpret what he was saying. So I stopped and just left it. I finished about a third of the book. But that one book I attacked many times in middle school. I think I finally got through it in seventh or eighth grade. And so once I finally got through that, I dug up some books we had in our house, some really interesting things like *White Holes* by John Gribbin. He's slightly out of the total cosmologists' mainstream, but he had really interesting ideas, and I was fascinated with these ideas. I read things like *The Ring of Truth* by Philip Morrison. And basically a lot of different science popularizing books that were a challenge for me at the beginning, but since I was always interested in them, I would always get through them. And then I would be really interested and I would go around and try to engage my friends in conversation about it and sometimes they would listen and sometimes they would ignore me entirely, but that was that.

Once I got to about ninth grade I started reading lots of science books and I was very interested in physics, the theoretical part of physics, which is from *A Brief History of Time*. I actually reread that three or four times just because there's so much good stuff in it and I got more stuff out of it each time. But then I started reading other things like Martin Gardner, who's a recreational mathematician who wrote some really interesting stuff. And then sophomore year I got a whole list of books that I started reading. Things like *Genius*, which is a biography by James Gleick. It's a biography of Richard Feynman, and Gleick was a good enough writer that he was also able to explain the science, the very complex quantum electrodynamics, and all sorts of complicated things that Feynman came up with, and I was able to understand them just from the biography. I have to say it's the most interesting biography I've ever read. I also was reading lighthearted things like *The Cartoon Guide to Physics*, which is actually very useful, I must say, by Larry Gonick. It's really funny. He has a whole series of these that are actually very very useful. I think I learned a great deal of physics just reading that. And then other books, like *The Refrigerator and the Universe* by Martin and Inge Goldstein, about entropy, which has always interested me. I think I finally almost have a handle on that. And of course there are other things, like *Gödel, Escher, Bach*, which is [Douglas] Hofstadler, and has an enormous amount of information that he ties together and a lot of math and physics and almost philosophy. It was really interesting and I still haven't got all the way through it. Over last summer I was also reading a lot. I was reading things like *Fourth Dimension* by Rudy Rucker. He's a mystic mathematician who talks about the fourth dimension in an interesting way. And other things like *Hyperspace*. I'm actually reading that now, by Michio Kaku. It's very advanced, the newest theoretical physics, the newest ideas, explanations, fundamental theories. And another book by Stephen Synbert, called *In Search of a Final Theory*. Other books like *The Quark and the Jaguar*, by Murray Gell-Mann, which again is about simplicity and about fundamental particles and simplicity. All of these I've really enjoyed.

Another excellent student I had started out with mysteries, and then diverged into nonfiction business and political books, magazines, and newspapers. Here's an excerpt from his interview:

When I was a kid I would read the usual cartoons and little story books, Alfred Hitchcock mystery series, the Hardy Boys. Toward middle school, things started to change a little bit. I started getting into reading the paper before I went to school every day, and I started reading more and more business-related stuff. Also my interest in computers and stuff started to grow, so I'd always be reading stuff like *PC Magazine*. I'd always be keeping up to date.

Basically I like reading everything, but what I always find most interesting are books on politics, history, business, or even biographies of certain people in history. One of the books I read was *Official and Confidential*, by Anthony Sommers, about the secret life of J. Edgar Hoover. This book absolutely fascinated me, and it catapulted me into reading stuff about Nixon, like Carl Bernstein's *All the President's Men*. Then I started reading *The Wall Street Journal* and I'd get interested in certain characters, and one that always fascinates me is Bill Gates of Microsoft Corporation. History was also very big for me, and I've read books like *Truman*, by David McCullough, and all kinds of stuff about the Kennedy assassination.

What basically happens is that something catches my eye, maybe it's in a newspaper or in a movie or some issue that's really happening, and I just go out and get a few books on it and I read them, and I think that's where my interest for this type of book grows.

But most of the Path 4 readers I know are high school boys who read very little until they discovered that there were actually books about sports or music or military heroes. What follows are excerpts from student writing I've gotten over the years describing the kinds of books they've now discovered they like:

I believe that in order to enjoy reading, you must like the book and the topic itself. I myself will tear through a sports book in one day, but a novel such as *Hard Times* [Charles Dickens] would be lucky to get opened. For me reading is hard and I really don't like it, but if there is a book or something that interests me, I will read because I *want* to and I'm willing to go through a bit of struggle, for I can read on the topic that I enjoy. Reading books about my sports heroes allows me to build my impression of them further. I see it as the same way as watching them on television, but instead I watch them in my own head. I loved *Fab Five* [Mitch Albom], *Fall River Dreams*, *The Last Shot*—about inner-city kids trying to make it out through basketball—and *The Long Hot Winter*, about a year with the Portland Trailblazers.

Another young man discovered books about rock stars:

> *Hammer of the Gods* [about Led Zeppelin, by Stephen Davis] is the hardest book I've ever read *that I love*. I've read every page of this book with a smile on my face. [He then read *Come as You Are: The Story of Nirvana*, by Michael Azerrad.] The book was so hard to put down that during Thanksgiving vacation, during my free time, I actually found it entertaining to read, for the first time in my life. [He then moved on and tried a sports book.] I couldn't resist finally starting up *Drive*, by Larry Bird. This book was great! It talked about not only Larry Bird but the Boston Celtics team. He told about every player he's ever played with, and he talks about his favorite games. His brightest and his worst moments.

Another young man I had in class read nothing until he discovered military aircraft books. He started with *Flight of the Intruder*, by Stephen Coonts.

> I have really liked this book and loved the descriptions in it. [He then read *Phantom Leader* ("very good and very realistic"), and part of *Steel Tiger*, both by Mark Berent, and then got a copy of *The Intruders*, the sequel to *Flight of the Intruder*, and loved it.] It [*The Intruders*] is so good because there is no time wasted telling about the characters because you already know about them from the previous book. [He then found a book on the Vietnam War called *Chickenhawk*, by Robert Marson.] I read *Chickenhawk* for a while. It was a very good book, but I got *Armored Law* by Tom Clancy for Christmas and could not wait to read it. . . . I hate to put the book down.

# Bibliography of Titles and Authors Mentioned in the Interviews

What follows is a list, alphabetical by author, of authors, book titles, and series names that were mentioned in the preceding interviews. Probably the fastest way to find the author of a series is to look up the series in the index to locate it in this bibliography. You should be aware that not all of the books listed below were recommended by my students. Sometimes they mentioned books they disliked. It is simply a list of all books mentioned. For a fuller description of most of these books, the most popular ones, you should consult the index in my first book, *Parents Who Love Reading, Kids Who Don't.*

**Aiken, Joan.** A mainstream relationship writer.

**Albom, Mitch.** *Fab Five.* Basketball book.

**Alexander, Lloyd.** Chronicles of Prydain. *Book of Three.* A fantasy series for science-fiction, fantasy, and magic readers.

**Alfred Hitchcock** mysteries. Four authors write these: William Arden, Robert Arthur, M. V. Carey, and Nick West. The titles all start *Alfred Hitchcock* and the *Three Investigators in the Mystery of...* For adventure mystery readers, especially boys.

**Andrews, Julie.** *The Last of the Really Great Wangdoodles.* Loved by relationship and magic readers.

**Andrews, V. C.** *Gates of Paradise. Fallen Hearts. My Sweet Audrina.* Relationship books featuring such major problems as abuse, incest, and child-selling. Popular with readers who like lots of action in their relationship books.

**Angelou, Maya.** *I Know Why the Caged Bird Sings.* Poetry. An African-American writer popular with readers who like relationship books, or who are interested in the African-American experience.

**Anthony, Piers.** Xanth series. First title: *A Spell for Chameleon.* A series popular with both pure science-fiction and fantasy readers and relationship readers who like magic.

**Appleton, Victor.** Tom Swift. Adventure series.

**Asimov, Isaac.** The Foundation series. *Caves of Steel. The Naked Sun.* Path 3 and occasional Path 1 readers.

**Atwood, Margaret.** Writes mainstream relationship books.

**Auel, Jean M.** *The Clan of the Cave Bear.* For readers who like history or historical fiction.

**Austen, Jane.** *Pride and Prejudice.* An eighteenth-century comic love story. Very popular with readers of classics who like relationship books.

**Azerrad, Michael.** *Come As You Are: The Story of Nirvana.* Rock star book.

**Banks, Lynn Reid.** The Indian in the Cupboard series. Path 1 and Path 3 readers, especially girls who love magic and dolls.

**Baum, L. Frank.** The Oz books. For fantasy and magic readers.

**Beauvoir, Simone de.** *Memoirs of a Dutiful Daughter.* For readers of classics and women authors.

**Bellairs, John.** Writes children's mysteries.

**Bellow, Saul.** *The Adventures of Augie March.* Only for sophisticated readers of classics.

**Berent, Mark.** *Phantom Leader* and *Steel Tiger.* Military airplane books.

**Bernstein, Carl, and Bob Woodward.** *All the President's Men.* An account of the Watergate affair. For readers who like history or political science.

**Bird, Larry, with Bob Ryan.** *Drive.* About the Boston Celtics.

**Blume, Judy.** *Tales of a Fourth Grade Nothing.* For relationship readers who like realistic books.

**Bradbury, Ray.** *The Martian Chronicles.* Science-fiction readers.

**Bradley, Marion Zimmer.** Darkover. Fantasy series.

**Braun, Lillian Jackson.** The Cat series of mystery books (*The Cat Who Went into the Closet, The Cat Who Talked to Ghosts,* etc.). For mystery readers, especially those who like modern mysteries.

**Brontë, Charlotte.** *Jane Eyre.* For relationship readers who like books set in the past.

**Brontë, Emily.** *Wuthering Heights.* For relationship readers who like psychological studies.

**Brooks, Terry.** The Shannara books. Landover books. For fantasy readers.

**Burroughs, Edgar Rice.** *Princess of Mars.* One of the Mars series. For science-fiction readers.

**Choose Your Own Adventure.** Various authors, depending on the subject. There are some fantasy titles (Paths 1 and 3) and some mystery/adventure (Paths 2 and 4).

**Christie, Agatha.** Mystery writer. Mostly Path 1 but some Path 2 readers.

**Clancy, Tom.** *The Sum of All Fears. Without Remorse. Armored Law.* For readers who enjoy military adventure books. Good for high school Path 4 readers.

**Clark, Mary Higgins.** Relationship suspense novels.

**Clarke, Arthur C.** *2001: A Space Odyssey.* Many other works. Classic science fiction. Path 3 and some Path 4.

**Cleary, Beverly.** The Ramona series. Popular with readers who like comic relationship books.

**Cochran, Molly.** *The Forever King.* For fantasy readers.

**Conrad, Joseph.** *Victory. Heart of Darkness.* For readers who enjoy realistic adventure.

**Conroy, Pat.** *The Prince of Tides. The Lords of Discipline.* Tragic-comic modern novels that most good readers like.

**Cook, Robin.** *Terminal. Vital Signs. Mutation.* Medical mysteries for readers interested in medical or suspense novels.

**Coombs, Patricia.** The Dorrie, the Little Witch series. For magic readers.

**Cooney, Linda A.** Class of '89 series.

**Coonts, Stephen.** *Flight of the Intruder. The Intruders.* Military airplane books.

**Cooper, Susan.** *Over Sea, Under Stone. The Grey King.* These are part of a series that starts with *The Dark Is Rising.*

**Crichton, Michael.** *Jurassic Park. The Andromeda Strain. Rising Sun.* Suspense books with a technological, medical, or science-fiction twist. For readers of those paths.

***Cricket Magazine.*** A magazine containing stories by well-known children's authors.

**Dahl, Roald.** *The Witches. Matilda. Charlie and the Chocolate Factory.* All of his children's books, for all readers. *My Uncle Oswald* for adult readers of comedy and classics.

**Davis, Stephen.** *Hammer of the Gods: The Led Zeppelin Saga.* Rock singer biography.

**Dickens, Charles.** *Great Expectations.* For sophisticated classics readers only.

**Dillard, Annie.** Essay writer. Two popular books are *Pilgrim at Tinker Creek* and *An American Childhood.* Enjoyed by Path 1 and 2 readers.

**Dixon, Franklin.** The Hardy Boys mysteries. For mystery readers. Usually only boys like them.

**DragonLance books.** Fantasy series by various writers. Margaret Weis and Tracy Hickman wrote the initial books: *Dragons of Despair, Dragons of Winter Night.* Other writers include Nancy Varian Berberick and Mark Anthony. For fantasy readers and Dungeons and Dragons players.

**du Maurier, Daphne.** *The Strand.* Mainly Path 1, although her *Rebecca* is so good it picks up Path 2 readers as well.

**Duncan, Lois.** *Gift of Magic.* For magic readers.

**Dungeons and Dragons books.** Various authors such as Rose Estes. Game modules can be found in hobby shops.

**Eager, Edward.** *Half Magic.* For relationship and magic readers.

**Ende, Michael.** *The Neverending Story.* Good for fantasy and magic readers.

**Enright, Elizabeth.** *Four Story Mistake. And Then There Were Five.* For family readers and readers of historical fiction.

**Esquivel, Laura.** *Like Water for Chocolate.* Mostly Path 1 with some Path 2 readers.

**Fitzgerald, F. Scott.** *The Great Gatsby.* This jazz age novel is good for most advanced readers.

**Follett, Ken.** Espionage books for suspense and perhaps history readers. *Pillars of the Earth* is a favorite.

**Frey, Darry.** *The Last Shot: City Streets, Basketball Dreams.* Great Path 4 book.

**Frost, Robert.** A very accessible poet for classics readers, but you might give a gift volume to any reader.

**Gell-Mann, Murray.** *The Quark and the Jaguar: Adventures in the Simple and the Complex.* For science and math readers.

**Gibbons, Kaye.** *Charms for the Easy Life. Ellen Foster.* Path 2 and some Path 1 readers. (*Ellen Foster* is too realistic for some Path 1 readers.)

**Gleick, James.** *Chaos: Making a New Science. Genius: The Life and Science of Richard Feynman.* For readers of science and science fiction.

**Goldstein, Martin and Inge.** *The Refrigerator and the Universe: Understanding the Laws of Energy.* For science-fiction and science readers.

**Gonick, Larry.** *The Cartoon Guide to Physics.* For science and maybe science-fiction readers.

**Grafton, Sue.** The alphabet mystery books: *A is for Alibi,* etc. Enjoyed by contemporary mystery readers.

**Gribbin, John R.** *White Holes: Cosmic Gushers in the Universe.* For science readers.

**Grisham, John.** *A Time to Kill. The Client.* Legal suspense for action and relationship readers.

**Hargreaves, Roger.** The Little Miss series: *Little Miss Bossy, Little Miss Broadway,* plus more. Good Path 2 books.

**Hawking, Stephen W.** *A Brief History of Time.* For science, science-fiction, and history readers.

**Heinlein, Robert.** *The Red Planet. Stranger in a Strange Land.* For science-fiction readers.

**Herbert, Frank.** *Destination Void. Dune.* For science-fiction readers.

**Herriot, James.** *All Creatures Great and Small.* Path 1 and other readers who like animals.

**Hillerman, Tony.** Writer of southwestern mysteries. Mostly Paths 2 and 4 readers.

**Hobbes, Thomas.** *Leviathan.* For readers of politics and history.

**Hofstadter, Douglas.** *Gödel, Escher, Bach.* For science and history readers.

**Holman, Felice.** *Slake's Limbo.* Teenage novel about a homeless boy, frequently taught in junior high schools. Not popular with students interviewed.

**Homer.** *Odyssey.* For classics and mythology readers.

**Hope, Laura Lee.** The Bobbsey Twins series. For readers of relationship books.

**Howe, Deborah.** The Bunnicula books. For magic readers.

**Hubbard, L. Ron.** Science-fiction books.

**Irving, John.** *The World According to Garp. The Ciderhouse Rules.* For readers who like relationships or comedy. Sports readers also like *Garp.*

**Jacques, Brian.** The Redwall series. Loved by readers of fantasy and magic.

**Jordan, Robert.** For fantasy readers.

**Kaku, Michio.** *Hyperspace: A Scientific Odyssey Through Parallel Universes, Time Warps, and the Tenth Dimension.* For science readers.

**Keene, Carolyn.** The Nancy Drew mystery series. Popular with almost all mystery readers.

**King, Stephen.** *Gerald's Game,* many others. For horror readers. Especially popular with Path 2 and some Path 4 readers.

**Kingsolver, Barbara.** *The Bean Tree* and others. Books for family and relationship readers. Especially enjoyed by readers who like contemporary women writers.

**Kundera, Milan.** Writes relationship books. Path 2.

**Kurtz, Katherine.** The Deryni series: First title, *Deryni Rising.* For fantasy and magic readers.

**Langton, Jane.** Writes mysteries set in New England.

**Lawrence, D. H.** *Sons and Lovers. The Rainbow.* For relationship readers.

**Le Guin, Ursula.** The EarthSea Trilogy. For fantasy readers.

**L'Engle, Madeleine.** *A Wrinkle in Time* and others. For fantasy and magic readers.

**Lewis, C. S.** The Narnia series: First title, *The Lion, the Witch, and the Wardrobe.* A series popular with almost all readers, but especially Paths 1 and 3.

**Lovelace, Maud Hart.** The Betsy-Tacy series. For readers of relationship books set in the past.

**Lowry, Lois.** The Anastasia books. For relationship readers.

**MacDonald, Betty.** The Mrs. Piggle-Wiggle books. For readers who like magic and comic relationships.

**Márquez, Gabriel García.** *One Hundred Years of Solitude.* For classics and history readers.

**Marson, Robert.** *Chickenhawk.* A true war book.

**Martin, Ann.** The Baby-sitters Club series. For relationship readers who like books set in the present.

**Massie, Robert K.** *Nicholas and Alexandra.* Nonfiction for history readers.

**Maupassant, Guy de.** Short stories.

**McCullough, David G.** *Truman.* Nonfiction for history readers.

**McMurty, Larry.** *Lonesome Dove.* Classic western.

**Mitchell, Margaret.** *Gone With the Wind.* Path 1 and some Path 2 readers.

**Montgomery, L. M.** The Anne of Green Gables series. For relationship readers who like books set in the past.

**Morrison, Philip.** *The Ring of Truth: An Inquiry into How We Know What We Know.* For science and perhaps history readers.

**Morrison, Toni.** *Beloved.* Relationship book featuring African-American characters.

**Mowat, Farley.** Writes animal and nature books.

**Nesbit, E.** *The Phoenix and the Carpet.* For magic readers.

**Pascal, Francine.** The Sweet Valley books. For relationship readers who like modern stories.

**Paterson, Katherine.** *The Great Gilly Hopkins. The Bridge to Terabithia.* For relationship and family readers.

**Peck, Robert Newton.** *A Day No Pigs Would Die. Soup* books, such as *Soup and Me.* Especially good for readers of family books. Loved by readers of relationship books.

**Pike, Christopher.** Teenage horror books.

**Plath, Sylvia.** *The Bell Jar.* Relationship story of a young woman's breakdown.

**Plato.** *The Republic.* For history and political readers.

**Potter, Beatrix.** The Peter Rabbit books.

**Rawls, Wilson.** *Where the Red Fern Grows.* Very popular book. For readers of adventure, family, and animal books.

**Reynolds, Bill.** *Fall River Dreams: A Team's Search for a Town's Soul.* Small-town basketball book.

**Rice, Anne.** *Interview With a Vampire. Lasher. The Witching Hour. Taltos. The Mummy. Belinda.* Very popular with magic and relationship readers. Liked by some science-fiction, fantasy, and mystery readers.

**Robinson, Edwin Arlington.** A major American poet.

**Rucker, Rudy.** *The Fourth Dimension: A Guided Tour of the Higher Universe.* For science readers.

**Seuss, Dr.** All of his books for all readers.

**Shakespeare, William.** *Richard III. Henry V. Romeo and Juliet. A Midsummer Night's Dream. Much Ado About Nothing. Twelfth Night.* For readers of classics, drama, and, sometimes, history.

**Siddons, Anne Rivers.** Relationship and family books.

**Silverstein, Shel.** A comic poet for children. Fondly remembered by relationship readers.

**Smiley, Jane.** *A Thousand Acres.* A family relationship book. Especially interesting for readers who like women authors.

**Star Trek books.** Various authors, including Alan Dean Foster and Michael Jan Friedman.

**Steel, Danielle.** Many love and family novels for relationship readers who like contemporary stories.

**Steinbeck, John.** *The Grapes of Wrath. East of Eden.* For readers who like historical fiction, classics, or relationship books.

**Stevenson, Robert Louis.** *Treasure Island. Dr. Jekyll and Mr. Hyde.* Adventure books.

**Sweet Dreams Romances.** Published by Bantam Books. Various authors. Great Path 2 books.

**Synbert, Stephen.** *In Search of a Final Theory.* For science readers.

**Tan, Amy.** Writes books about the experiences of Chinese Americans.

**Tolkien, J. R. R.** *The Hobbit.* For relationship, magic, and science-fiction and fantasy readers. The Ring Trilogy. For science-fiction and fantasy readers.

**Twain, Mark.** *A Connecticut Yankee in King Arthur's Court.* For readers who like classics. A difficult book.

**Tyler, Anne.** *Searching for Caleb.* For readers of family books by women authors.

**Voight, Cynthia.** Writes young adult relationship books. Path 2.

**Walker, Alice.** *The Color Purple. Possessing the Secret of Joy.* Relationship books featuring African-American characters.

**Watson, James.** *Molecular Biology of the Gene.* For science readers.

**West, Nick.** Writes some of the Alfred Hitchcock Three Investigator books.

**Wharton, Edith.** *Ethan Frome.* A book loved by English teachers and often disliked by students. *The Age of Innocence* is more popular.

**White, E. B.** *Charlotte's Web. Trumpet of the Swan.* For relationship, animal, and magic readers.

**Wilder, Laura Ingalls.** The Little House books: First title, *Little House in the Big Woods.* Path 1 and some Path 2 readers.

**Wodehouse, P. G.** The Jeeves series about the British upper class. Comic relationship books.

**Woolf, Virginia.** *To the Lighthouse. Mrs. Dalloway.* For relationship readers.

# Index